D1139044

THE PUBLIC MANAGER'S GUIDE

THE
PUBLIC MANAGER'S
GUIDE

Donald P. Crane

William A. Jones, Jr.

The Bureau of National Affairs, Inc., Washington, D.C.

Library of Congress Cataloging in Publication Data

Crane, Donald P.
  The public manager's guide.

  Bibliography: p.
  Includes index.
  1. Government executives—United States.
  2. Public administration.   I. Jones,
William A., 1934-   II. Title.
JK723.E9C7   353.07'4   81-21654
ISBN 0-87179-361-X   AACR2
ISBN 0-87179-375-X (pbk.)

Printed in the United States of America
International Standard Book Number: 0-87179-361-X (hardcover)
0-87179-375-X (paperback)

Preface

As teachers in a multi-disciplinary graduate program in public administration, we perceived the need for a text which balanced administration (management) and politics (policy). At the same time, we felt that the existing texts were weak on relevance for practicing public managers, especially those at middle-management levels. To respond to these needs, we developed a text with a pragmatic orientation. We attempted to convey the excitement and complexity of public management in a straightforward, easy-to-read style. The focus is on what public managers actually do and there are numerous examples of practical application. In addition, the book emphasizes the primary *concepts* of the public-management field and current issues which may influence public managers' performance.

The Public Manager's Guide is written to reach practicing public managers as well as students. It would be appropriate for academic courses at the graduate and undergraduate levels and, especially, for use in governmental training programs.

We would like to thank the "blue ribbon committee" of public managers who helped us in various ways. Their reactions, suggestions, and examples were of great value. We also hasten to absolve them for any errors or shortcomings in the final text; those are totally our own. Helping us in this capacity were:

Ms. Elizabeth Berrier, formerly with the Georgia Department of Human Resources and now Associate Regional Director in the southeast for Planned Parenthood Federation of America

Mr. Jack Caldwell, formerly with the U.S. Office of Personnel Management and now Chief of the Academic Specialties Staff for the U.S. Immigration and Naturalization Service at the Federal Law Enforcement Training Center

v

Mr. Richard Gensel, Projects Control Manager for Cobb County, Georgia

Dr. Paul Hirsch, Director of Field Instruction for the College of Public and Urban Affairs at Georgia State University

Dr. Don Meyers, formerly with the U.S. Postal Service and now Associate Professor of Management at Winthrop College

Ms. Willieboyd "Mac" Saddler, formerly Regional Comptroller for the U.S. Department of Health, Education, and Welfare and now Director of Program Review and Management Support for the southeastern region of the U.S. Office of Civil Rights

Mr. Charles Storm, Commissioner of the Georgia State Merit System

In addition to our "blue ribbon committee," we are also indebted to several other persons who helped in various ways. One who was particularly helpful was William Fitchpatrick of the U.S. Office of Personnel Management. In addition to suggestions and examples, he threw in some needed inspiration. The assistance of Ron Hoskins as co-author of Chapter 8 was invaluable. Tom Lauth of the University of Georgia and Vicki Quigley of the University of Louisville also helped in a variety of ways. Our sincere thanks go to all of these people.

January 1982   Donald P. Crane
                                               William A. Jones, Jr.

Contents

1

The Job of the Public Manager

Key Concepts

Public Management
  Public Manager
    Government
      Public Goals
        Public Management Categories
          Politics and Administration
            POSDCORB
              Duties of the Public Manager
                Unique Aspects of Public Management
                  Roles of the Public Manager

In May 1961, President John F. Kennedy proclaimed as a national goal that the United States "send a man to the moon and return him safely to earth before the end of this decade." In 1969, this goal was accomplished when three astronauts traveled to the moon. Neil Armstrong took a "small step for mankind" and was joined on the moon's surface by Edwin Aldrin; then the three spacemen returned to planet earth. In less than nine years the nation's goal became a reality.

An impressive feat by modern technology? Absolutely. Equally impressive was the performance by American public managers. Before establishing this national goal, President Kennedy did some checking to make certain the required technology was available. He then assumed the capacity of public managers to make it happen. Outstanding performance of public managers in the past had earned the confidence of the President in their future capabilities.

Public management is the link between government goals and government accomplishments. Goals translate into actions only through the coordinated application of human effort and economic resources. This process of translation is the essence of the public manager's job. For government's work to be accomplished:

▶ Policies, plans, and organizations must be created.

▶ Money must be obtained, budgeted, and expended.

▶ People must be hired, trained, assigned, and supervised.

▶ Programs must be monitored, evaluated, and guided.

Whether the goal is traveling to the moon, protecting the environment, or paving a street, public management is a crucial component. When we look to government to do anything, we are looking toward public managers.

Contrary to what seems to be a popular view, governmental organizations generally are managed quite well. This does not negate the continuing need to seek improvement. Just as we want business to be well run to provide a good product for a reasonable price, we want efficient and effective returns for our tax dollars.

This book is about American public managers in the last few decades of the twentieth century. The purpose of the book is not to provide a detailed and definitive exposition. Rather, the authors seek to capture the nature and flavor of the public manager's job and to stimulate the reader's appetite for further investigation into the subject.

Public management in the United States is an extremely diverse enterprise. It is a part of all three branches of government—executive, legislative, and judicial. It is a part of all levels of government—national, state, and local. Beyond these traditional categories, public management is a part of newer governmental categories which have emerged in recent years— special districts, councils of governments, regional planning commissions, and others. All of these categories of public agencies, both traditional and contemporary, provide the means through which society pursues its goals.

SOCIETAL GOALS AND THE PUBLIC MANAGER'S ROLE

To exist in proximity to others, we form governments. In an effort to make our governments work, we constantly attempt to define our public goals—a process commonly referred to as politics. Political scientist Harold Lasswell termed this process of politics a matter of "who gets what, when, how" as a result of governmental practices, policies, and goals. In our opening example, three men took a very long trip. Thousands of other people received jobs in order to make this trip possible. Millions of people were involved in paying for the round-trip ticket.

While the details and dollar amounts vary, this same general process holds true for all of the things we ask government to do. A few examples are useful to illustrate the diversity. Government—

▶ provides for the national defense

▶ inspects elevators and chickens

▶ builds public housing

▶ fights fire and crime

▶ regulates the stock market

▶ educates us

▶ requires a health warning on cigarettes

▶ conducts foreign relations

▶ maintains public roads and sells automobile tags

▶ licenses us for driving, hunting, and fishing

▶ researches health problems

▶ and, last but not least in our brief list of examples, taxes us!

This list could no doubt be extended for several more pages. The jurisdiction and complexity of modern government are such that an enumeration of things where government is not involved would probably yield a much shorter list. Governmental complexity is one reflection of the nature of modern society.

All of the governmental activities listed above are actions in response to a specific goal that has become established in society. Much of the literature of political science deals with the various ways in which goals come into existence. Without detouring to explore this literature, it should be noted that public goals evolve in many ways; they may have varying degrees of clarity, they may even be contradictory, and they may remain in effect when we no longer need them.

Alternative Ways to Pursue Goals

While our central concern is with public managers and their efforts to achieve public goals, action in relation to goals can be achieved in other ways. One alternative would be for government to choose "no action" on a particular matter. The President, mayor, governor, Congress, city council, or other pertinent person or group could decide that a problem is temporary, unimportant, or for some reason an item not requiring action. Inaction might also be government's response because the involved persons are unable to decide, or to agree, on what to do.

Assuming agreement to take action can be reached, a range of choices is possible. This range can be depicted on the following scale, with each point representing an increase in the amount of government involvement:

Level 1— Government acts to inform private persons who then may or may not take appropriate action (example, a government pamphlet urges mothers to keep dangerous items out of baby's reach).

Level 2— Government provides financial assistance to influence private action (example, a small business loan).

Level 3— Government regulates the behavior of private organizations (example, approval of freight rates charged by trucking companies).

Level 4— Government at one level financially supports a government agency at another level (example, the U.S. Department of Housing and Urban Development provides support to state and local government housing agencies).

> Level 5— Government creates an agency to pursue a par-
> ticular goal or goals (example, the U.S. Depart-
> ment of Energy).

One central point is evident from this scale. No matter how little or how much government chooses to become involved, public managers are required at every level. Whether the action involves a small staff to work on public information announcements, or an entire new agency, public managers are required if government is to act. The more action desired, the more public managers will be required.

The Variety of Public Managers

As noted in the preceding discussion, public managers are found in every branch, level, and function of government. To add an additional element to this frame of reference, the reader should keep in mind the range of activities in which public managers are engaged. Examples of the diverse job categories of public management include the following:

- personnel administration specialists
- budget analysts
- casework supervisors
- city managers
- program or project monitors
- research administrators
- investigators
- grant makers
- hospital administrators
- police chiefs
- park and forest managers
- inspectors
- public information officers
- and, of course, tax collectors

These and other public management categories will be used as examples throughout this text. Despite the obvious diversity of the jobs of public managers, however, there are also many commonalities in their roles. These commonalities are the primary concern of this book.

NATURE OF THE PUBLIC MANAGER'S JOB

It would be convenient for both the reader and the authors were it possible to begin with a clear and simple definition of the term "public manager." Unfortunately, repeated efforts by many writers have failed to produce such a definition. Attempts to develop definitions have usually centered on efforts to define "public administration." After years of such efforts, it almost appears that we are now less able to define this term than we were at the close of the nineteenth century. The earliest writers seemed to be the most confident about their definitions.

Dimensions of Public Management

In the first recognized article on public administration, Woodrow Wilson argued in 1887 that:

> "The field of administration is a field of business. It is removed from the hurry and strife of politics; it at most points stands apart even from the debatable ground of constitutional study. It is a part of political life only as the methods of the counting-house are a part of the manufactured product."[1]

While Wilson viewed public administration as the "latest fruit of the study of politics," he called for administration to become a science. The conventional interpretation of Wilson's position is that he was asserting that politics is politics, and administration is administration—that the two are essentially separate activities. Politics tended to be equated with the making of policy while administration referred only to its implementation. Some scholars, however, have drawn different conclusions from Wilson's essay. Political scientist Herbert A. Simon, for example, argues that Wilson was making a normative claim rather than reporting an empirical observation about the way

---

[1]Woodrow Wilson, "The Study of Administration," *Political Science Quarterly* (June 1887), p. 209.

things were (are) in government. According to Simon, Wilson meant that governmental administration "ought to be" an activity removed from the strife of politics.[2] According to this interpretation, Wilson's essay should not be understood as a naive claim that administration and politics are separate; rather, it should be interpreted as one of the early reform statements on behalf of neutrality in administration aimed at improving the capacity of the executive branch to provide responsive and responsible government. Regardless of how one interprets Wilson's view of politics and administration, one thing is clear. His essay called attention to the importance of administration as a central activity of government. That is its most important legacy.

While academicians may debate Wilson's position, Frank Goodnow asserted throughout his *Politics and Administration* that administration could and should be separated from policy making and partisan political activity.[3] More recent writers have demonstrated the importance of politics in the administrative process.[4] Through interaction with clientele groups, the exercise of discretion, and the development of expertise, public managers are involved in politics and policy making that is difficult, if not impossible, to distinguish from administration.

In 1937, classic management writer Luther Gulick took quite a different approach to developing a definition of administration. He began by asking what is the work of the chief executive? What does he or she do? Gulick identified the answer as POSDCORB. This is his acronym using initials which stand for the following activities:

> *"Planning*, that is working out in broad outline the things that need to be done and the methods for doing them to accomplish the purpose set for the enterprise;
>
> *"Organizing*, that is the establishment of the formal structure of authority through which work subdivisions are arranged, defined and co-ordinated for the defined objective;

---

[2]Herbert A. Simon, "The Changing Theory and Changing Practice of Public Administration," in Ithiel de Sola Pool, ed., *Contemporary Political Science: Toward Empirical Theory* (New York: McGraw-Hill, 1967), pp. 87–88.

[3]Frank Goodnow, *Politics and Administration* (New York: MacMillan, 1900).

[4]A few examples include: Dwight Waldo, *The Administrative State* (New York: Ronald Press, 1948); Francis E. Rourke, *Bureaucracy, Politics and Public Policy*, 2nd ed. (Boston: Little, Brown, 1976); John Rehfuss, *Public Administration as a Political Process* (New York: Charles Scribner's and Sons, 1973).

"Staffing, that is the whole personnel function of bringing in and training the staff and maintaining favorable conditions of work;

"Directing, that is the continuous task of making decisions and embodying them in specific and general orders and instructions and serving as the leader of the enterprise;

"Co-ordinating, that is the all important duty of interrelating the various parts of the work;

"Reporting, that is keeping those to whom the executive is responsible informed as to what is going on, which thus includes keeping himself and his subordinates informed through records, research and inspection;

"Budgeting, with all that goes with budgeting in the form of fiscal planning, accounting, and control."[5]

In his approach, Gulick emphasized the generic nature of the executive role. He was less interested in searching for unique aspects of the "public" executive's job.

Paul Appleby, a distinguished practitioner and scholar in public administration, saw government work as emphatically unique. He considered government to be completely different from every other activity in society. He saw "so big a difference that the dissimilarity between government and all other forms of social action is greater than any dissimilarity among those other forms themselves."[6] He pointed to three related features of government. These were its breadth and impact on all citizens, its political character, and its public accountability.

In their book *Modern Public Administration,* Felix and Lloyd Nigro point to the fact that administration is "cooperative group effort in a public setting."[7] The Nigros suggest that not only are public and private organizations different, but there are great differences among various organizations within each of these categories. In general, they subscribe to Appleby's distinctions and further note that today much of government's work is accomplished by a public-private partnership. Our

[5]Luther Gulick and L. Urwick, *Papers on the Science of Administration* (New York: Institute of Public Administration, 1937), pp. 12–13.

[6]Paul Appleby, *Big Democracy* (New York: Knopf, 1945), p. 1.

[7]Felix and Lloyd Nigro, *Modern Public Administration,* 4th ed. (New York: Harper and Row, 1977), p. 18.

earlier reference to the space program is, again, a good example. While NASA did much of the research and development, actual manufacturing and other tasks were performed by numerous private corporations under government contracts. The Nigros correctly see the contemporary scene as one where the public-private dividing line is so blurred that "it is difficult to tell where government leaves off and private business begins."[8]

A Working Definition

There is no one best definition of public administration or public management. The ground covered so far suggests that public management involves such things as:

▶ working with and through other people

▶ striving to achieve public goals

▶ applying management skills and knowledge

With the above review as background information, it is necessary to enumerate the dimensions of a definition that we can use—and build upon.

This book will focus on *the public manager* rather than on public administration or public management. Its purpose is to emphasize the role and responsibilities of *individuals* working in the field of public administration. Much of the current literature tends to focus on defining public administration and on listing and dissecting its various dimensions and elements. While such a focus has merit, it is different from the perspective of this book. Many who study public administration hope to be (or already have become) public managers. Others hope to gain an understanding of public managers and their behavior. Regardless of which goal motivates the reader, this book should enable him or her to better understand the world of the practicing public manager.

Public managers are the persons who must, in the final analysis, do the work of government. Legislators enact laws, judges judge, and presidents proclaim; but until public managers swing into action, little will actually be accomplished. Whether the objective is to put someone on the moon, to

---

[8]*Id.*, p. 17.

enforce civil rights legislation, to collect taxes, or simply to pick up the garbage, public managers must perform.

The largest single public employer is the federal government. According to U.S. Civil Service Commission figures, as of June 30, 1978, there were 2.8 million civilian federal employees, representing a payroll cost of $44 billion annually. (Effective January 1, 1979, the U.S. Civil Service Commission became the U.S. Office of Personnel Management as a result of the Civil Service Reform Act of 1978.) On January 29, 1974, in its *Federal Personnel Manual Letter Number 412-2*, the U.S. Civil Service Commission defined what is meant by a "managerial position" in the federal government service. While this definition may not meet every sophisticated test that could be designed, it is both helpful and workable, and needs to be paraphrased only slightly to become equally applicable to positions in state and local governments.

Three dimensions are stressed in this definition which we have adopted for this book. Each incumbent of a managerial position must be—

1. involved in directing the work of a governmental organization

2. accountable for specific programs, functions, activities, or projects

3. involved in monitoring and evaluating progress toward organizational goals and in making appropriate adjustments based on this evaluation

As part of these three basic dimensions, the public manager must perform most of the following duties:

▶ develop goals and plans, either jointly with higher management or independently

▶ contribute significantly to determining resource needs and their allocation, and account for their effective use

▶ recommend or make important changes in the organization, such as basic structure, key positions, or operating costs

▶ consider such broad factors as legislative relations, public policy, economic impact, public relations, and labor-

management relations, when making (or recommend-
ing) decisions

▶ coordinate agency programs and efforts with the activities of other agencies

▶ assess the impact of organizational development on the
agency and its programs, on other government units,
and on the private sector

▶ establish organization policies in determining program
emphases and guidelines

▶ understand and communicate agency policies and
priorities throughout the organization

▶ deal with personnel policies and decisions affecting the
organization and key employees, or deal with matters
having possible serious repercussions

▶ delegate authority to subordinate supervisors and hold
them responsible for the performance of their units

Careful reading of these duties gives considerable added depth
to the three dimensions mentioned above, all of which will be
discussed in following chapters.

SOME UNIQUE ASPECTS OF PUBLIC MANAGEMENT

Many people would argue that "management is management is management." To a degree, our working definition
accepts that there is much validity to such a statement. Management is a "people" process and all organizations are, by
definition, conglomerations of people. The organization may
be public or private, large or small, centralized or decentralized.
Its goal may be profit, service, control, religion, or other. Whatever the distinction, the manager's concern in every instance
is to foster cooperative interactions and contributions toward
matters of organizational concern. In each case the manager
must develop "people" skills, such as communicator, analyzer,
motivator, persuader, and strategist.

Why Management in the Public Sector Is Different

Our working definition also recognizes that despite the
generic aspects of the role performed by all managers, manage-

ment in government also has its unique dimensions. The writings of political scientist Frederick Mosher are especially helpful in emphasizing these. He agrees that many jobs are similar, or even identical, in both government and business organizations. He then notes that transfers from one to the other are frequent, and that training and experience requirements may be similar. Beyond these similarities, however, Mosher emphasizes the special aspects of the public sector. Some of these he sees as differences in degree while others are more basic differences of kind.[9]

As the first point of departure from the private sector, the sovereignty of government should be emphasized. Government represents the highest power in a particular society or jurisdiction; it derives its authority from "the law of the land." Government managers are expected to swear or affirm a special kind of loyalty to their employer and to the authority that the employer represents.

A second distinct feature of employment as a public manager is the concept of political neutrality. Some top management positions in government jurisdictions are political appointments. Appointees are usually active participants in the politics of the mayor's office, of the governor's office, or of the president's office. However, a much larger number of managers hold nonpolitical, or career, appointments. These managers, who are the major concern of this book, are generally expected to refrain from active political involvement. Since the late 1930s such activity has been prohibited by the federal Hatch Act and similar legislation on the state and local level. (There are efforts currently underway to modify such laws, see Chapter 6.) The public manager is expected to serve the people and the cause of public programs, but to avoid seeking political influence. While the complexity of modern society makes it increasingly difficult, the public manager is expected to be politically neutral while occupationally competent.

A third feature of the public manager's job is political responsiveness. This requires the manager to strive for goals established by the appropriate political bodies. Carried to an

[9]Frederick C. Mosher, "Features and Problems of the Federal Civil Service," in Wallace S. Sayre, ed., The Federal Government Service, 2nd ed. (Englewood Cliffs, N.J.: Prentice-Hall, 1965), pp. 163–172.

extreme, this concept would suggest a distinction between policy making and policy implementation which simply does not exist. We expect to find policies and goals set by legislative bodies, chief executives, and the judiciary, while managers strictly implement them. There obviously is no such distinction. Managers recommend to and otherwise interact with legislative, executive, and judicial bodies as they reach their decisions. Managers also set policy and establish goals as an integral part of the implementation process. Despite the haziness of jurisdictional distinctions, the public manager must respond to the basic political goals and directions set by his elected superiors. Consequently, political responsiveness is a prerequisite for the successful public manager.

A fourth feature of public service suggests that it should be representative of the total population. Representativeness requires an equitable distribution of employment throughout society, and equal representation with regard to policy-oriented phases of the management process. Ideally, all levels of an agency would contain a mixture of race, color, creed, and national origin proportionate to the population of the geographic area it serves. Bureaucracies may be said to be representative in yet another way—to the extent that their policy decisions conform to what is believed to be prevailing public opinion. As important as demographic representativeness in selection and promotion of personnel may be from a human rights perspective, it is not certain that agencies representative in this sense of the larger society will be more representative of public opinion in their policy decisions—nor should it be inferred that they will be less representative.

Government has been dubbed by some as a goldfish bowl. While this is not exactly true, the nature and degree of public scrutiny, or the possibility of it, is an endemic part of public management. Mosher suggests that public employment may be as much related to social purposes, and in some cases more so, as it is to getting the job done in the most efficient way. Government programs to reduce unemployment, rehabilitate the handicapped or disabled, and even veterans' preference in employment are examples. In addition, government has some degree of responsibility to lead the way as a "model employer" setting an example for other employers. The use of merit systems, emphasis on equal employment and treatment, minimum wages, and retirement systems are relevant examples.

When a team of private executives worked with New York City's welfare administration to help reform the system a few years ago, they characterized the work environment as almost a "foreign culture." These businessmen observed that government differs from the private sector in structure, motivation, definition of personal achievement, and modes of conducting the organization's affairs. They concluded that managing in the public environment calls for "tremendous versatility."[10]

Some would argue that these features which distinguish public management are becoming more important with the passage of time. Others would oppose such a view and perceive all large organizations becoming more and more alike. Regardless of the position one takes, the precise meaning and importance of these features change over time. Despite this, however, each feature exists and demands our awareness.

SELECTED ROLES OF THE PUBLIC MANAGER

The focus of this book is on the various roles of the public manager. Chapters 4 through 9 describe how public managers carry out tasks and responsibilities in the various roles they must assume. The following is a brief synopsis of these roles:

Policy Maker. As society's delegate the public manager interacts with the larger political environment to influence policy and to integrate environmental matters into the public organization.

Planner and Organizer. The public manager must set objectives, plan strategy, and make decisions to guide the organization toward desired results. Plans are then implemented within an organization whose activities are coordinated and directed toward the effective achievement of specific objectives.

Personnel Manager. A key to the public manager's success is the effectiveness of the people within the organization. The public manager operates in a systematic fashion to establish

---

[10]Arthur H. Spiegel III, "How Outsiders Overhauled A Public Agency," *Harvard Business Review* (January-February 1975), p. 116.

expectations for employee performance, to determine and improve personnel capabilities, and to influence productivity in order to achieve overall personnel effectiveness.

Labor Relations Manager. With the growing influence of labor unions in the public sector, the role of the public manager in labor relations has become a significant aspect of the work. Negotiating contracts, settling disputes between unions and agencies, maintaining employee discipline, and implementing the provisions of labor-management agreements are typical of the labor relations responsibilities in this role.

Financial Manager. In this role the public manager controls and/or influences the use of public funds. Various techniques for a rational approach to budgeting, financial analysis, and control are available, but the public manager's financial role is complicated by the politics involved in the process.

Controller and Evaluator. The role of controller involves program evaluation and control, including goal setting, and measurement and evaluation of program results. Here, again, the political dimension of the controller and evaluator roles presents a challenge to the public manager.

The Public Manager as a Professional. The nature of the public manager's jobs requires meaningful role integration and orientation. For men and women to be successful in public management, they must take a professional approach to their work. In this regard, careers in public management require adequate preparation, continuous self-development, psychological commitment, and additional personal qualities and skills.

WHY STUDY PUBLIC MANAGEMENT

There are personal and professional reasons why almost everyone should spend some time studying public management. As government increasingly pervades our society, it touches every individual. The activities of public managers influence, coerce, reward, or control almost everyone in some way. Public organizations, and the management of them, are a significant part of our life.

It is easy to criticize "big government," "red tape," or "bureaucracy" without thought of the need for public organizations. Our modern way of life simply could not exist without them. The task before us, either as citizens or as managers, is to find ways to make our public organizations more proficient—to make them responsive and responsible to our needs, and effective in their performance.

Persons who are concerned about the state of the world today, or about "the human condition," must take special interest in public organizations. If we are to make major improvements (progress, if you will), we must understand, and work through, organizations. Even when we dislike organizations, we find that we must "organize" to fight successfully for change.

Much of our knowledge about public management also applies to business, religious, and other kinds of organizations. The study of public management is especially concerned with organizations that are large. Governmental organizations are definitely not alone in this category. Large-scale business organizations—such as IBM, GM, AT&T, and others—are in many ways like public organizations. It is impossible, for example, in such structures to use profit as the focus for measuring the performance of individual managers. The process and problems of managing such organizations differ little from those of IRS, HUD, and other public agencies.

Finally, it is necessary to encourage capable people to study public management and managers, in the hope that they will aspire to be public managers. The needs and challenges of government are continuing to grow, as is the need for competent public managers. To make public organizations work—indeed, to make government and society work—nothing is more important than the quality of these managers.

SUMMARY

There is consistency in the roles played by public managers. According to the U.S. Office of Personnel Management, public managers are involved in directing the agency's work, accounting for results, and evaluating progress toward organizational goals. In this respect they are universally involved in activities such as planning, organizing, directing, coordinating, reporting, and budgeting.

However, several dimensions of the public managers' jobs are unique. Government managers are expected to affirm loyalty to their employer; they are expected to serve the public; they influence the making of public policies; and their agencies are purported to be representative of the populations they serve. Public management is constantly subject to public scrutiny.

CASE STUDIES

1. Crisis in Micropolis

In her 10 years as the City Manager of Micropolis, Betty Kelley had never been under such intense pressure as she now faced. Her suburban bedroom community seemed to be in an uproar and all five city council members were in an unpredictable mood. Things were unsettled all over, even in next-door Central City, but Betty knew that her immediate need was to "save her own skin" and to protect her reputation as a good public manager.

Betty recognized her dilemma as one that is easy to describe, but very hard to solve. Increasing prices, taxes, and inflation had driven the local citizenry to the point of a tax revolt. The cry for *relief* was growing louder and election time was getting closer. None of the current council members were interested in retiring from political life, but that prospect seemed to be more and more likely.

Betty had analyzed the situation again and again. There was no possibility of further increasing taxes or obtaining other revenue; there was also no way to avoid the increased costs of maintaining the city's current level of public services.

With increased costs a certainty and no possibility of new revenue, Betty calculated her own position to be "squarely in the middle." Local citizens were trying to survive an increasingly tight cost-benefit squeeze. Members of the city council were getting ready to fight a cost-vote squeeze. One answer for both groups might be to find a *better public manager*—to fire Betty and bring in a new face—one, for example, who could bring more *business efficiency* to running city hall.

With all of this in mind, Betty had been able to think of only one possible solution—turn over one or more of the city services to the private sector. Over the years Micropolis had become the provider of the full range of local government services, such as police and fire protection, water and sewerage, and garbage collection. Maybe the time had come to withdraw from some of these activities. Betty decides to present such a proposal to the council at its next meeting.

As her Assistant Manager, Betty needs you to prepare a detailed plan immediately. You must determine which local government activity might best be contracted to a private company, prepare the argument for such a change, and anticipate the arguments Betty will hear from whatever opposition might develop. As is so often the case in public management, Betty must have your recommendation by the close of business today. It is now 3:45 p.m. The council meeting is tonight.

2. The "Success" of I.M. McDougal

I.M. was proud of his past accomplishments and eager for the challenges that he saw ahead. Fifteen years ago, fresh out of college with a B.B.A. degree, he had opened a small fast-food restaurant. His specialty, and trademark, was ,"the good old American hamburger."

From the beginning he was a very successful businessman and within 10 years his restaurants were located in 31 different states. A total of 75 restaurants had been opened and not one had failed. I.M. was also happy that none of these were franchised locations. He had complete ownership and control over the restaurants, and each one proudly displayed both the American flag and I.M.'s personally designed hamburger pennant.

About five years ago, having become quite comfortable financially, I.M. began to develop an interest in politics. His initial interest grew out of an annoyance with government licensing, inspection, taxes, and red tape. As he became more informed about government, his involvement grew both deeper and broader. He began to attend political party meetings and to contribute to election campaigns.

This involvement continued to develop and over the last year I.M. had played a prominent role in the gubernatorial campaign. His candidate won an overwhelming victory and was now the Governor-elect. He would take office in two weeks and had just appointed I.M. to be secretary of the state's Department of Health and Human Services. I.M. was anxious to experience a period of public service. He visualized such an opportunity from a dual perspective. It would give him a chance to repay society for all the success he had enjoyed, and he knew he could improve the efficiency of this state agency.

I.M. has now approached you because of your reputation as a public management consultant to advise him about the post he will soon assume. What suggestions and recommendations can you offer?

2

The Public Environment

Key Concepts

Politics
  Pluralism
    Elitism
      Political System
        Official Actors
          Inputs
            Outputs
              Feedback
                Functions of Government
                Structure of Government
                Picket Fence Federalism
                Ideas and Values

     To understand public management one must first understand the context within which it takes place. This context is, in a word, politics. It is the arena in which decisions are made that affect the entire society, decisions that carry the force of law, decisions that can be legitimately carried out by force if necessary. Government can be viewed, depending on the perspective, as synonymous with politics or as the primary *result* of politics. Both politics and government are often discussed as though they were contemporary forms of American sin. In reality, of course, both have always been pervasive parts of all group life. By definition, the basis for every nation is its government and the most descriptive term, rather than sin, would be necessity. The governing process provides every society with mechanisms to:

▶ decide on common goals

▶ provide for the common defense

▶ promote the common welfare

In the United States, we pride ourselves on having a democratic form of politics. The Founding Fathers are seen to have developed a government based on equality and representation. While the study of American history actually reveals this to be largely a myth, it is one we like to perpetuate. The central point, however, is that every nation has its own particular political form and process. To understand public management in a given nation, we must begin by looking at the nature of the political, governmental, or public environment.[1]

THE NATURE OF AMERICAN GOVERNMENT AND POLITICS

Government and politics are favorite subjects of discussion for Americans, and few avoid them entirely. Like sports and sex, they are mainstays of conversation. In all instances, it is correct to say that people will talk about things that are important to them and to their self-interest.

As mentioned earlier, government has a monopoly in its ability to make and enforce rules that apply to everyone in the society. Force can be used if necessary, and its use is legitimate. The real key to government's survival is, of course, the acceptance of it by its citizens. The application of force could rapidly lose its legitimacy if it were to be applied too often.

Government is important to every citizen because it can, and does, provide for and take away from everyone. It offers services such as streets, mail service, national defense, parks, social security, and disease control. In return, it makes demands upon citizens such as taxes, restrictions, and controls. Sales and income taxes, driving and fishing licenses, and the penalties prescribed by government for crimes are examples of

---

[1]The reader will find a review of the U.S. Constitution to be useful companion reading with this chapter.

these. Government acts to protect, regulate, license, tax, and inspect in a variety of ways. Its objective is to provide important services for society at large. To achieve this objective requires that some rights be taken away. Citizens find it much easier to get accustomed to the services than they do to the costs.[2]

Pluralism and Elitism

In times of war or other national (or local) emergency, the primary challenge of government becomes quite clear. The citizenry can quickly rally to the common defense when there is general agreement on how it is defined. This is not to say that there are no difficulties and complexities in such cases but rather that in normal everyday government, consensus may be more difficult and complex to attain.

Governing is a process of competing, trading, bargaining, and compromising. Some hold that this process is widespread and functions through the many groups and organizations in American society. Individuals and groups are seen to be well-represented in the political process through their membership in various organizations and larger groups. This view is popular in modern political science and is labeled as pluralism.

Pluralism perceives the American political system as over-lapping economic, religious, ethnic, and geographical group-ings competing for and sharing power. The political process serves as the mechanism for dynamic interaction among these groups. Pluralism is seen to benefit minorities as well as major-ities, and decision-making activities are seen to be divided among many competing groups.

Congress, state legislatures, and other legislative bodies are composed of people who represent a variety of interests. Legislators depend on votes to get elected, and they are especially sensitive to the concerns of the groups within their constituencies.

Supporters of pluralism argue that it opens up the decision-making process to the vast majority of the electorate. Each citizen is seen supporting the interest groups that are consistent with his or her beliefs; the groups then evolve consensus views

---

[2]A.J. Wilson, "It's Easier to Give Than Take Away," *Public Management* (March 1977), pp. 2–5.

and air them in political forums comprised of other interest groups. Final decisions are seen as representing a compromise of diverse interests.

The elitism perspective divides society into two groups, the elites and the masses. Persons with power, prestige, and money are elites and everyone else is considered to be the masses. Decisions are seen to flow from the actions and interactions of society's elites. The larger population, or the masses, is seen to have little meaningful participation in governmental decision making.

A significant part of the total political science literature deals with arguments for and against pluralistic or elitist interpretations of American democracy.[3] While interesting reading, the two explanations can probably best be labeled as opposing ideologies. Both views are probably right in part, but they also represent some degree of distortion of reality.

A Systems View

Political scientist David Easton has developed a useful way to visualize how American government functions.[4] Easton's "systems" approach or model has enjoyed great popularity in political science and serves as a framework, or overview, within which more specific kinds of information can be added. Figure 2.1 is a representation of Easton's model.

While Easton's model can be depicted very simply, it is based on a number of important ideas. Some of these are included in the following:

▶ A "system" is composed of various units, or parts, and each unit plays a unique role.

▶ The different units of the system interact to produce outcomes.

▶ Actions and interactions of units are affected by information, resources, and demands that flow into the system from the surrounding environment.

---

[3]See Robert A. Dahl, *Pluralist Democracy in the United States* (Chicago: Rand McNally, 1967); Peter Bachrach, *The Theory of Democratic Elitism* (Boston: Little, Brown, 1967).

[4]David Easton, *A Framework for Political Analysis* (Englewood Cliffs, N.J.: Prentice-Hall, 1965).

Figure 2.1.   Key Elements of the Political System

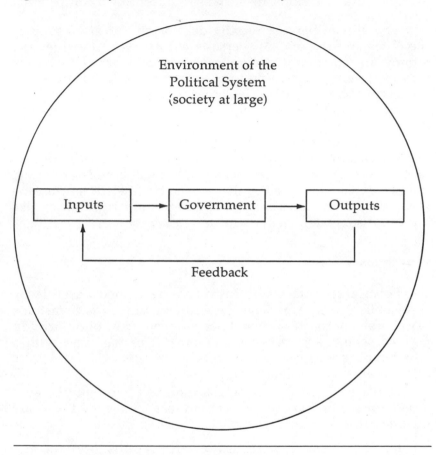

▶ System outputs filter through the environment and feed back into the system as new inputs.

By using this model as a simplification of reality one is better able to get a grasp on American government.

Public managers are central elements in this systems model. They deal with governmental inputs and produce outputs which flow back into society. Other figures in this center role as official actors are:

▶ the elected chief executive (e.g., president, governor, mayor)

- ▶ political appointees (e.g., commissioner, secretary)
- ▶ elected legislators (e.g., senators, representatives, council members)
- ▶ judges

These five sets of actors make up what we call the government.

A variety of inputs constantly flow into government. Some support the system and others demand from it. Support inputs include:

- ▶ elections and voting
- ▶ payment of taxes
- ▶ jury duty
- ▶ military service

Demands on the system also take a variety of forms, such as:

- ▶ filing a social security claim
- ▶ writing a letter of complaint to an elected official
- ▶ applying for a federal grant
- ▶ forming organizations to get government action on environmental problems

It should be remembered that demands and supports come from both individuals and organizations. Organizations can range from a "save the oak tree in front of city hall" group to a multimillion dollar interest group that is highly organized and well financed. Also of special significance on both the demand and support sides are political parties and the mass media.

A continuous flow of supports and demands shapes the thoughts and actions of government actors. Most of these actors are also aware of latent demands and supports in the society. These represent the unspoken boundaries of governmental action. For example, a taxpayer revolt begins to take hold at a certain point; aggression by a foreign nation results in citizen support for the military; or corrupt actions by a politician force his resignation.

Outputs are government's response to assorted problems in the society, which are the items we read about in the daily newspaper: inflation, housing, health and welfare, education, energy, pollution, and urban problems. These matters are constantly on the government agenda because of their common or public nature. They are acted on by government repeatedly— government rarely deals with a problem only once.

The output side of the system yields such things as:

▶ laws, rules, and regulations

▶ expenditure of government dollars

▶ policy objectives and preferences

Now that some key dimensions of the systems model have been surveyed, the illustration can be revised as shown in Figure 2.2, depicting the overall political system. (In Chapter 3, the public manager will be shown to function within a management system which is a microcosm of this political system.) The reader should note that this represents only small steps toward a full analysis of the model. For example, legislatures are usually divided into two houses and various committees; interest groups are of many types and function in varied ways; political parties have similarities and differences. The important role of the various communications media has not been developed. The model is still very much a simplification of reality.

Although simplified, the model is a useful tool in helping to locate the public manager within the governmental system. Some of the important units and forces that surround the typical public manager can be seen more clearly. The interaction of all components of the system is the political process. The public manager is at the center of this process and has a complex role. A multiplicity of interest groups, with various expectations, are anxious to influence public managers.

It is helpful to think of society as a collection of systems constantly interacting. One can, for example, identify the American public education system, business system, communications system, transportation system, religion system, and others. Each of these can be described in terms of their multiple subsystems or parts. Many examples can be used to illustrate the interactions among them. Teachers (as members of the education system), for instance, actively seek pay raises by

Figure 2.2.   The Political System

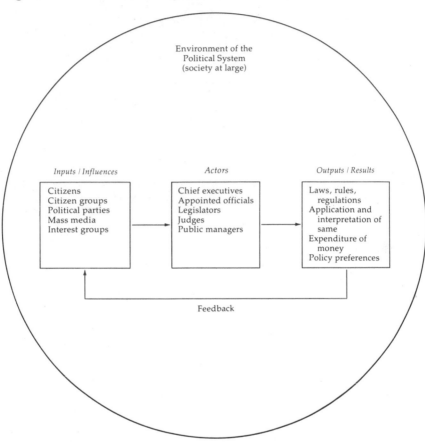

lobbying in the legislature (the political system). At a higher level, society can be viewed as an interactive organism composed of multiple systems, as shown in Figure 2.3 in simplified form.

Various people, depending upon their backgrounds and biases, assign different degrees of importance to these systems, although for the present purpose, they are considered equal in the total scheme of society. Interactions are given center stage to indicate their pervasive nature—moving in all directions at once.

Figure 2.3   Society as a Group of Systems

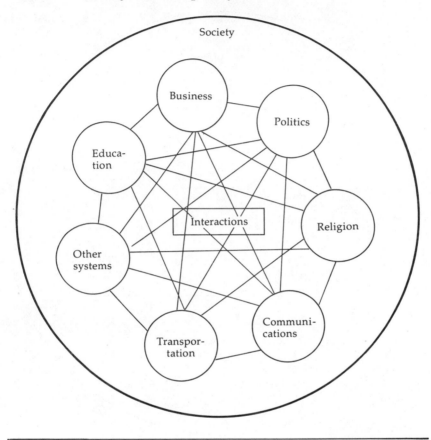

FUNCTIONS OF GOVERNMENT

One primary difficulty with the systems view is that it is too neat and organized. While useful as a device to help develop a perspective or orientation, it fails to capture the complex and fragmented nature of a system. It is a good snapshot, but does not convey the dynamic operation of the political process over time. Political activities and outcomes are as diverse as the content of our daily newspapers. Despite this, there are some specific functions being continuously performed.

Decisions, for example, are constantly made through the workings of the political system or process. Conflict is continually resolved through the activities of politics. As issues and opportunities become public, decisions are made about them. Often these decisions are made slowly, perhaps painfully, and in some instances not made at all. This too is a decision. Political and/or other forces may be unable to agree for any number of reasons. For example, knowledge limitations can severely restrict decision making on such key matters as the energy crisis, inflation, unemployment, criminal justice, health, environmental concerns, or urban problems. Individuals and groups will often disagree as to what ultimate goal is sought. How much should government do, for example, and how much should be left to private interests.[5]

In addition to providing the mechanism for society's collective decision making, government makes it possible for private persons and organizations to function. A monetary system makes commerce possible; courts and legal provisions make it possible to negotiate and enforce private contracts; public roads encourage the private production of automobiles; a social security system helps to relieve older persons of financial burdens; military protection reduces the threat of outside agression. Many things become possible by virtue of the fundamental services that government provides for the society.

In making public decisions and facilitating private ones, government acts in a variety of ways. For example, government *promotes and encourages* scientific progress, home ownership, rural electrification, minority business, international trade, and airport construction. Government also *regulates and controls* interstate commerce, nuclear energy, television, and automobile emissions. The direct market activities of government *buying and selling* is also significant—it makes huge purchases of land, vehicles, buildings, aircraft, ships, rockets and missiles, pencils, and paper clips. In addition, sales are made continually, including postage stamps, TVA electricity, water and sewage, and military equipment sold to foreign governments.[6]

---

[5]For an analysis of democracy from the perspective of an economist, see Anthony Downs, *An Economic Theory of Democracy* (New York: Harper and Row, 1957).

[6]The ideas in this paragraph are explored in Lloyd D. Musolf, *Promoting the General Welfare: Government and the Economy* (Chicago: Scott, Foresman, 1965).

Another constantly debated function of government is that of guardian of the morals of society. Some argue that cigarettes and liquor should be heavily taxed because they can be harmful. Sunday blue laws, pornography, dangerous drugs, and prostitution are other areas where the role of government is debated.

It should also be noted that building support for itself becomes an important function of every government. This reflects the self-interest of each person within the system. Politicians want to be reelected, high officials desire to be reappointed, administrators and staff hope to be promoted, and so forth. While we talk about a government of laws, first and foremost we have a government of people—and people aspire to be successful and to get ahead.[7]

THE STRUCTURE OF AMERICAN GOVERNMENT

The reader should keep in mind the fragmented nature of power in the U.S. system of government. The Founding Fathers were careful to avoid establishing a strong, central source of power. While the events of history have moved us rapidly in that direction, fragmentation is still the most distinguishing feature of the American government.[8]

Framers of the Constitution sought to establish and maintain a separation of power in governmental organization through a system of checks and balances. By separating the government into branches, they ensured that each holds the power of the others in check. The chief executive can veto bills enacted by the legislature; the legislature can override the veto, and it has the authority to review major appointments of the president; the judiciary has the right to review the constitutionality of the actions of the other branches. Any member of these branches can be removed from office by impeachment should he or she act improperly, and political pressures can be brought to bear within a branch or by another branch to force

---

[7]An interesting case study is presented in A. Lee Fritschler, *Smoking and Politics: Policymaking and the Federal Bureaucracy*, 2nd ed. (Englewood Cliffs, N.J.: Prentice-Hall, 1975).

[8]While space limitations preclude a lengthy discussion here, some readers may find it useful to review an American government text such as Kenneth Prewitt and Sidney Verba, *Principles of American Government*, 3rd ed. (New York: Harper and Row, 1980).

the recall or resignation of an elected official. The House and Senate Watergate hearings forced the resignation of President Nixon in 1974, and Senator Wayne Hays was influenced to step down in 1976 when his colleagues found evidence that Elizabeth Ray, supposedly a secretary, was being paid a government salary to perform sexual favors.

Further control over power in government has been maintained through a bicameral legislature (the federal House and Senate) where measures passed by one body must be reviewed and approved by the other. In addition, elected officials are the ultimate authority in administrative agencies; program implementation is defined by law; and Congress and the chief executive must approve proposals for new or revised programs. Similarly, the budgeting process follows legislated procedures that must be approved by officials in legislative and executive branches.

State governments have an even more complicated separation of power. Governors must work with officials who are elected or appointed by boards or commissions in making their own appointments of department heads. State legislatures are also constrained in their activities. Short sessions limit the depth and scope of the bills they can enact; and constitutions, federal legislation, and commissions restrict their borrowing and spending.

The greatest diversity of organizational and power arrangements appears at the local level. Of the estimated 80,000 local governments, the mayor-council form is the most common. The executive and legislative branches share power, department heads are appointed by the mayor, and budget requests of the various departments are acted on by the council. The commission form departs from the typical local organization because elected officials who comprise the council perform both the executive and legislative functions, and the council administers the affairs of the municipality. About 40 percent of cities of 5,000 or greater population use the council-manager form. With the increasing complexity of social and economic problems faced by cities and counties, the use of professional managers may become more prevalent.

Persons interested in a particular activity of government—such as health, transportation, or criminal justice—usually find that it is dispersed throughout the national, state, and local levels of government. Intergovernmental relations, or federalism, has become a major topic, and a considerable body of literature has developed.[9] Political scientist Deil S. Wright has provided a useful representation under the label "picket fence federalism."[10] An illustration of Professor Wright's schematic approach is provided in Figure 2.4.

The picket fence is designed to show the flow of money, program authorities, and guidelines from the national to local governments. Grover Starling has suggested that each cross slab (the governments) "holds the pickets in line [but] it does not bring them together."[11] Like the systems view, the picket fence is a device to help grasp the notion of federalism or intergovernmental relations. Again, it is a "still" view and should be thought of as a place to begin developing an under-standing—not as the definitive picture. Many of the problems of our society, for example, are found in urban areas. When we examine a metropolitan area, we will find, for example, that:

▶ The "local" social security office is operated by the fed-eral government, the employment service office by the state, and the welfare office by the county.

▶ The sewerage and water systems may be parts of local government or they may be "special districts" estab-lished apart from city and county government.

▶ The school system and the local hospital may also be "special districts", or part of either city or county government.

▶ The financial support for each of these comes from a "dukes mixture" of federal, state, and local government sources.

---

[9]Some useful works are William Anderson, *Intergovernmental Relations in Review* (Minneapolis: University of Minnesota Press, 1969); Morton Grodzins, *The American System* (Chicago: Rand McNally, 1966); Ross Clayton, Patrick Conklin, and Raymond Shapek, eds., "Policy Management Assistance—A Developing Dialogue," *Public Administration Review* (Special Issue), December 1975; James L. Sundquist, *Making Federalism Work* (Washington, D.C.: Brookings Institution, 1969); Michael D. Reagan, *The New Federalism* (New York: Oxford University Press, 1972).

[10]For further detail, see Deil S. Wright, "Intergovernmental Relations: An Analyt-ical Overview," *The Annals of the American Academy of Political and Social Science* (November 1974).

[11]Grover Starling, *Managing the Public Sector* (Homewood, Ill.: Dorsey Press, 1977), p. 54.

A useful project for the interested reader would be to attempt the development of a systems view of a particular urban area, or of a governmental activity such as welfare or agriculture. The interdependent, or fragmented, nature of governmental activities would quickly come into focus.

Figure 2.4.   Examples of "Picket Fence Federalism"—Highways and Education

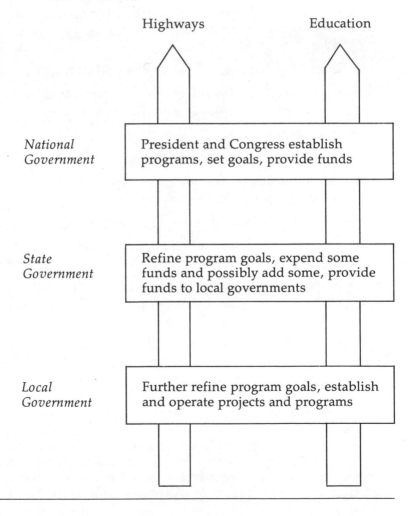

THE IMPACT OF IDEAS AND VALUES ON PUBLIC MANAGEMENT

Politics and public management are culture-bound activities. The ideas and values that pervade society set definite boundaries for the governmental process in a representative, democratic society. Such a society strives to fulfill human needs that cannot be met individually, and to do so in a collective manner that reflects the society at large. A number of contemporary phenomena have had major impacts upon the prevailing ideas and values of American society. A few of these are:

▶ a movement toward larger size, bigness, in many sectors—government, business, labor, religion, and others

▶ population changes in both size and composition

▶ increases in white collar and service-related jobs and decreases in agriculture and manufacturing

▶ consumerism

▶ environmental and energy concerns

▶ decline in authoritarianism and greater interest in consensus/group decision making

▶ organized efforts to achieve greater equality

▶ increased interest in "professionalism" in almost all occupations

▶ belief that analysis and planning can yield solutions to most problems, and that people can control their own destiny

Phenomena such as these are constantly forcing individuals and groups to reassess their value systems and beliefs. As change occurs, evolution in ideas and values is reflected in the nature of governmental systems.

In this century, a leading notion has been that public managers should not be involved in politics or policy making. This idea calls for public management to be purely an instrument or tool for routine policy execution. Like any other instrument, it is expected to be competent and efficient in its use, but neutral regarding important decisions. As pointed out earlier, this concept is not realistic in modern government. Legislative bodies, chief executives, judges, political candidates, and others commonly invite or require nonpartisan public managers to become involved in the policy process. This takes such forms as drafting new laws and regulations and serving as knowledgeable witnesses in various areas. When a public issue develops in a particular field, it is quite natural to ask the persons working in that field to become involved. Unfortunately, experts in government service, like their private counterparts, do not always agree. Even when they do, political evaluations often dictate amending their advice. Regardless of the outcome in particular cases, public managers will often find themselves involved in policy issues. This might occur at any stage in the governmental process—from problem identification to evaluation of a completed program.

Public managers also find that laws, policies, and rules developed through the political process are usually far from complete. In administering a public park or forest, for example, the public manager may well have to balance conservation and recreation interests. At a more elementary level, the traffic policeman must decide how specific he must be in enforcing the speed limit on a suburban street.

Closely related to the notion that public managers should not be policy makers is the admonition that public managers always act in the public interest. While this phrase has a nice ring, it is impossible to define it for purposes of day-to-day application. In the example above, for instance, how does one balance the conflicting goals of conservationists and recreationists in terms of the public interest? (The public manager's impact upon the political process and policy making is discussed in Chapter 4.)

SUMMARY

All citizens need to understand their government. Those who wish to become public managers will find this need to be critical. Only by first comprehending the world within which public managers function can one comprehend their activities. The public, or political, environment is complex. It is unique in every nation, and it sets the stage for the nature and character of public management.

Such ideas as the systems model and picket-fence federalism are useful ways to organize our thoughts. By understanding the central ideas and values that pervade the society at
large, public managers are better prepared to balance conflicting goals in the management of government.

CASE STUDIES

1. On the Firing Line

Jack Sanderson is fully aware that his task is going to be
difficult. After many successful years of dealing with complex
problems as a public manager, he is about to face an audience
that, in some ways, will be one of his toughest. This audience,
the Young Entrepreneurs Club, is almost totally antigovern-
ment. The members are outspoken and quite aggressive in
their view that "the only good government is no government."
Their position is essentially that citizens should be left alone
and allowed to function without governmental interference.

Jack has never taken time to think about this basic issue.
He began his public-sector career at an early age and has always
accepted government as a given part of society. His college
work was in psychology, and he is now wishing that he had
studied government.

As his new staff assistant, and one who has studied public
management, your task is to provide Jack with eight or ten
central ideas for his presentation. Jack doesn't expect to convert
the Young Entrepreneur membership, but he does hope that
they will better understand the role and importance of government at the national, state, and local levels. Perhaps some of
them can even become convinced of the need to participate in
the political process. In preparing your material for Jack, be
sure to spend some time anticipating the questions and criti-
cisms he will likely receive.

2. Getting the Real Story

The political campaign had been a hard fight for Eleanor
Lopez. Now it looked as though her electoral battles were just

a warm-up for even bigger challenges. In winning a seat on the city council, she had repeatedly promised to lower the cost of government services.

Before becoming interested in a city council post, Eleanor had not had a lot of information about governmental operations and their costs. Like many citizens, she simply felt that all taxes and related government charges and fees were too high. As the owner of a local tavern, she had the opportunity to talk to many people about her opinions and found a lot of support for her conviction that the cost of government could be lowered. During the campaign, her opponents had accused her of being simplistic and charged that she didn't understand the problems of government. Even Eleanor now had some tendency to agree with this. At her first city council meeting, she was truly surprised and shocked by what she learned about local government. Police services, fire protection, the city hospital, parks and recreation, garbage collection, and other activities were far more complex and costly than Eleanor had imagined.

In reflecting on the dilemma of what to tell the voters, Eleanor began to be aware of some of the very basic problems of democratic government.

▶ How can citizens understand and control a complex governmental system?

▶ Who are the "experts" and what is their role in a democracy?

▶ What is the meaning and significance of "majority rule"? Is it practical in reality?

▶ Can politicians be made to "deliver" on their promises?

Identify several additional fundamental questions and then try your hand at some responses.

3

The Management Environment

Key Concepts

Organizations
  Bureaucratic Model
    Organizational Structure
      Managerial Functions
        Behavioral Theories
          Organizational Development
            Systems Approach
              Management-by-Objectives
                Policy
                  Contingency Theory
                    New Public Administration

The nature of our society and the political influences that interact with government bodies create a complex and sophisticated environment. The management environment operates within a political system and continuously interacts with it. The various components comprising the management environment are discussed in this chapter to aid the reader in understanding the operation of public organizations.

To understand the operation of public organizations, we need to appreciate the uniqueness of government administration. As discussed in Chapter 1, public managers are different from those in the private sector. They are continuously subject to public scrutiny, and their actions must consider a myriad of special and general interests as well as the possibility of investigation. Persons inside or outside the organization may become disgruntled with their performance. Paul Appleby, a longtime public servant, appropriately described this uniqueness:

> "Other enterprises may ignore factors remotely related to their central purposes, but not the government of the United States; it is supported, tolerated or evicted on the basis of a balance involving the sum total of everything in the nation. No other institution is so publicly accountable. No action taken or contemplated by the government of a democracy is immune to public debate, scrutiny, or investigation. No other enterprise has such equal appeal or concern for everyone, is so equally dependent on everyone, or deals so vitally with those psychological intangibles which reflect popular economic needs and social aspirations. Other institutions admittedly, are not free from politics, but government *is* politics."[1]

ORGANIZATIONS AND THE MANAGER'S ROLE

Organizational theorists generally agree that organizations provide the vehicle for accomplishing *goals or objectives*, operate through human relationships that are divided into *roles* which contribute to the attainment of goals, and contain *hierarchies of authority* that direct, limit, and control the activities of lower-level members toward goals. The definition of the organization contains each of these elements: *Organization consists of a group of individuals with specific roles and defined authority who interact to coordinate their efforts toward the accomplishment of articulated objectives*. The need for a hierarchy of authority makes management the key to the functioning of organizations. But why are they formed in the first place?

Since the beginning of recorded history, people have formed organizations to satisfy needs that could not be satisfied independently. People engage in cooperative group efforts when the benefits promise to outweigh the costs. Today, organizations range from informal, ad hoc gatherings to formal, highly structured bureaucracies. Formal military groups have been organized to protect the populace; governmental agencies have been developed to accomplish specific tasks; and voluntary associations have attracted members for social, religious, recreational, philanthropic, or a variety of other reasons.

---

[1]Paul Appleby, *Big Democracy* (New York: Knopf, 1945), p. 7.

Organizations cannot act by themselves; they require management by people in positions of authority within them. Managers are needed to coordinate and integrate human, financial, and physical resources for the accomplishment of objectives.

When Roy Ash served with the Office of Management and Budget, he observed that in any organization, management is a rare and prized commodity. He lamented that a lack of managerial talent coupled with the complicated nature of governmental organizations had led critics to argue that our government may have become ungovernable.[2] John Miner's research on the "motivation to manage" concluded that there has been a general decline in this motive among younger managers and students which will eventually lead to a critical shortage. But even more alarming is his finding that "The government managers typically have less overall motivation to manage than business managers . . . ."[3]

As this condition becomes acute, the opportunity for the aspiring (and managerially motivated) manager to rise in government service will greatly increase. This phenomenon admonishes any upwardly mobile public manager to develop to the limit of his or her potential. Enlightened agencies are expanding development opportunities through such programs as Certified Public Manager, educational leave, management development seminars, and numerous other activities. (Specific recommendations for manager development are given in Chapter 10.)

Let us examine the nature of organizations in general, and more specifically, the elements that comprise public organizations. Perhaps this discussion will enlighten managers on the organizational aspects of their jobs and will inspire others to seek public management responsibility.

NATURE OF ORGANIZATIONS

Organizations can be viewed in terms of the results they achieve, and can be deemed effective if they achieve their

---

[2]Roy L. Ash, "Good Management—A Prized Commodity," *Civil Service Journal* (October–December 1973), p. 1.

[3]John B. Miner, *The Human Constraint* (Washington, D.C.: The Bureau of National Affairs, Inc., 1974), p. 65.

intended results. But effectiveness is diminished unless it is attained efficiently; at a low, or at least a reasonable cost. If the United States wants to land a scientific exploration team on Mars, an organization will be needed to accomplish the task. Any number of organizations could carry out the mission at different costs in money, time, manpower, and materials, but only a limited number could carry it out efficiently. We can conclude from this that different types of organizations are appropriate for different tasks.

The nature of organizations can be viewed as a continuum. At one extreme there are organizations that perform routine or programmed tasks such as statistical recording or monitoring where efficiency is a primary concern. These types tend to focus on the task and, hence are inclined to be "mechanistic" or "closed." At the opposite extreme are "open" or "socio-technical" organizations, in which creativity and flexibility are emphasized because of the varied and non-routine nature of the work. Organizations that deliver services, e.g., health care, to the public exemplify this type of organization. In the middle are organizations that have attributes of both the predictable/routine and the creative/flexible, or that fluctuate between these two extremes. They lean toward closed or open organizations depending upon various factors, such as the work being performed at the time, the philosophy of the ranking managers, and the nature of the people in the organization. Personnel staff organizations which maintain employment records as well as deliver services—training, testing, collective bargaining— might be an example of this middle category.

The nature of organizations also can be classified depending on their fundamental orientation. Gulick and Urwick in their classic *Papers on the Science of Administration*[4] identified four categories of organization: (1) Organizations oriented toward accomplishing a specific purpose, such as a sanitation department that maintains a city's or county's cleanliness. (2) Process organizations which perform certain tasks. A city law department, for instance, has a group of lawyers who serve other departments (one might represent the city's urban

---

[4]Luther Gulick and Lyndal Urwick, *Papers on the Science of Administration* (New York: Institute of Public Administration, 1937), p. 15.

renewal—another defend the city's public works department).
(3) Organizations classified as *place* because they service a specific geographic area. The regional bureaus in the U.S. Department of State are good examples of this type. Five Assistant
Secretaries are responsible for foreign affairs activities in major
regions of the world. (4) Finally, there are clientele-oriented
organizations designed to serve a particular group of people.
The Bureau of Indian Affairs that handles needs of American
Indians throughout the nation is typical of this type of
organization.

    Public organizations can be classified by a variety of
schemes as indicated in this discussion. However, the one
characteristic they all have in common is their bureaucratic
nature. Federal, state, and municipal agencies, by and large,
follow the bureaucratic model originally espoused by Max
Weber. Because of its widespread adoption in public management, it is perhaps the core of the conceptual framework of the
management environment. The Weber model is summarized
in the following section.

Bureaucratic Organizations: The Weber Model[5]

    Max Weber was raised in an affluent and politically influ-
ential German family. As professor, editor, author, and consultant to government, he exemplified the leading scholar at
the turn of the century. Through his writings he sought to
influence the adoption of a rational basis for the management
of large-scale enterprises and he conceived his bureaucratic
model as the ideal approach.[6] Weber attacked the traditional
use of political control and favoritism in emerging capitalistic
economies, particularly in Germany. He felt that bureaucracy
would emphasize rules and competence and would lead to a
high degree of efficiency and reliability in management.
Although Weber's writings on bureacracy did not emerge in

---

    [5]For a complete description of the bureaucratic model, see *From Max Weber: Essays
in Sociology*, H.H. Gerth and C. Wright Mills, eds. and trans. (Fair Lawn, N.J.: Oxford
University Press, 1946).

    [6]In the "ideal type," organizational characteristics are a matter of definition rather
than a matter of incipient fact. Organizations observed in the real world may only
approximate the bureaucratic model.

America until the late 1940s, they are credited with having a profound impact on organization theory.

The Weberian model of the ideal bureaucracy contains the following elements:

▶ Fixed, clearly defined, and divided jurisdictional duties that are given sanction by laws or administrative regulations.

▶ A system of graded authority organized in a hierarchy in which the lower offices are supervised by the higher.

▶ Authority clearly defined and limited to the functions necessary to carry out the organization's task. (Weber claimed that this form of "rational-legal" authority was the basis for a bureaucracy.)

▶ Members of the organization—except elected officials— selected and appointed on the basis of their technical qualifications verified by formal examination, and/or by certification of expert training and education.

▶ Materials and written documents comprise the files for the operation of the bureau or office.

▶ Managers (administrative officials) work for fixed salaries on a career basis. They are subject to strict rules of conduct and controls that are consistently and uniformly applied.

To Weber, management meant the exercise of control on the basis of knowledge. Qualified by their technical competence, managers lead their organizations by rationality rather than by whim, by ability rather than by favoritism. Rationalism in modern management expresses itself in constant self-appraisal. How often have you heard managers ask "How does this promote our mission?" The growing influence of scientific and technical professionals in organizational decisions also contributes to this spirit of rationalism.

The hierarchical nature of bureaucracies creates a factoring of goals into subgoals and specialization (even routinization) of organizational activity. Operationally, the bureaucratic model gives the appearance of plodding inefficiency because an activity has to go through many procedural steps before it is finalized. It may also appear impersonal because of the formal specialization of functions. Perhaps the latter points up an inherent deficiency in the "ideal" blueprint, and even Weber recognizes that it is impractical to expect any organization to reach that ideal. Dysfunctional consequences, the behaviorists point out, become evident when the idiosyncracies of people come into play. It follows logically that organizations do not operate like well-oiled machines. Consequently, public managers would be well-advised to assign a high priority to the human factor in the organization.

The bureaucratic model applies to both private and public organizations. One unique feature of public management, as previously pointed out, is that its environment operates within a political environment. A few comments about this relationship might be appropriate.

MANAGEMENT—POLITICAL ENVIRONMENT RELATIONSHIPS

In Chapter 2 it was noted that public managers play a political role and affect public policy through their participation in the formulation as well as implementation of programs. In public organizations there is a dependence upon other organizations (agencies, legislative and executive bodies, citizen groups, and so on) for goal definition, resource allocation, jurisdiction, and exertion of influence.

Political disagreements often center in these areas. For example, public dismay over the alleged mismanagement of the health and welfare agency of one state led to its reorganization and the dissolution of several of its units. Thus, the degree to which politics are a positive or negative influence depends on how well managers establish linkages with other organizations. By acting the role of "boundary agent" the public manager attempts to reconcile the political and management environments to reduce the threats of uncertainty posed by dependence on other organizations.

Politics also exist within organizations as evidenced by struggles for personal survival, power and prestige. Hence, the public manager's success often depends on his or her skill at real politics—the ability to determine who gets what, when and how. The internal political system consists of groups and individuals who compete for power to decide policy and gain favors. As shown in the Weber Model, bureaucracy is designed to deal with politics through a clear division of labor, a hierarchy of authority, clearly defined rules, and impersonal and rational modes of behavior. Bureaucracy, by promoting opportunities for its people to advance and by minimizing unfairness and favoritism, decreases what Stephen Robbins, a writer on administration, characterizes as "dysfunctional politics."[7] The values and beliefs of top managers determine what behavior will be rewarded by the organization. Watergate is one example of what can occur when higher level managers abuse the system and influence others to conspire with them in dysfunctional political activities. Bureaucracies are not immune from such behavior, but the organizational environment makes it more visible and consequently more difficult.

There are no hard-and-fast rules for gaining power and influence within one's organization; but successful public managers recognize early in their careers that sensitivity to the internal and external political environments is crucial to their effectiveness. This is especially true in local government. At this level public managers are closest to their constituencies and more responsive to the pressures within the political environment. In addition to politics, a variety of other elements comprise the management environment. Each of these elements is discussed in detail in the following section.

COMPONENTS OF THE MANAGEMENT ENVIRONMENT

Figure 3.1 depicts the management environment and its various components. We see the management environment functioning in a political setting. The management environment itself consists of the organizational structure, functions performed by managers, people, management systems, physical factors, and policy. At the focal point is the public manager who is responsible for goal achievement with and through the various components of the environment.

Organizational Structure

Classical management theory contends that organizational objectives can be accomplished through the efficient structur-

---

[7]Stephen P. Robbins, *The Administrative Process: Integrating Theory and Practice* (Englewood Cliffs, N.J.: Prentice-Hall, 1976), p. 31.

Figure 3.1.   The Management Environment

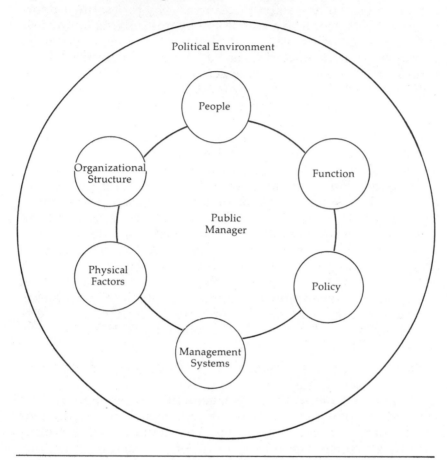

ing of tasks. Organizations are viewed as products of rational thought that perform coordinated tasks and that are governed by a hierarchy of authority.

In his classic text, *The Functions of the Executive*, Chester Barnard[8] presented a model of the formal organization. The model stressed that people were key to the functioning of organizations. Their cooperation in achieving the organiza-

---

[8]Chester I. Barnard, *The Functions of the Executive* (Cambridge, Mass., Harvard University Press, 1938), pp. 70ff.

tion's objectives was gained through communicating what performance was expected of them and what satisfactions would be gained from their accomplishments. Barnard's model emphasized that executives, or managers, were key to the successful implementation of the model.

The classical school also defined other principles related to organizational structure. In a hierarchy of graded authority, individuals normally report to one superior for any given assignment (unity of command); the work to be performed is clearly defined and divided jurisdictionally; managers must be given authority commensurate with responsibility to accomplish their assigned duties (parity); and they must be made accountable for the results. With the enactment of the Civil Service Reform Act in 1978, all levels of government rededicated themselves to making managers accountable for *results*. From this stemmed the need for reliable performance data to judge managers' efficiency and effectiveness in utilizing people and other resources to accomplish designated goals. Consequently, agencies have been developing quantitative data from work measurement, productivity, and cost systems in order to gauge performance against established goals and provide a basis for evaluating the effectiveness of public managers. Some of the specific methods for implementing this include:

▶ *Cost/benefit analysis* to measure efficiency—the emphasis being on more and better output per dollar invested.

▶ *Unit cost information* to appraise resource utilization, compare operations, and analyze personnel requirements. Agencies' accounting systems often record obligations and disbursements for appropriations, programs, functional activities, and organizational segments by object class (e.g., salaries, travel, equipment).

▶ The *budget process* to facilitate accountability by enabling a comparison of expected performance with actual performance.

▶ *Performance standards* to serve as expectations for managers' performance. For instance, managers can be required to state that their units will produce a certain number of units of output for a given dollar level.

▶ *Appraisal and review* to incorporate all the above methods. By consulting descriptions of the manager's duties, the manager and his or her supervisor can identify key result areas of the job and set goals for definite accomplishments within each area. Chapter 6 covers the performance appraisal in more detail. For this discussion, suffice it to say that the performance appraisal is an essential tool for managerial accountability.

In practice, public agencies exhibit many of the structural attributes of classical management paradigms. However, certain unique conditions, such as political involvement, size, and constitutionality present a real challenge to their managers. The following discussion of the structure of public organizations demonstrates some of the problems in translating theory into practice. It should give public managers a greater appreciation for the management environment and make them more keenly aware of the principles associated with structuring organizations.

Political Involvement

In public agencies at all levels of government, elected officials and career managers must function together in the same organization. The elected officials often act in a manner that conflicts with the managers' operational effectiveness because these officials have political obligations. They must satisfy or appease their constituents if they desire to be reelected. In a similar vein, legislative committees and the chief executive might send conflicting directives to a manager which can easily create a conflict of loyalty. Such multiple loyalties within an agency can upset the manager's control over the agency and inhibit control by either the chief executive or by the legislature.

Size

As government agencies expand, their management becomes increasingly difficult. Critics of government's size cite program proliferation, overregulation, and burdensome reporting requirements. The federally funded social programs have demanded astronomical growth of state and local payrolls and employees. In 1980 there were 16.2 million people working in government compared to only 3 million in 1930. Payroll dollars soared from a total of less than $1 billion in 1940 to more than $16.5 billion in 1975. Equally dramatic is the growth in total government expenditures ($680 billion in 1977) from 12 percent of the gross national product in 1929 to 38 percent in 1977. Figure 3.2 illustrates the growth of government employment as a percentage of total U.S. employment.

Governor of New York State William Carey points out that there are over 80,000 units of state and local government. He warns: "This tangle must be thinned out and rationalized. The welter of states, counties, cities, municipalities, townships, special districts, and miscellaneous clutter serves only to produce a web of redundancy."[9]

Perhaps some of the hodgepodge and confusion stems from the very nature of governmental organization. Within the labyrinth of bureaus and agencies, some exist by design, some by mistake, and still others by evolution. To capsulize the structure as it was originally intended, this discussion will cover the components shown in Figure 3.1.

Functions

According to classical management theory, all managers perform common managerial functions in carrying out their roles. They *plan* by developing forecasts, by establishing objectives and policies for the organization, and by detailing plans of action that will achieve their objectives. Then they *organize* to determine the functions necessary to operate the organization, divide labor into specific tasks, combine the functions into departments or units, and delegate the necessary authority.

Managers also *direct* the efforts of other people and coordinate their activities so that they contribute optimally to the organization's objectives. Directing involves staffing the organization with competent people, evaluating the performance of individuals, establishing systems conducive to employee motivation and recognition, and communicating information

---

[9]William D. Carey, "New Perspectives on Governance," in The Conference Board, *Challenge to Leadership: Managing in a Changing World* (New York: Free Press, 1973), p. 85.

Figure 3.2.   Government Jobs As Percentages of Nonagricultural Jobs, 1920-80

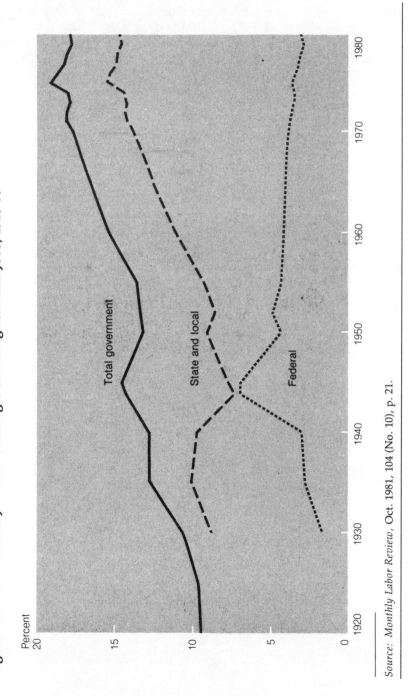

Percent

Source: Monthly Labor Review, Oct. 1981, 104 (No. 10), p. 21.

up, down, and across the organization. Finally, to verify that the process functions as planned, managers *control.*

Schools of management and special management development programs teach people how to perform these functions so that they can be more effective managers. Since the basic principles, concepts, and techniques of managing have some general applicability to management situations and can be learned in a classroom, public managers can take the initiative to become educated in management. Schooling alone, however, does not make a manager; there is no substitute for broad-based, in-depth experience. Only by performing these functions does the practitioner develop managerial capabilities.

People

It takes people to run organizations. One of the keys to public managers' effectiveness is their ability to get people in the organization to support its mission willingly and enthusiastically.

Considerable insight into the ways people behave in organizations has resulted from the studies of behavioral scientists. Research in human behavior in organizations was stimulated by the Hawthorne experiments of 1927-32 undertaken by a team of Harvard social scientists. They found that social and psychological influences in the work environment had a significant influence on performance. Since that time sociologists have studied group dynamics, cooperation, and conflict in organization. Psychologists have developed theories of motivation, leadership, and human behavior patterns.

The body of literature that emerged from these studies formed the behavioral school of management thought.

According to behavioral theory, behavior is influenced by an individual's needs, wants, and desires, and people form associations (informal organizations) with others who have mutually supportive or common needs and interests. In directing the work force, then, the public manager can influence the behavior of employees by exercising leadership and by providing an environment that stimulates desired performance. One manifestation of behavioral theory that many public managers have found useful is *Organization Development (OD).*

The OD approach attempts to bring about organizational change and effectiveness by involving people in problem solving and planning. OD depends on the support of employees who understand how the manager wants to effect change. It is a continuous and overall effort that increases organizational effectiveness by integrating individual desires for growth with organizational goals. Managers systematically plan and implement change by sharing power. Specifically, OD locates problem-solving responsibilities as close to the grass roots as possible, builds trust and creates harmony through collaboration, encourages employees' self-direction and self-regulation, and introduces a system to reward the attainment of individual and organizational goals.[10]

Formal processes are implemented in OD to create social conditions that encourage employee contribution to organizational objectives. Such methods include:

▶ team building activities, such as intra-agency problem-solving meetings

▶ intergroup sessions to discuss changes or to work out common concerns

▶ action research involving data gathering

▶ corrective action and feedback

▶ training programs, such as laboratory (sensitivity) training

▶ development of specific skills such as decision making or development of positive attitudes

▶ feedback on survey responses

▶ activities among groups for problem resolution or training

Several years ago, the city of Dallas, Texas implemented an OD system. Initially, it conducted a dialogue between management and employees to gain both commitment to and involvement in the program. The city used a written instrument to measure participants' perceptions of how their departments looked the previous year, its present state, and a realistic assess-

---

[10]For a detailed discussion of the application of OD in government agencies, see Robert T. Golembiewski and William B. Eddy, eds., *Organizational Development in Public Administration* series (New York: Marcel Dekker, 1978).

ment of future expectations. Next, it involved management and supervisory personnel in an intensive four-day seminar on personal and organizational development which focused on team building and behavioral skills. Then questionnaires and interviews were used to collect data about the organization. The information gained from this process formed the basis of a report to management covering problem areas and their causes and making recommendations for change. Finally, OD teams of employee representatives from major job classifications and selected first-line supervisors developed an action plan which identified problem areas and recommended cost-effective strategies to improve operations. Key to the process was the involvement of the organization's human resources.[11]

Systems

The systems concept or approach views the organization as a network of components that work in a coordinated manner toward goal achievement. The essence of this approach is operations research that utilizes mathematical models to quantify organizational problems and facilitate planning and control functions. Computers enable managers to use systems models to simulate real-world conditions and to manipulate extraordinary amounts of data in order to arrive at more objective decisions. The systems approach also is viable for addressing behavioral, social, and political problems in the management environment.

As an illustration of the systems approach we might envision the management environment system. Essentially, it is a microcosm of the political system discussed in Chapter 2. The management environment works as a system in the following manner:

Inputs to the management system include the resources— human (people), financial, and physical—and the information and regulations that influence the public manager in working toward the achievement of the organization's goals. The manager then interacts with other actors within the environment. For example, an elected or appointed official may serve as

---

[11]John W. Cutsinger, "Organizational Development in Dallas," *Public Management* (April 1974), pp. 3-4.

liaison with the political environment and often influences the manner in which the public manager functions. In addition, the public manager's functions involve the direction of people over whom he or she has authority, as well as communication and coordination with peer managers and higher-level officials within the organization.

The public manager also interacts with the management environment at large to achieve system results. One example of the public manager interacting with the environment is the process of cooptation. In cooptation new elements are absorbed into the leadership or policy-determining structure of an organization as a means of averting threats to its stability or existence. At the Tennessee Valley Authority, through its grass roots policy, local agricultural interests were able to influence major changes in overall policies on public land management and conservation, as well as participate in specific activities, such as fertilizer distribution. TVA shared with agricultural interests the exercise of authority over a segment of its operation.[12]

Outputs are the programs produced by the system in response to demands. Citizens continue to demand more and more from the government in protection, housing, health care, education, economic growth, public works, stability, technology, and an ever-widening array of services. And the system responds, with the result that costs soar and government continues to grow. The options seem to be, consequently, to cut services or to increase taxes, but in a national policy statement issued in 1976 by the Committee for Economic Development, a third option was suggested: "that more intelligent use be made of existing resources to achieve desired goals; that is, increase government productivity."[13]

However, many services provided by the government defy objective measurement, and the outcome of many programs is not completely predictable. The Medicare program is a classic

[12]Philip Selznick, "TVA and the Grass Roots: Guiding Principles and Interpretation," in Albert H. Rubenstein and Chadwick J. Haberstroh, eds., *Some Theories of Organization* (Homewood, Ill.: Richard D. Irwin, 1966), pp. 110ff.

[13]Committee for Economic Development, *Improving Productivity in State and Local Government* (Summary of a Statement on National Policy by the Research and Policy Committee of the Committee for Economic Development). (New York: Committee for Economic Development, March, 1976), p. 11.

example. According to figures published by the Social Security Administration, May 1981, Medicare covers about 26.7 million people at a cost exceeding $29 billion. The duration of incapacitation of elderly Americans covered by Medicare has been reduced from an average of eight days a year to five days a year. But the program resulted in the federal government becoming the leading purchaser of health care. Doctors responded by raising their fees, causing a significant jump in the cost of medical care. The unanticipated consequence has been the imposition of controls on the ways doctors practice medicine. The Federal requirement for peer review of physicians in federally assisted hospitals, for example, threatened to close down almost one third of the hospitals in the state of Oklahoma because there were not enough doctors to make up the review boards.

Feedback provides the system with a dynamic environment for the public manager. Programs and services produced by the organization have an impact on individuals and groups inside and outside of the organization. Through various means, e.g., public opinion or scientific measures, the outputs are recorded, measured, and evaluated. The results elicit citizen response in the form of praise, protest, and so forth, which place further demands on the system. This response becomes the influence and information that cause change in priorities and goals and eventually affects the operation of the organization. Feedback introduces dynamism to the system—constant and changing demands maintain a state of flux. Thus, the system components of public demands, of management, and of programs interact to affect an original purpose. Similarly, the outputs (programs) of the system are a reflection of the inputs (resources). Evaluation of the results (outputs) forms a basis for appraising the performance of the inputs—this is especially true for appraising people's performance.

Applications of the systems approach. Concern for better government has resulted in a number of systems applications pertinent to public organizations. Productivity programs are making major inroads at all levels of government. Basically these programs serve to identify and analyze problems and to monitor progress toward performance improvement. Systems applications are used to measure efficiency, e.g., calculating ratio of work accomplished to inputs; introducing engineered

work standards; and utilizing effectiveness–measurement procedures through citizen or client ratings of various service characteristics, or through use of predeveloped rating scales.[14]

There are a variety of productivity programs in effect. For
example, the City of Detroit has a Productivity Center that
implements a continuing productivity effort through an expert
staff; Phoenix performs program analyses and reviews through
a Planning-Programming-Budgeting System; and Tacoma,
Washington's program for productivity improvement involves
extensive use of OD.[15] In state government, Washington
involves citizen task groups in planning future programs, all of
which involve productivity programs; and Wisconsin has
decentralized its productivity efforts in order to actively involve
and stimulate each manager throughout the state. In the federal
government, through the National Center for Productivity and
Quality of Working Life, there is a systematic review of all
federal activities that affect the performance of the economy as
well as a national productivity policy.[16]

Policy

The impact of public policy on organizations and the ways
that public managers influence public policy was discussed
earlier in this chapter and in Chapter 2. Similarly, organizational policies guide the operation of the organization. They
emanate from organizational objectives and implement the
intent of the formulators, e.g., the managers. Policy making is
an integral part of the planning function of management, and
policy, both public and organizational, has a significant bearing on the management environment.

Physical Factors

This component of the management environment refers to
every physical condition within the organization. Technology

---

[14]Harry P. Hatry, "The Status of Productivity Measurement in the Public Sector,"
Public Administration Review (January–February 1978), p. 29.

[15]Frederick O'R. Hayes, "City and County Productivity Programs," *Public Administration Review* (January–February 1978), pp. 15ff.

[16]Walter L. Balk, ed., "Symposium on Productivity in Government," *Public
Administration Review* (January–February 1977), pp. 5ff.

plays a significant role in public management. Computers help managers retrieve information and manipulate data useful to decision making. Sophisticated equipment improves managerial and organizational performance. For example, video programs permit communications and training on a decentralized basis, and artifical organs help sustain patient life in health-care agencies. In recent years, environmental aspects of work locations have gained attention. Safe, healthy surroundings enhance performance; and comfortable temperatures, pleasing visual effects, and absence of distracting noises contribute to employee efficiency. Behavioral scientists have studied the effect of the physical grouping of people on productivity, and operations researchers have developed work-flow systems to enhance efficiency. Physical factors also include the materials and supplies available within the organization. Papers, pencils, forms, manuals, and files are essential to the operations of the bureaucracy. Information is recorded, communiques generated, and information filed to maintain a smoothly running organization. Even though government may be criticized for creating a paperwork jungle, agencies would cease to operate without some measure of it.

Integration of the Components: Contingency Theory

Public managers must consider myriad implications within a constantly changing environment. Each component of the environment interacts with others, and the entire environment in turn interacts with the political environment. Not only is each component variable, but there is a multitude of possible interactions among them. How then should public managers view the management environment?

Contingency management means that the style of management or the design of the organization depends upon variables and their interactions in the situation. The approach to leadership, motivation, or decision making would vary in different situations. Essentially, contingency theory stipulates that there is no single best way to manage—the environment or situation must be analyzed to determine an appropriate course of action.

Perhaps contingency management will be the integrating theory for the classical, behavioral, and systems approaches. It is a rational systemwide way of thinking; yet it includes behavioral, economic, and technological variables. The contingency approach makes sense for public managers who must operate in a dynamic environment.

SUMMARY

The managerial environment is lodged within a political system and contains components of functions, organizational structure, people, management systems, policy, and physical factors.

The term organization refers to two or more people engaged in a cooperative effort to satisfy collective needs or goals. Various theories have been espoused to explain how organizations function, but in public management Weber's bureaucratic model has had the most profound impact. He claimed that the ideal bureaucracy was based on clearly defined duties sanctioned by law and that they contained a hierarachy of authority in which people were appointed on the basis of qualifications and were assigned clearly defined roles.

This chapter explored various approaches to management. According to classical theory, all managers perform the common functions of planning, organizing, directing, and controlling. The behavioral approach focuses on informal organizations of people who associate to be mutually supportive of their needs and interests. The systems concept views the organization as encompassing components that are coordinated toward the achievement of a goal. Finally, contingency approach theorizes that the style or design of an organization varies with the situation.

CASE STUDIES

1. Whose Best Interest?

In late 1976 the Department of the Army was considering a request by the Chicago Bridge and Iron Company (CBI) for a public-work permit to dredge and dock on the Colleton River at Victoria Bluff near Hilton Head Island, South Carolina—a resort center. Public sentiment had become polarized to the extent that Assistant Secretary of the Army Victor Veysey visited the Island to hear both sides before making his recommendations regarding the permit.

Opponents, who were primarily residents of the Island, environmentalists, and resort developers, agreed that CBI would be a foot in the door for additional industrialization which is not compatible with resort living; construction operations would likely damage the aquifer, the primary source of fresh water for island residents; the additional tax revenues would not sufficiently offset potential loss of resort jobs that could result from industrialization of the area.

Proponents were county and city elected officials and representatives of minority groups. They felt that the CBI project would be in the public interest because it would provide skilled employment for local residents who traditionally worked in unskilled occupations for low pay. In addition, they maintained that aquifer damage was improbable as determined by engineering studies. The low-income segment of the county's population would benefit from the increased tax revenues and the potential source of employment.

▶ What are the various considerations that are relevant to this situation?

▶ What criteria should the Department of the Army use in making its determination?

▶ If you were Mr. Veysey, how would you recommend? Why?

2. The New Office Manager

When George Teasel retired as manager of the Social Security Administration's (SSA) district office in Metropolis, Loretta Compton was appointed as his replacement. Loretta had been the assistant manager in the Chicago office, so her appointment from outside the local office created quite a stir.

Mr. Teasel had been the Metropolis District Manager for the past ten years and he had worked his way up from field representative. He was a popular manager and most of his staff had been with him the entire time he was manager. The policy at SSA had traditionally been to promote from within, but a year ago it changed to one of selecting managers on a nation-wide basis. As might be expected, Metropolis staff was reluctant to accept the new policy; they were a tightly knit group with long service in SSA and most of them were middle-aged. John Stoner, the assistant manager, was particularly upset because he felt that he had been developed for the manager's position by George Teasel and that he was more deserving of the appointment.

SSA commissioned Loretta Compton to improve the productivity of the office. There was a substantial backlog of disability and health insurance claims which took sixty to seventy days to process (the national standard was thirty days), the error rate on claims forms processed by this office and detected by the payment center was the highest in the region, and complaints from clients were well above the norm.

Soon after she assumed her position as manager Loretta Compton met with her staff (clerical people, field and claims representatives, unit supervisors, and department managers) to brief them on the need to improve production and to solicit their cooperation. Everyone seemed to be in agreement with Ms. Compton's plans, which included performance improvement training program, rearrangement of the work flow on claims processing, and the institution of management by objectives.

Despite these efforts performance did not improve. Supervisors seemed to irritate employees in the way they initiated changes, absenteeism began to increase and the claims backlog got worse, not better. Loretta found herself working longer hours in an effort to correct the situation. After six months as manager she was wondering if she could ever get the full support of her staff and get the situation to turn around.

▶ What seem to be the underlying causes of the poor performance of the Metropolis office?

▶ If you had been in Loretta Compton's place, what action would you have taken initially?

▶ At this point in time (six months later), what would you recommend Loretta Compton do to remedy the problems?

4

The Public Manager as Policy Maker

Key Concepts

Public Problems
  Public Policy
    Democratic Values
      Policy Process
        Policy Actors
          Policy Role of the Public Manager
            Policy Analysis
              Policy Criteria
                Methods of Policy Analysis
                  Policy Making as Decision Making

Contemporary America is confronted with a broad assortment of major problems and opportunities. Daily newspapers devote much of their space to such items as the energy crisis, environmental and pollution concerns, inflation, unemployment, health and welfare, urban problems, and a multitude of other public concerns. The "public" nature of such issues inevitably forces them onto the agenda of government.

As our daily lives have become increasingly complex in the twentieth century, so have the agenda and activities of our many governments. We see more demanded of the public sector, whether it be local, state, or national government. In addition, many demands turn into paradoxical situations. Even when sufficient consensus develops and government takes action, the result may not solve the problem. In fact, the ultimate result will probably be a change in the nature of the problem. We want a cleaner environment, for example, but we also want to increase production and consumption. We want lower taxes, but we also want defense, police, health, parks, and better roads. Most conflicts that come to government for resolution have no easy or simple solutions. In addition, it is rare when government is able to act on a particular issue with finality.

None of the public managers' roles is more unique, or more important, than that of policy maker. The public manager is deeply involved in policy making at two interrelated levels. First, and most obvious, is the making of policy about the internal operation of his or her agency. Decisions must constantly be made about practices and procedures within the agency. Second, but perhaps less obvious, is the manager's participation in policy that directly affects the world outside the confines of the agency itself. This second category, "public" policymaking, is the primary concern of this chapter.

Historically, public managers were seen as implementing, but not making public policy. Today's understanding is considerably revised, enlarged, and more realistic than this earlier view.

A BROAD VIEW OF PUBLIC POLICY

While the central interest of this chapter is the implementation of societal goals and policies through public management, this interest must be viewed in a broader context. Two important aspects to keep in mind are:

▶ the overall nature of politics and policy making within our total political system

▶ the fact that public agencies represent only one of the many ways society can choose to deal with a public problem

A complete review of the ways in which policies develop would require a thorough exposition of the American political system. The existence of our particular democratic system is itself the result of an evolving public-policy process. All political systems stem from ethical assumptions; democracy is no exception. A primary assumption is that the individual is the basic unit of value, thus government should facilitate the pursuit of individual needs and interests. Political scientists Dye and Ziegler discuss democracy in terms of five values or policy preferences. Paraphrased somewhat, these include:

1. popular participation in decisions that shape the lives of persons in society

2. majority rule

3. recognition of minorities' rights to try to become majorities—including such specific rights as freedom of the press, of speech, to form opposition parties, to assemble, and to run for office

4. commitment to individual dignity and to preserving the values of life, liberty, and property

5. commitment to equal opportunity for all persons to develop their capabilities[1]

Our Constitution sets forth fundamental elements of how these policy preferences are attained. From time to time the Constitution has been amended to clarify or change policies or the ways they can be achieved. The public manager needs to have a clear understanding of the assumptions about democracy. While there is much distance between the Constitutional framework and the operation of specific agencies, it must be remembered that public agency goals and policies arise within the context of the political system under which we live.

Alternative Ways to Pursue Public Policies

A governmental system can choose to address problems or needs in various ways. Establishing a public agency and setting in action a public management process is only one possible outcome. In response to a particular problem, there is a range of choices available to government; it can—

1. decide to do nothing

2. encourage voluntary action by citizens

---

[1]Thomas R. Dye and Harmon Ziegler, *The Irony of Democracy*, 4th ed. (N. Scituate, Mass.: Duxbury, 1978), pp. 7–8.

3. give individuals tax credits or other specific incentives to take individual action

4. contract with private organizations to accomplish the desired action

5. provide grant-in-aid dollars to lower governmental levels (i.e., from federal to state and/or local)

6. create a new program within an existing agency

7. create a new agency

Each of these options represents a basic policy direction taken with respect to a particular need or problem. All seven can easily be found in our society. Government actions in such areas as tobacco, automobile safety, environmental issues, health, and international relations provide a wide range of examples. In general, as a problem becomes more visible and more severe, and as politicians and others (including voters) begin to agree on what should be done, there is a movement from item 1 toward item 7.

The Public Agency Choice

Public agencies are obviously established for the purpose of pursuing public policies. For such agencies to function effectively, however, more than broad policy is required. The Congress or state legislatures may legislate, and the president or governors may approve, a new program. It becomes a reality only as organization charts are developed, goals for component units are established, office space is secured, and staff is hired. As these steps are taken, more precise policies (or goals) are created—aimed at operationalizing the original broader policy.

This process of policy making is depicted, in a simplified form, in Figure 4.1.

In viewing this process, the reader should try to identify additional "primary actors" at the various levels. A few moments of reflection on the nature and significance of interaction between levels would also be very useful. This simplified view is equally applicable in considering local, state, or federal government. It is also applicable to whatever function of government one considers—from aviation to zoos.

Figure 4-1. A Simplified View of Government in Action

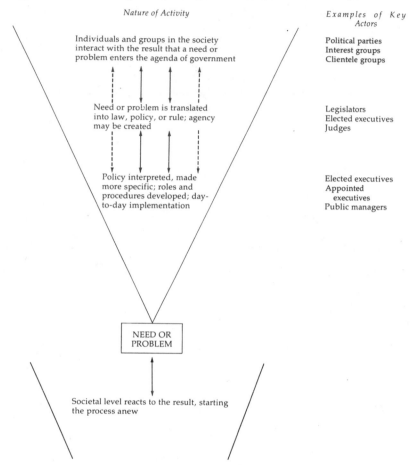

Nature of Activity

Individuals and groups in the society
interact with the result that a need or
problem enters the agenda of government

Need or problem is translated
into law, policy, or rule; agency
may be created

Policy interpreted, made
more specific; roles and
procedures developed; day-
to-day implementation

NEED OR
PROBLEM

Societal level reacts to the result, starting
the process anew

*Examples of Key
Actors*

Political parties
Interest groups
Clientele groups

Legislators
Elected executives
Judges

Elected executives
Appointed
    executives
Public managers

Note: While the large arrow indicates the direction of movement, smaller arrows point
out the continuing interactions between the various levels.

POLICY MAKING AND THE PUBLIC MANAGER

Policy is defined in various ways in the literature of public
management. One author has called it "a big decision govern-

ing how a cluster of little decisions will be made."[2] Another refers to public policy as "whatever governments choose to do or not to do."[3] Both of these writers are correct. Policy is essentially government's steering process. It has to do with moves, made or not made, and with the resultant course and direction that is charted.

The charted course is a central output of the political system described in Chapter 2. All of the societal systems identified there participate in the policymaking process. Key actors in the policy arena include:

1. elected and appointed government executives

2. legislators

3. judges

4. career public managers

5. political party leaders

6. media persons in the press, radio, and television

7. lobbyists and special interest groups

8. religious leaders

9. clientele served by government agencies (e.g., veterans, farmers)

10. community leaders and citizens

11. leaders in professions and occupational groups (e.g., business, education, law, science)

While the first four on this list are the official actors, directly and legally responsible for government actions, the other seven also play important parts. The influence of individuals and groups in the policy process depends upon many factors, including:

▶ the general nature of the subject matter (changing the social security program as compared to building a highway or a park)

[2]Robert S. Lorch, *Public Administration* (New York: West, 1978), p. 273.

[3]Thomas R. Dye, *Policy Analysis: What Governments Do, Why They Do It, and What Difference It Makes* (University, Ala.: University of Alabama Press, 1976), p. 1.

▶ the intensity of feeling about an issue or problem

▶ the resources available to the interested parties (e.g., money, voters, expertise, time)

▶ success in attracting other persons and groups as allies

▶ luck and circumstance

The degree of success of persons and groups in influencing policy is illustrated in almost every daily newspaper or news broadcast.

Why Public Managers Are Policy Makers

In addressing the public manager's role as policy maker, it is useful to begin, in a sense, at the end. How does the policy activity of the public manager ultimately affect the average citizen? While the impact has been diversely illustrated by authors, none have caught the essence better than political scientist William Boyer:

"A typical day in the life of an average person illustrates the importance of administrative policies. If he drives his car to work, it is probably equipped and maintained to satisfy minimum requirements and specifications as determined by an administrative agency. His car is insured by a company regulated by an administrative agency. He must abide by administratively created traffic regulations involving such matters as speed zones and stop signs. If he should travel by bus, trolley, or railway, he must pay a fare fixed by a regulatory agency.

"If he works in an office building, he probably ascends to his office in an elevator constructed and maintained in accordance with an administrative code. The building itself was probably planned by a licensed architect and constructed under the supervision of registered engineers pursuant to the administrative regulations of a building code; it was wired as prescribed by an electrical code, heated and ventilated according to another code, and equipped and fitted with plumbing fixtures as required by plumbing code. He lunches at a restaurant where the equipment complies with health rules. The food he eats was produced and marketed under agricultural regulations, transported by means of regulated carriers, and processed according to administrative food standards."[4]

---

[4]William W. Boyer, *Bureaucracy on Trial: Policy Making by Government Agencies* (New York: Bobbs-Merrill, 1964), p. 3.

Although the role of the public manager is pervasive in this example, this is only part of the story. In addition to conducting the day-to-day affairs of government, public managers are central actors in the long-range decision and policy-making process. Francis Rourke has been in the forefront of the scholars articulating the public managers' policy role.[5] He has concentrated, first, on the sources of power of the public manager in the policy process and second, on the uses of that power. As to the sources of their power, Rourke gives particular attention to the variety of skills that managers bring to the policy process. These include skills that are necessary both for making and for implementing policy decisions. Rourke notes that the purpose of creating large organizations is to enhance human competences by providing for a division of labor. The resulting opportunity for concentrated attention gives public managers significant advantages over political officials who deal with a variety of matters, spending relatively little time on any one. In this sense, public managers often have a near monopolistic control of information about the area in which they work. In addition to specialized knowledge, their continuity in dealing with particular matters leads to further development of their expertise. Public managers have many opportunities to use their specialized knowledge. They are often asked, or required, to advise chief executives and legislators in the deliberation of policy issues. In addition, as the example above suggests, laws and policies generally leave room for discretion to those who implement them. The city council, for example, may determine the speed limit for a particular street, but the real policy is determined by the decisions of the police chief and his or her staff in enforcing the ordinance.

Rourke also notes that most legislation passed by Congress is drafted in the offices of various executive agencies. This is common practice whether the draft is requested by the President or the Congress. Both tend to look for the most knowledgeable agency when a proposal is needed.

Another source of power cited by Rourke is the political support acquired and developed by public managers. Many agencies have their particular group, or what may be called

[5]Francis E. Rourke, *Bureaucracy, Politics, and Public Policy,* 2nd ed. (Boston: Little, Brown, 1976).

attentive public that has great interest in the agency's activities. Agencies in areas such as labor, agriculture, and the veterans affairs will rarely take a stand opposing the interest of the group they serve. The interest and support of outside groups obviously translates into political support, and appropriations in the Congress.

Political support can be sought in any one, or in any combination of, three centers:

1. the executive branch itself—the president, governor, mayor, or other highly visible and/or powerful person(s)

2. the legislative body—influential individuals or groups who have special interest in any agency and its work

3. the public—interested, and politically active outside groups, or the public at large

In seeking political support, one source of danger for an agency is the potential cost associated with it. Support-seeking can become deference to particular persons or groups, and the agency can find that a high price is exacted in the political arena. In return for support, political persons and groups often want to influence the agency's decision-making process.

In the final analysis, public managers are involved in the policy process because they are needed. They bring critical knowledge and expertise in their particular field to the policy process. Few know as much about the work of government agencies as the people who manage them. If a chief executive, or a legislative body, seeks information on transportation, housing, or conservation, what better and more accessible place to look than in the agency itself?

The public manager's knowledge and expertise are based on a combination of education, training, and experience. Tenure and continuity are important dimensions. Often the public manager has seen his or her field evolve through many policy changes. This enables the manager to develop a significant grasp of particular public problems, of the agency's capacity for dealing with such problems, of what has worked and what has failed. As the size and complexity of government have grown, so has the importance of the public manager's knowledge. To achieve governmental purposes the public manager must, by the nature of his or her task, be a significant and continuing participant in the making of public policy.

POLICY ANALYSIS

In recent years political scientists, economists, and others have become increasingly interested in policy analysis. Interest has focused on "the examination and improvement of the policymaking process itself, as well as the evaluation of policy choices and outcomes."[6] This reflects a change in emphasis from the way politics and government traditionally have been studied.

Historically, the "institutions and structures of government. . . political behavior and processes" have been the central concerns.[7] Policy analysis strives to achieve an interdisciplinary approach and to focus on society's activities and problems. While some persons pursue policy analysis as scholarly research or out of personal curiosity, more people are interested in policy analysis for action-oriented reasons. They hope to bring a higher degree of rationality and scientific analysis to the process of making public policy. The analyst likes to think of his or her work as objective, rigorous, and important. The result of such analyses may well be all of these, however, and still not be used or usable.

While policy analysts and evaluators focus on issues and problems, political actors are more concerned with people and with creating "new options or frameworks that are of mutual advantage to competing groups."[8] While the analyst may believe that he or she is the "purveyor of truth," the politician may see him or her as "just another lobbyist."[9] This does not mean that the politician is anti-analyst, or even unappreciative of the work that has been done. It is simply a product of the politician's role under our form of government, and reflects the fact that "truth" as determined through the political process is a very subjective matter.

Policy analysis is concerned with several general areas. First, it is concerned with the assessment of policy impacts and outcomes. Second, it is concerned with the evaluation of fail-

---

[6]Felix A. Nigro and Lloyd G. Nigro, *Modern Public Administration*, 4th ed. (New York: Harper and Row, 1977).

[7]Dye, *supra* note 3, p. 2.

[8]John E. Brandl, "Evaluation and Politics," *Evaluation* (Special Issue, 1978), p. 7.

[9]*Id.*, p. 6.

ures and successes of policy on specific problems. Third, it must apply analysis to policy improvement and reform. Persons doing policy analysis might be guided by a list of policy evaluation criteria such as the following:

"1. The clarity and specificity of the objectives and goals toward which the policy is aimed

"2. The completeness and quality of the data on which the policy is based

"3. The independence of the analysts from any self-serving and protectionist influences exercised by those who are responsible for the policy and its administration

"4. Provision for evaluation findings to be received by policy makers and administrators and to be translated into appropriate policy changes

"5. The existence of adequate policy output indicators on the basis of which judgments can be made about the level of performance and productivity

"6. Consideration of policy impacts on such public values as democratic participation, equality of opportunity, political responsibility, managerial accountability, justice and equity, and humanness in internal and external relationships."[10]

Methods of Analysis

A basic problem in the analysis of public policy is how to do it in the most systematic and effective manner. To develop broad understanding of the policy process and its products, there is a need to develop methods to sort out and categorize information and to make certain the right questions are asked. Four approaches to the study of policy that currently are being used are:

1. case study

2. input-output analysis

---

[10]Ivan L. Richardson and Sidney Baldwin, *Public Administration: Government In Action* (Columbus: Merrill, 1976), p. 128.

3. criteria based evaluation

4. process approach

In the case-study approach the analyst becomes immersed in a selected policy matter to learn as much as possible about it.[11] This approach has the obvious advantages of detail and specificity. The biggest disadvantage is that many case studies must be completed and compared before general conclusions can be reached.

The second method, input-output analysis, attempts to apply the systems model outlined in Chapter 2. The goal is to explain policy output by analyzing system inputs. Thomas Dye, for example, conducted extensive statistical comparisons of the spending patterns of the 50 states.[12] His goal was to determine whether spending decisions on such programs as education and welfare were related to socioeconomic and political variables such as the extent of urbanization and industrialization, income levels, degree of voter turnout for elections, and amount of political party competition. Research of this type has produced mixed results, which in general support the importance of socio-economic considerations. Some deviant cases have also been identified providing useful clues for further analysis.

The third approach, criteria-based evaluation, attempts to identify and apply "yardsticks" or measures that are deemed relevant. Political scientist Yehezkel Dror has provided a good list of the most frequently used criteria:

1. past quality (are we doing better?)

2. quality of other systems (how do we compare?)

3. desired quality (is the result what we hoped for?)

4. professional standards of quality (how do the experts in this area view our result?)

---

[11]Among the many excellent case studies available are A. Lee Fritschler, *Smoking and Politics: Policymaking and the Federal Bureaucracy,* 2nd ed. (Englewood Cliffs, N.J.: Prentice-Hall, 1975); J. Clarence Davies, *The Politics of Pollution* (Indianapolis: Bobbs-Merrill, 1970); Robert J. Art, *The TFX Decision: McNamara and the Military* (Boston: Little, Brown, 1968); and Hugh Heclo, *A Government of Strangers: Executive Politics in Washington* (Washington: Brookings, 1977).

[12]Thomas R. Dye, *Politics, Economics, and the Public: Policy Outcomes in the American States* (Chicago: Rand McNally, 1966); See also Ira Sharkansky, ed., *Policy Analysis in Political Science* (Chicago: Markam, 1970).

5. survival quality (can we, or the organization, continue at this level?)

6. planned quality (is this the result we paid for?)

7. optimal quality (how far are we from the "ideal"?)[13]

As Dror points out, standard 7 is the most desirable measure to use. Unfortunately, it is also the most difficult to achieve and often the least practical.

The fourth approach, analysis of the policy process, will probably provide policy makers the best understanding over time. It has the advantage of breadth, and the potential for integrating the other three methods discussed above. Policy analysis has been defined by scientist and public manager Jacob Ukeles as "the systematic investigation of alternative policy options and the assembly and integration of the evidence for and against each option. It involves a problem-solving approach, the collection and interpretation of information, and some attempts to predict the consequences of alternative courses of action."[14] Although policy analysis has many of the earmarks of rational decision making, it does not attempt to arrive at an optimum selection and may have the purpose of merely screening out the worst possible alternatives.

Although policy analysis has been criticized by classical public policy-makers, it is one of the five major subject areas in public affairs programs specified by NASPAA (National Association of Schools of Public Affairs and Administration). Ukeles concludes that "The field appears to have staked out a useful middle ground between those who have condemned political policy-making as irrational, and those who have scoffed at the irrelevancy of research and analysis in the political arena."[15]

A scholar who has provided a useful synthesis of the policy analysis approach is Charles Jones. He develops a model that includes:

▶ how problems develop and get on the agenda of government

---

[13]Yehezkel Dror, *Public Policymaking Reexamined* (Scranton, Penn.: Chandler, 1968), pp. 58 ff.

[14]Jacob B. Ukeles, "Policy Analysis: Myth or Reality?" *Public Administration Review* (May–June 1977), p. 223.

[15]*Id.*, p. 227.

▶ what happens within government

▶ government's response to the problem

▶ the result and feedback which follows[16]

In developing his ideas, Jones emphasizes the never-ending nature of the policy process. Issues and problems change and evolve, but rarely is a policy matter dealt with and dispatched once and for all.

Policy Making and Decision Making

As the study of the policy process has developed, many writers have emphasized the importance of policy making as decision making. Political scientist Gerald Caiden, for example, has suggested that "policy making is probably the most important aspect of decision making."[17] A number of authors have attempted to analyze and explain decision processes and outcomes.[18]

Yehezkel Dror provides a useful summary of the prevalent decision models. He identifies five different types of decision, or policy making. Briefly, these include:

1. *Purely rational*—establish a complete set of goals, consider all alternatives, calculate all possible results from each alternative.

2. *Extra-rational*—go on intuition, hunches, etc.

3. *Satisficing*—opt for a satisfactory rather than an optimal decision.

4. *Sequential*—break decisions into smaller parts and search for additional information at each step.

---

[16]Charles O. Jones, *An Introduction to the Study of Public Policy*, 2nd. ed. (Belmont, Calif.: Wadsworth, 1977).

[17]Gerald E. Caiden, *The Dynamics of Public Administration* (New York: Holt, Rinehart and Winston, 1971), p. 75.

[18]Two leading examples are Charles E. Lindblom, "The Science of 'Muddling Through,'" *Public Administration Review* (Spring, 1959), and Amitai Etzioni, "Mixed-Scanning: A 'Third' Approach to Decision-Making," *Public Administration Review* (December 1967).

5. *Incremental*—make changes slowly and cautiously (somewhat similar to type 4 above).[19]

Dror argues for the development of another model—the optimal model. He sees the need for meta-policy—policy about how policy is made. Dror perceives a wide gap between the available knowledge of how policy can best be made and the way policy actually is made. While Dror's suggestion may be overly optimistic, he appears to be correct in emphasizing the need for study in this area.

The study and understanding of the policy process and policy analysis are, in many respects, at an underdeveloped stage. Few topics in the social sciences are more challenging than the matter of public policy, and the role of the public manager in that process.

SUMMARY

Policy making is a reality of the public manager's job. The manager affects public policy through participation in the formulation and development of programs, and in the exercise of discretion in their implementation. Such actions have far-reaching effects, both within government itself and throughout the society. No citizen is beyond the reach of politics, the policy process, or the public manager.

CASE STUDIES

1. A Policy Problem in Dawson City

Members of the City Council of Dawson City continue to receive citizen complaints about police actions on Memorial Drive. This controversy has been going on ever since this street was built and opened 3 years ago. Approximately 50 percent of

---

[19]Dror, *supra* note 13, pp. 129ff.

the complaints are from citizens who have received speeding tickets. The other 50 percent complain that not enough tickets are being given.

Memorial Drive was developed to serve as a link between two state highways that pass through Dawson City. Both commercial and residential development has grown along the new street.

The controversy has become the number one policy problem of both the Police Chief and the City Manager. Prepare a plan of action that they can use to work toward an appropriate speed limit—a workable public policy.

2. Teaching With a Case Study

As a professor concerned with teaching current, and future, public managers about policy making, you firmly believe in the value of case studies. Your use of case studies has become well known among public managers in the area and you have received several awards for teaching excellence. As a result, you also have become a frequent speaker at meetings of local civic clubs and service organizations.

The League of Women Voters has asked you to present a case study at their next meeting. They expect to have 25 to 30 people in attendance and would like a case study that will provoke discussion. They also would like the case to illustrate potential interaction between the League and managers of public agencies in the area.

Prepare the case study you will present. To ensure that key points will be brought out, prepare 5 or 6 questions you can ask the group as they discuss the case.

5

The Public Manager as Planner and Organizer

Key Concepts

Planning
  Organizing
    Effectiveness
      Management Philosophy
        Objectives
          Principles
            Strategies
              Decision Making
                Organization Design
                  Span of Control
                    Unity of Command
                      Delegation
                        Authority
                          Responsibility
                            Line-Staff Relationships
                              Organizational Restructuring

In the early stages of World War II, an armament company that was a key factor in Germany's war machine had an urgent need for a quart of alcohol to complete a technical project. In order to receive the alcohol from a local supplier the company was required to follow purchasing procedures. Thus, it requested a requisition slip from the Reich Monopoly Bureau, but the company was referred to the Economic Group who would issue a "certificate of urgent need." The matter was referred to the Regional Office which, after six weeks of feverish activity, announced that the request had been approved and forwarded to the Reich Monopoly Bureau for final action. Finally, eight weeks after the initial request, the requisition approved "for technical purposes only" was issued and a company messenger was sent to pick up the alcohol. But on his arrival the messenger was informed that a certificate first had to be obtained from the Food Rationing Board, a Division of the Agriculture Department. When frustrated company officials inquired, the Food Rationing Board informed them it could license alcohol for drinking purposes only and not for manufacturing or technical uses. So, after more than two months, the Company abandoned all hope of ever receiving its urgently needed alcohol.[1]

While this is not a typical example, it does illustrate the inefficiencies of bureaucratic mismanagement. Proper planning and organizing will not absolutely guarantee against such incidents, but they can contribute significantly to the efficient and effective management of public organizations. This chapter will describe the managerial functions of planning and organizing together with the techniques attendant to each function.

PLANNING—ORGANIZING RELATIONSHIPS

Planning is concerned with the development of objectives and their accompanying programs, and organizing makes possible the accomplishment of activities necessary to achieve the planned objectives. Planning is future oriented in that a manager decides in advance what is to be done, how and when it is to be accomplished, and who is to be responsible. It is a conceptual process that involves anticipation of future events that can be predicted. Because these events are generally affected or often even imposed by factors beyond the control of the manager, they cannot be predicted with absolute certainty. In this respect, planning includes an exchange process between the organization and its environment in which the organization attempts to work the exchanges to its advantage. Planning

---

[1]Based on a true incident from Albert Speer, *Inside the Third Reich* (New York: Avon Books, 1971), p. 673.

presumes the existence of alternatives—even for circumstances beyond the control of the manager—from which objectives can be selected. Thus, the planning process provides a rational approach to the determination of the organization's objectives.

Organizing involves the grouping of activities necessary to attain objectives, the assignment of each grouping to a manager with appropriate authority for its administration, and provision for coordination of people's efforts throughout an organization. Key to the success of the organizing effort are objectives which give meaning to the roles people play. When each employee understands his or her role and how it relates to others there is a greater likelihood that they will cooperate toward the attainment of the established objectives.

Planning also provides the basis for controlling operations. With measurable objectives the managers can clearly determine how well programs are moving toward their intended ends. Thus, both planning and control look to the future; planning attempts to anticipate future events and control helps to insure that those events occur as they were planned.

Importance of Effectiveness in Public Programs

Although plans do not guarantee the success of a program they do greatly enhance the probability of success. When desired results are conceived in advance of the performance of activities, experience has shown that the results are far better than when a haphazard unplanned approach is taken. Effectiveness and efficiency in public programs are far more likely to occur when objectives are carefully thought out and prioritized, and strategies with supporting activities are delineated in advance of implementation.

When public programs fall short of their intended purpose, society suffers. Since 1969, this country has endured three recessions in quick succession. In recent years, the unemployment rate has hovered near 8 percent and according to many economists, inflation is reaching crisis proportions. These adverse conditions have given rise to a push for centralized, comprehensive economic planning. On another dimension, several years ago the U.S. Army recognized a lack of effectiveness in its "people" capabilities, i.e., poor leadership, lack of meaningful and challenging work, a pervasive rejection on the part of some soldiers of individual responsibilities, and other shortcomings. The Army instigated a remedial program for Organizational Effectiveness, and the centralized planning effort corrected many of the deficiencies.

Society expects its public agencies to be effective and this expectation places the onus on public managers to deliver the necessary goods and services. Managers are accountable to society for the performance of their organizations. It is from society that managers derive their authority because society, e.g., taxpayers, supplies the resources for the operation of the organizations. From society's viewpoint, effectiveness is the degree to which a public agency achieves its objectives given the resources available to it. But, as discussed in Chapter 3, efficiency is a corollary to effectiveness. The manager must achieve the organization's ends, but at a reasonable cost. Effectiveness without efficiency is still untenable. For example, if the costs of protecting health and safety become excessive, citizens will demand that alternative or replacement programs be developed. Obviously, this would mean replacing the management of the inefficient program.

Achieving organizational effectiveness is especially challenging for public managers because they often must show results in a relatively short time, attain massive objectives with limited resources, and operate with people whose careers may be outside of their control. Despite these and other constraints, many public managers have helped their organizations achieve effectiveness. The first appointed head of the Environmental Protection Agency, William Ruckelshaus, managed to achieve the standards promulgated in the Clean Air Act within a relatively short time. Similarly, the widely respected former administrator of New York City's Health Service Administration, Gordon Chase, involved the medical establishment and the voluntary sector in an effective program to combat a host of social and environmental dangers that affected enormous numbers of people. The key to the effectiveness of these public managers was that they were able to influence the purpose, structure, and people of their organizations by developing clearly stated, measurable goals that were politically acceptable. In the words of Harvard professor Joseph Bower, "To be effective in the public sector, you must be a politician. But (perhaps what they have argued is wise) you must not play for political power. Rather, it is through use of analytic and operating skills, supported by staff, that a substantive program can be developed and implemented."[2]

THE PLANNING PROCESS

The planning process is depicted graphically in Figure 5.1. It has its basis in a management *philosophy*. Emanating from the philosophy are the organization's *objectives,* the ends toward which activities are directed. To implement these objectives managers are guided in their decision making by *policies,* but they must develop *strategies* that direct activities toward the attainment of objectives. Lower-level managers then disseminate *procedures* that detail the intended methods of handling these activities. *Rules* are promulgated to delineate specific required actions to support the activities or programs. Each of these elements of the planning process is a type of plan itself because it is chosen from among alternatives; it is oriented toward the future, and it helps determine the results of the organization. In the same regard, a budget is also a plan; it expresses expected results in numerical terms. Because they are such an important planning tool budgets are treated in detail in Chapter 7.

Determining a Management Philosophy

Although the management literature does not yield a consistent definition of the term "management philosophy," the one offered by administration theorist Ralph C. Davis appears to be most widely accepted. He contends that a philosophy is a "body of doctrine . . . [which] refers to any formal statement, either express or implied, of objectives, ideals, principles, points of view, and general modes of procedures."[3] For a manager, a philosophy helps bridge the gap between theory and practice. It becomes a way of thinking that influences the way

---

[2]Joseph L. Bower, "Effective Public Management," *Harvard Business Review* (March–April 1977), p. 140.

[3]Ralph C. Davis, *The Fundamentals of Top Management* (New York: Harper & Row, 1951), p. 804.

Figure 5.1.   The Planning Process

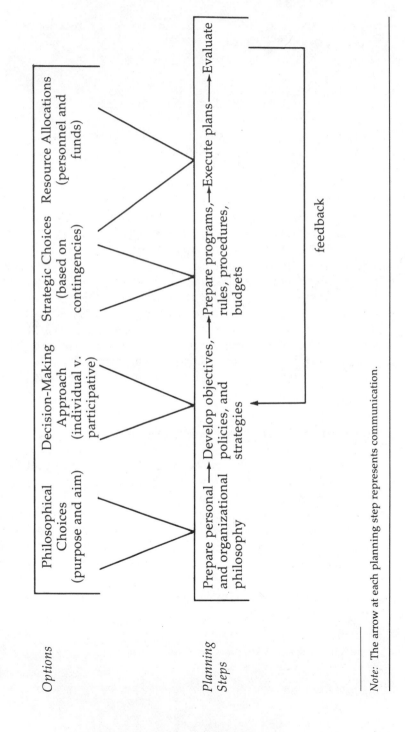

Note: The arrow at each planning step represents communication.

an individual behaves as a manager. Thus, organizational efficiency is facilitated because managers with well-defined philosophies can focus on specific desired ends. And when top management's philosophy is articulated in writing, it guides the organization in the development of objectives and of supporting plans and programs. Since the environments in which public managers operate are dynamic in nature, the development of a management philosophy logically becomes a continuous self-development process.

The process of developing one's management philosophy is portrayed graphically in Figure 5.2. The process involves the following:

Assimilation of thoughts from a vast reservoir of ideas derived from theory, beliefs about practices, and attitudes of the manager. Even the experienced practitioner with a pragmatic outlook would be well advised to integrate the theoretical dimension with the practical and personal dimensions.

Conception, or the formulation of a mental image or impression that can be translated into a model to serve as a framework or design. This is the most difficult phase of the process. It requires the manager to identify the key elements that form his or her way of thinking about the job of managing the organization. These might be classified into sets of thoughts that become the primary components of the philosophy. Defining the relationships among components integrates the philosophy into a tentative model. Once the model is described, the manager can test it against existing conditions. Time devoted to developing a strong, clear concept can pay important dividends when the thoughts are reduced to writing.

Description involves the written articulation of one's philosophy. This is the step between concept and reality. There is no prescribed format for a written philosophy. It can take the form of an essay, a concept paper or a pronouncement. But whatever form it takes, a written philosophy is an essential first step in the planning process.

One example of a public management philosophy is the following excerpt of the FY '77 Annual Posture Statement of the Department of the Army made by General Fred C. Weyland: "Simply put, the Army's role, its purpose, and its reason for existence, is to serve the United States interests in this uncertain and unsettled world. Among those interests are National survival and the freedom of interaction with people of the world

**Figure 5.2   A Process for Developing a Personal Management
Philosophy (A Manager's Way of Thinking About
the Job of Managing an Organization)**

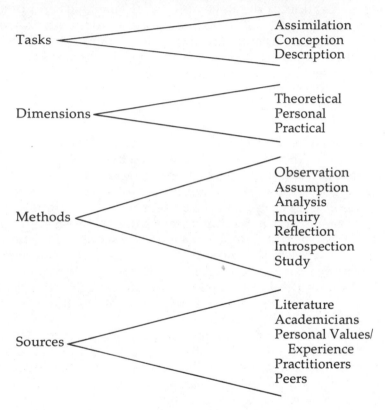

Source: Adapted from: *Army Command and Management: Theory and Practice* (Carlisle
Barracks, Penn.: U.S. Army War College, 1979), p. 116.

in peaceful pursuits."[4] Were there an "official" Army philosophy the statement would be substantially expanded to include
the details necessary to relate the various parts into a unitary
whole.

[4]General Fred C. Weyland, *FY'77 Annual Posture Statement*, Department of the
Army.

A search of the literature on the basic criteria for a philosophy of management, indicates that essentially a management philosophy should—

▶ be practical and workable

▶ be based on an acquired body of knowledge in conjunction with personal experience

▶ incorporate the functions of management

▶ be based on sound evidence from other disciplines

▶ be flexible to take account of changing environmental conditions

▶ consider and be congruent with existing organization objectives

▶ enhance the general welfare of the organization and its personnel

▶ be communicated openly

▶ be based on equity, morality, and human dignity

▶ have an orientation toward the future

Setting Objectives

It has already been noted that setting objectives is an essential step in the planning function that guides the organization toward specific, intended results.

Regardless of the approach one takes to establishing objectives, the essential point is that a definition of objectives is the critical first step in making rational decisions.

Policies. Policies are guidelines for action. They emanate from organizational objectives and implement the intent of the formulators. Properly conceived policies consist of two parts: first, a principle or a group of related principles, and second, rules of action. Together, these two parts support the objectives toward which they are directed.

Principles. A principle is a significant truth that is usually stated as a cause-and-effect relationship. Years of experience with organizational problems have led to generalizations about effective administration; these generalizations have become the principles that channel organizational activities. Principles in organizations increase efficiency and crystallize the nature of management, but most important, they explain the intent of the policy. Examples of principles related to public management might include:

▶ Public employees perform better when they have a voice in determining matters that affect them.

▶ The authority, duties, responsibilities, and relationships of everyone in the organization should be clearly and completely spelled out in writing and communicated so that everyone's efforts can be directed toward a common goal.

▶ A public manager's performance is determined by the quality of service his or her agency delivers to its constituents.

It should be emphasized at this point that these examples are not absolute. Managers have operated successfully in violation of some principles. For example, matrix organizations violate the principle of the unity of command yet are a viable form of organization.

Rules. When policies are implemented in the form of rules and procedures, the principle is only implied. If the reason behind a rule is not explained, the rule becomes an edict. As the public service employs increasing numbers of younger, better-educated people who tend not to obey orders blindly, agencies find it necessary to explain the reasons behind policy statements. Employee understanding and acceptance of the meaning of rules are essential in eliciting cooperation.

A statement of principle can clarify the meaning of a rule. Take, for instance, this rule on attendance: "The workday begins at 7:30 a.m. All employees are expected to be at their duty station and ready to work promptly at the beginning of the workday." Such a matter-of-fact announcement is likely to elicit a negative response from employees. However, if management explains the principle behind the rule, voluntary conformity is much more likely to result. Consider this version of the rule: "The public relies on us to serve their needs. A starting time of 7:30 a.m. has been designated so that we can be prepared when our clients call. Experience has shown that a 7:30

a.m. starting time allows us to provide the best possible service. You are, therefore, asked to be at your work station promptly at 7:30 a.m."

Systems analysts Hinricks and Taylor[5] have devised a scheme of systematic analysis, a decision-making process which focuses on utilizing limited means to achieve unlimited ends. They propose to convert societal values into objectives, or quantified desired outputs that are measurable or prioritized. Setting these objectives is no easy task, but it calls for answering questions such as: What are the "wants" of society? What are its primary values? The alternative choices in setting public managerial objectives include:

1. *Maximize*. Ignore special interests and attach value only to common needs of individuals.

2. Insure that *everybody gains* in welfare, e.g., satisfaction and achievement of individual preferences.

3. Insure that at least *one individual gains and nobody loses*.

4. Insure a *net gain*, e.g., gains outweigh losses.

5. *Maximize the minimum possible gain*. For example, U.S. defense strategy could be premised on achieving a minimum effective deterrent.

6. *Minimax*, or minimize the maximum possible loss.

Achieving Objectives

Strategies. Traditionally, the military utilized the concept of strategy to develop plans in light of the adversary's anticipated movements. From a public-management standpoint strategy is a plan of action that specifies the resources and the allocation of those resources required to achieve organizational goals.

The U.S. Army has a national objective that seeks to reduce the chance and risks of war with emphasis on prevention of

---

[5]Harley H. Hinricks and Graeme M. Taylor, *Systematic Analysis* (Pacific Palisades, Calif.: Goodyear, 1972) pp. 111 ff.

nuclear war. It also desires to maintain a general freedom of action in international relations. The military strategy to support that approach is based upon collective security, deterrence, forward defense, and flexible response. The Army's concept of strategy in that overall scheme is flexibility, usability, and visibility of force—these being the characteristics of land warfare.

The concept of strategy implies competition and one might argue that public agencies are not viewed as competitive. Yet public agencies do compete for programs and for the funds to support them. As mentioned in the previous discussion of the public environment, political considerations cause some programs to be adopted while others are dropped. Consequently, the public manager needs to think strategically in order to promote the continuation of desired programs.

Here is an example of strategic thinking that paid off. A large metropolitan area that was designated a prime sponsor under the Comprehensive Employment and Training Act (CETA) included in its strategy for implementing its manpower program (1) a detailed forecast of local industry's employment needs, and (2) a Labor Market Advisory Committee that included executives from a representative sample of local firms. The Committee guided the CETA staff in developing programs that would be meaningful to local industry. The large number of CETA program graduates who subsequently were hired attested to its success.

Procedures. We are all familiar with manuals that contain procedures detailing the manner in which an activity is to be carried out. While policies are broad guidelines for managerial thinking, procedures are step-by-step methods to guide action. An agency might have a policy on reimbursement for official travel expenses; the procedure would detail the method for filing for reimbursement and describe how to fill out and process the necessary forms.

Program. The ultimate step or outcome of the planning process is a program. Programs seldom stand by themselves. To carry out a plan of action, a complex array of programs is usually required. Any one program affects and depends on others. The interdependence of programs calls for coordination and timing so that each program will be supportive of the other.

DECISION MAKING

Regardless of their classification or level in the hierarchy, public managers are required to make decisions either individually or as members of a decision-making group. In each managerial role (planner and organizer, controller, personnel manager, and so forth), the public manager is called on to make decisions. Decision making is especially relevant to the planning process because the manager must select appropriate objectives for the organization and must determine the appropriate courses of action to achieve the objectives. Public decision making is a dynamic process because the solution of one problem often gives rise to another. For example, as managers seek to correct environmental problems, they may find that unemployment increases. Or as federal funds are expended on welfare programs, the resulting strain on the economy may increase the risk of inflation. Consequently, today's solutions do not resolve tomorrow's problems.

Conceptual, or decision-making, skill is one of the basic skills of a successful administrator, or manager. Conceptual skill relates to the ability to recognize the relationships among the social, economic, and political elements in the management environment and to take action that advances the welfare of the organization. This skill is perhaps the most difficult to apply. It involves making decisions whose outcomes are extremely uncertain.

In any government agency, there is a maze of clientele groups that have a basic influence over the organization. For instance, county governments must be mindful of citizen needs when planning programs. However, they are also influenced by state legislation and administrative guidelines, and by basic requirements of federal funding sources. In addition, the internal politics of the organization impinge on the decision-making process. Each of the clientele groups has its own expectations as to the outcome of the programs being planned or replanned by the county, so that the ultimate decision must, somehow or other, consider— or at least not violate— the wishes of each of the clientele groups. This is more easily said than done.

Group Decision Making

Considerable controversy surrounds the issue of group decision making. Proponents claim the approach is conducive to employee involvement in decisions that affect them and yields a high degree of commitment. They also find an advantage in encouraging creative thinking through maximization of a variety of inputs. The group approach gains much of its support from the popular notion that it is good management style to have your people participate in the decision-making process.

But there are also disadvantages to the group approach. Conflicts are likely to occur especially when diverse interests are present in a group. Consequently, a consensus may be the product of the most vocal, but not necessarily the most knowledgeable, members. All of this activity is time consuming, may be frustrating to some members of the group, and may not produce desirable results. Furthermore, when groups make decisions, if the desired outcome does not materialize, there is a tendency to "pass the buck" rather than accept responsibility for the decision.

An alarming but interesting phenomenon related to group decision making behavior was identified by social commentator Irving Janis. He studied a number of fiascos (e.g., the Bay of Pigs, the Cuban Missile Crisis, the Korean War, and the escalation of the Viet Nam War) that resulted from high-level political decision making. His studies led to the coining of the phrase "group think," which refers to "a mode of thinking that people engage in when they are deeply involved in a cohesive in-group, when the members striving for unanimity override their motivation to realistically appraise alternative courses of action."[6]

Many of the drawbacks of group decision making can be overcome to make the process more effective. Various research studies provide the following pointers for facilitating group decision making.

1. Clear definition of objectives. Public managers involved in decision making should be knowledgeable of the group's goals. In a similar sense, when any group, whether it be employees or citizens outside the agency, participates in the decision-making process, the outcome is more likely to be positive when it understands the goal to be achieved. For example, if the group is a coalition on urban housing, the goal would be

---

[6]Irving L. Janis, *Victims of Group Think* (Boston: Houghton Mifflin, 1972), pp. 9 ff.

stated in terms of a certain number of additional low-cost housing units to be disbursed throughout the area. The coalition
then might decide how to accomplish building and locating the
units given the resources of the group.[7]

2. Accountability. Public managers who have experienced
success with group decision making cite accountability of the
group as a key. When the group recognizes that it will be held
accountable for its action, self-imposed peer pressure helps
bring deliberations to an action stage within a reasonable time
and each member of the group seems to accept the decision as
if he or she had made it alone.

3. Size of group. Although research findings are not consistent on the optimum size of a decision-making group, it
appears that in general such groups function best with five to
seven members. One researcher claims the ideal size is five.[8]
Other research findings[9] support the conclusion that "if the
quality of the group's solution is of considerable importance,
it is useful to include a larger number of members, e.g., seven
to twelve, so that many inputs are available to the group making
its decisions. If the degree of consensus is of primary importance, it is useful to choose a smaller group, e.g., three to five
so that each member can have his concern considered and
discussed."[10]

Participative Decision Making

The participative approach to decision making is one in
which subordinates in a particular situation are allowed and
encouraged to participate in decisions which will affect them.
The participative approach is evident throughout government

[7]Donald P. Crane, "The Case for Participative Management," *Business Horizons*
(April 1976), p. 20.

[8]A. C. Filley, "Committee Management: Guidelines from Social Science Research,"
California Management Review (Fall 1970), p. 19.

[9]George E. Manners, Jr., "Another Look at Group Size, Group Problem Solving
and Member Consensus," *Academy of Management Journal* (December 1975), p. 723.

[10]L. L. Cummings, G. P. Huber, and E. Arendt, "Effects of Size and Special
Arrangement of Group Decision-Making," *Academy of Management Journal* (December
1974), p. 473.

where legislative bodies rely on committees and subcommittees to draft legislation and where administrative agencies encourage group participation and often call on coalitions of public managers and citizen groups to develop recommendations on specific problems. In New York State, for example, the energy crunch resulted in the formation of local citizen groups which have had considerable influence on the location of public utility facilities. Controversies have become polarized, and issue-based coalitions have arisen to counter the power companies, especially when environmental issues are involved. Whether participation by larger segments of the citizenry is viewed as positive or negative, one thing is clear—the trend, in the New York area and elsewhere, is toward greater involvement of citizens in governmental decisions that affect them.[11]

Decision-Making Techniques

In making decisions, public managers like to think of themselves as "rational" decision makers. The decision maker does not have a high degree of control over the decision-making situation, especially within the realm of public decisions; however, current emphasis on official conduct that is in the "public interest" admonishes public managers to endeavor to be rational in their decision making. Public managers' responsibility depends on rationality and decision makers can act responsibly only if their actions are based on actual and fully developed information and alternatives. And ethical responsibility can exist only where there is a sufficient cognitive base.[12] Essentially, the rational model incorporates the following elements:

1. *Identifying the problem,* or articulating a pervasive or priority problem.

2. *Developing* facts and information relevant to the problem.

---

[11]Joan B. Aron, "Decision-Making in Energy Supply at the Metropolitan Level: A Study of the New York Area," *Public Administration Review* (July–August 1975), pp. 340 ff.

[12]Norton Long, "Public Policy and Administration: The Goals of Rationality and Responsibility," *Public Administration Review*, Vol. 14 (Winter 1954), pp. 22-31.

3. *Evaluating and prioritizing* alternative viable solutions to the stated problem.

4. *Choosing a course of action* that will satisfactorily solve the problem. At this juncture the decision maker faces several basic considerations such as:

   a. *Consequences.* High risk or high cost decisions obviously deserve longer and more careful deliberation.

   b. *Time constraints.* Deadlines have to be met, but a snap decision can have dire consequences and good judgment may dictate that "no decision is better than a wrong decision."

   c. *Nature of the problem.* The source of the problem, its complexity, impact, and the decision maker's familiarity with it all have a bearing on how it is handled.

   d. *Availability of delegation.* When competent resources (personnel) for delegation are available, problems can often be referred to them for action.

   e. *Report of action.* The recipient of the report and those affected by the consequences have a bearing on the decision maker's actions.

5. *Implementing,* or translating the decision into action calls for gaining the support of those responsible for implementation, programming to insure efficiency and effectiveness, and follow-up procedures to get feedback from implementors of the decision, e.g., program managers.

6. *Evaluating feedback,* or a continuous process to detect deviations from objectives and to make necessary changes in the program, or even in the objectives themselves.

Writers in the field of public decision making have criticized the rational model as being impractical. They claim that it contains inherent limitations, for instance, in the amount of information that the decision-maker has at hand for any given problem; and that the myriad problems confronting the public manager permit only partial attention to each problem.

Many of those who reject the rational approach subscribe to the strategy of "disjointed incrementalism" or "muddling through" espoused by economist Charles E. Lindblom, or the "mixed scanning" approach advanced by sociologist Amitai Etzioni.

Disjointed incrementalism or muddling through, Lindblom[13] asserts, considers the limited perceptive abilities of decision makers and reduces the disadvantage of having to process excessive amounts of information. The steps in this approach can be summarized as follows:

1. The manager analyzes only values and policies which differ marginally from existing policies.

2. A drastically limited means-ends analysis is undertaken on only a few alternatives, ignoring their possible consequences and values.

3. A succession of limited comparisons continually redefines the problem and achieves incremental changes. Thus, decision makers analyze past sequences of policy steps to acquire knowledge for further steps and to rectify past errors.

The "muddling through" approach is designed to correct immediate public problems rather than to promote future social goals.

The mixed-scanning approach advanced by Etzioni provides a specific procedure for information gathering called scanning, a strategy for the allocation of resources, and guidelines for the relationships between the two.[14] This approach focuses on problems similar to those that occurred previously and on those which might deserve attention if they arose unexpectedly. Mixed scanning combines various levels of scanning and provides criteria for situations requiring emphasis at one level or another. In this approach managers make fundamental decisions by exploring in an overview fashion the main alternatives they consider to be relevant to the goals, and they also make incremental decisions within the context of the fundamental ones.

---

[13]Charles E. Lindblom, "The Science of 'Muddling Through'," *Public Administration Review,* Vol. 19 (Spring 1959) pp. 79-88.

[14]Amitai Etzioni, "Mixed-Scanning: A 'Third' Approach to Decision-Making," *Public Administration Review,* Vol. 27 (December 1967) pp. 385-392.

Perhaps the ideal approach to problem solving in public policy making would incorporate mixed scanning and disjointed incrementalism with rational thinking. However, the serious-minded public manager would do well to master the techniques inherent in the rational approach. Then, the application of more intuitive approaches will serve to strengthen the decision.

IMPLEMENTING PLANS THROUGH ORGANIZING

Organizations are designed to carry out the plans developed to achieve their objectives. When managers structure an organization, they usually proceed in the following fashion:

▶ Understand the *objectives* and their priorities.

▶ Identify the *functions* that need to be performed.

▶ *Group* similar or related activities into departments or units.

▶ Assign a group or grouping to a *manager* with the appropriate authority to manage it.

▶ Provide for *coordination* vertically and horizontally throughout the structure.

Finally, the organization must be *designed* so that (a) everyone in it knows his or her specific duties and responsibilities and how they relate to those of other members; (b) assignments are clearly understood; and (c) there is a communications network to facilitate the accomplishment of the organization's objectives.[15]

Writers on the subject of organizational design have identified a continuum of organizational design patterns. At one extreme is the *mechanistic* pattern that incorporates the traditional pyramidal structure. In this type of organization, all elements are highly structured to attain machine-like efficiency—tasks are highly detailed, communication is formalized, and decision making is centralized at the top. At the other extreme of the continuum is the *organic* pattern. It is an "open"

---

[15]Harold Koontz and Cyril O'Donnell, *Essentials of Management* (New York: McGraw-Hill, 1974), p. 137.

design where roles are ambiguously defined and constantly changing. Decision making is decentralized and interactions among organizational units are flexible and informal; work groups may even be autonomous. One writer suggests that organizations be designed according to the task and the type of people involved: the mechanistic pattern is most suited to stable, unchanging environments and a staff that prefers certainty, whereas the organic pattern is most suited to an unstable, uncertain environment and people tolerant of ambiguity.[16]

The function of organizing is based on a number of concepts, often referred to as principles of management. Those most applicable to the public manager as an organizer are discussed below.

Span of Control

The concept known as the "span of control" is based on the premise that there is a limit to the number of people a manager can effectively direct. As the number of individuals reporting to a manager increases arithmetically, the number of personal relationships increases geometrically.[17] Thus, with one person reporting to a manager there will be two relationships. But, if one additional person is added, the number of relationships increases by four—from two to six! Since the manager must work with people and their relationships rather than with people as raw numbers, the number of persons that can be effectively managed by one supervisor becomes limited.

Although writers in this field have attempted to identify a specific number that constitutes the most efficient span of control, empirical evidence indicates that the effectiveness of the span depends on a variety of factors. Essentially, a combination of the complexity, variety, and proximity of the tasks being supervised affects the width of the most effective span of control.

Highly complex or technical work obviously requires closer supervision than simple, basic work. Hence, complex tasks

---

[16]Michael B. McCaskey, "An Introduction to Organizational Design," *California Management Review* (Winter 1974), pp. 13 ff.

[17]V. A. Graicunas developed his theorem on the span of control through deductive reasoning. See V. A. Graicunas, "Relationship in Organization," in L. Gulick and L. Urwick, eds., *Papers on the Science of Administration* (New York: Augustus M. Kelly, 1937), pp. 183-187.

would tend to limit the span. A laboratory manager directing the efforts of serologists, virologists, and biological technicians might have only five or six people in the unit (because of the variety and complexity of the work), whereas an office manager might be able to supervise the work of 15 to 20 accounting clerks who perform basic work that is similar in nature. Finally, when the people being supervised are geographically dispersed, this factor places a constraint on the manager's capacity to direct the work. Conversely, close proximity of the work performed improves control.

Studies also have shown that such factors as the quality of training, the extent and pace of change in the work environment, adequacy of delegation of authority, and degree of objectivity in evaluating performance are additional determinants in the effective span of control.

Unity of Command

Soon after Moses led the Jews out of captivity he sat to judge the people. Seeing that Moses was not able to listen to all of these people by himself, Jethro, his father-in-law, gave him advice which he heeded. The Bible describes Moses' action:

> "And Moses chose able men out of all Israel, and made them heads over the people, rulers of thousands, rulers of hundreds, rulers of fifties, and rulers of tens.
> "And they judged the people at all seasons: the hard cases they brought unto Moses, but every small matter they judged themselves."[18]

Thanks to Jethro's advice Moses organized a hierarchy with a *chain of command* that freed Moses of "small matters" and permitted him to be more accessible to his constituency on the hard cases. Each of the "rulers," or managers had increasingly greater authority the higher their rank in the organizations. Rulers over thousands might compare with a colonel or an agency division director; rulers over hundreds, a major or department manager; rulers over fifties, a captain or unit manager; and rulers over tens, a lieutenant or first-line supervisor.

Implicit in Moses' organization is the principle of unity of command: for any given assignment an employee reports to

---

[18]*Exodus 18:* 25-26

only one manager. The logic behind this principle of organizing is that by answering to only one boss there should be better understanding and coordination of the assignment to be performed. As desirable as the unity of command principle may be, it is often violated, especially as bureaucracies grow in size and complexity.

Delegation

Through delegation, managers are able to accomplish more because persons lower in the hierarchy are given authority to accomplish specific assignments. Successful managers generally exhibit the ability and willingness to delegate authority. Their approach to delegation includes the following:

- ▶ *Competence.* They assess the employee's ability to carry out the assignment.

- ▶ *Parity.* They delegate authority commensurate with responsibility.

- ▶ *Clarity.* They make sure instructions are clear and that the employee understands the assignment.

- ▶ *Expectations.* They ensure acceptance of conditions for completion of assignment.

- ▶ *Accountability.* They make the employee accountable for results.

- ▶ *Control.* They provide for regular, periodic review of accomplishments to verify that the assignment is carried out properly and to correct ineffective performance.

- ▶ *Reward.* They evaluate results and provide for a system of rewards that will encourage effort.

Authority versus responsibility Authority, *not* responsibility is delegated. A manager is given the responsibility to carry out an assignment, and is held accountable for the results. Theoretically, the manager has been given enough authority to complete the assignment. But how many times have you heard someone complain "Oh, I sure do have a lot of responsibility around here, but they never seem to give me any authority to get the job done!"? This kind of problem stems from the confusion with the terms "authority" and "responsibility." Perhaps if public managers understand the difference they can be more effective at delegating.

Authority is a right. It may be the right to hire and fire or the right to expend specified sums of monies, and so on. The source of that right is usually some higher authority such as a manager's boss. In this case the manager's authority is a function of his or her position in the organization. Authority flows or is delegated from the top of the organization to the bottom. Theoretically, the higher the position in the organization, the more authority it carries. This type of authority is considered formal authority. But to be viable, such authority must be accepted by those under the command of the person exercising authority. Logically, if subordinates do not accept the authority of their boss, that authority becomes meaningless. This points up the necessity of public managers to gain the respect (acceptance) of their employees. Responsibility is accountability for the attainment of objectives; it is the obligation to exercise authority properly, efficiently, and effectively. Public Managers often are given responsibility that far outweighs the authority necessary to carry it out. According to the parity principle, any manager must delegate authority which is commensurate with the responsibility.

Line-Staff Relationships

As organizations grow in size and complexity the need for specialists becomes evident. Staff units are formed to support, advise, control, and provide services for line activities.

Line is distinguished from staff essentially by the nature of authority relationships. Line authority is a relationship in which the manager exercises direct supervision over employees—the authority relationship is in direct lines or steps. The nature of the staff relationship is advisory. In other words, the line has *direct* authority to carry out the organization's objectives, while the staff supports the line's efforts; staff is auxiliary to the principal operations. Under the concept that authority relationships determine whether a department or unit is line or staff, it is often difficult to categorize organizational units as purely line or staff. However, departments that predominantly advise, e.g., personnel, are viewed as "staff" departments, whereas those that directly carry out the organization's mission, e.g., police in a public safety agency, are considered "line." Figure 5.3 is an organization chart of the U.S. Department of the Interior which provides an illustration of the line and staff units in the overall organization.

How staff gets its power. The most obvious source of staff authority is direct delegation from the line. But why do some staff people seem to have more power or authority than others? Consider the following:

> "People accept the proposals of persons in whom they have great confidence. In any organization there are some individuals who, because of past performance, general reputation, or other factors, have great influence or authority. Their proposals will often be accepted without analysis as to their wisdom. Even when the suggestions of such a person are not accepted, they will be rejected reluctantly and only because stronger authority contradicts them."[19]

As staff people gain the confidence of the line organization as a result of quality performance, they tend to be granted more and more authority. Frequent contact with line managers develops in staff people an ability to sense or even to anticipate areas of need that they can accommodate. A knowledge of line people, coupled with willingness to help and accessibility when needed, creates an environment conducive to the development of confidence. By providing practical solutions to line problems, and presenting them in such a fashion that the line manager can accept or reject the proposal without further study (this is the *doctrine of completed staff work)*, the influence, or power of the staff is greatly enhanced.

Winning respect and gaining esteem through expertise and reputation is an additional source of power. This status results from the person's credentials, e.g., a law degree, a Ph.D. in chemistry, or a Master of Public Administration, and demonstrated expertise in his or her specialty. As a result of the staff person's particular area of knowledge, the line might delegate authority to him or her to make decisions or take actions in a particular area. This *functional authority* is a prime source of power for staff people. The highly complex nature of personnel problems has increased the influence of those who have

---

[19]Herbert A. Simon, Donald W. Smithburg, and Victor A. Thompson, "Authority: Its Nature and Motives" in David R. Hampton et al., *Organizational Behavior and the Practice of Management* (Glenview, Ill.: Scott, Foresman, 1968), p. 462.

Figure 5.3. Department of the Interior

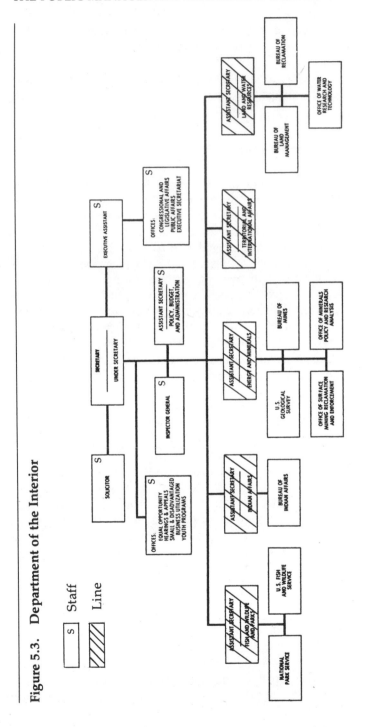

Source: *U.S. Government Manual 1981–82* (Washington: U.S. Government Printing Office), p. 832.

demonstrated expertise in the area of human resource management. Knowledgeable personnel professionals have been given wide functional authority to develop affirmative action plans, train public managers, negotiate agreements with unions, conduct team-building programs through the organization, and so forth.

Other Forms of Organization

Although line-staff type organizations are the predominant form in government, others are evident.

The *matrix* form of organization pulls together project groups in a temporary organization to accomplish a specific purpose. Individuals are assigned from functional departments of the traditional line-staff organization. Project personnel are under the authority of the project manager until the completion of the project, at which time they usually return to their original departments. NASA operated under the matrix form of organization to manage the Apollo and Saturn projects.

Other organizational structures found occasionally in government are based on function performed by various units of an agency and/or by clientele served.

ORGANIZATION CHARTING

Charts such as the one shown in Figure 5.3, are graphic representations of the organization structure at a given point in time. They show authority relationships as well as channels of communications. Charts are a useful tool for organizing because they depict departmental and unit relationships. Potential organizational conflicts and inefficiencies often can be circumvented by charting the relationships before the structure is made operational.

The chart also is a useful tool to plan the organization. It describes the location of various elements or units in the structure and can be useful in locating or relocating units within the organization. The drawback of organization charts is that they are diagrams. They oversimplify, whereas the "real" organization is a complex of formal and informal relationships that rarely operate as depicted in the chart. Furthermore, the chart represents a static picture whereas the organization is dynamic;

the relationships and organizational units are constantly changing. But despite these weaknesses, an updated organization chart is a useful planning and development tool. To enhance their usefulness Fraser[20] suggests applying a numerical value to each unit and subunit in the chart based on such items as budget size, floor space occupied, and/or selected personnel characteristics. The numerical values, he proposes, can be displayed with proportional square or rectangular symbols of varying sizes.

Organizational restructuring. Restructuring is now being viewed by public managers at all levels as key to making government responsive and accountable. However, few are naive enough to believe that restructure alone will accomplish this goal. Restructure is an evolutionary process, not a panacea. It requires careful analysis and understanding of the problem, a reshaping of attitudes and practices, a substantial commitment of resources, and a resolve on the part of the change agents to see it completed.

A congressional bipartisan study committee proposed to the 95th Congress a thorough overhaul of the committee structure including: a reduction of the number of standing committees to 15 from the existing 31; a reshaping of some committees, i.e., the Interior Committee would absorb the Aeronautical and Space Sciences Committee and all related transportation committees; and the Public Works Committee would be transformed into a committee on environment and public works.[21]

Early in his term President Carter received limited approval from Congress to restructure the executive branch. He started with a reorganization of the Office of the President and then directed his efforts toward eliminating a large number of the existing 1,300 plus federal boards and advisory committees. Through the initiation of zero-base budgeting he required each organizational unit to review its functions annually to ascertain whether or not it should be retained.

President Reagan hopes to reverse the Carter initiatives by cutting back on the size and number of government organiza-

---

[20]Ronald Fraser, "Reorganizing the Organization Chart," *Public Administration Review* (May–June 1978), pp. 280-282.

[21]"The Senate Braces for an Overhaul," *Business Week* (November 29, 1976), pp. 25-26.

tions and is focusing his reorganization efforts on disengaging government from the economy. President Reagan's actions demonstrate a philosophy on the role of government that is almost the antithesis of President Carter's.

This phenomenon of changing directions is even more prevalent in state and local organizations. Such changes can become intense at the local level because of the existence of multiple governmental jurisdictions, for example, schools, hospitals, and other activities are usually separate entities from the general city and county government. In addition, the national and state government directly administer many programs within most urban areas.

SUMMARY

Planning and organizing are basic functions of a public manager. In the planning function, the manager develops objectives and their accompanying programs. Organizing the group's activities assigns appropriate authority and provides for the coordination of effort toward the attainment of the objectives.

Conceptualization of desired program results in advance of their initiation is the essence of planning and helps insure effectiveness and efficiency. The process calls for deciding on the objectives and preparing policies to guide the organization. Strategies consider contingencies and help direct program efforts. Procedures and rules detail the methods for implementing programs.

The decision-making process for selecting organizational objectives and effective measures for their achievement is complicated by the political nature of public agencies. However, a rational approach is suggested as a viable complement of the more "intuitive" schemes. Either group or individual decision making is enhanced by the rational approach. And the group process, despite its inherent disadvantages, offers the benefit of allowing employees to participate in decisions that affect them.

The function of organizing requires an understanding of several basic concepts:

▶ *Span of control.* There is a limit to the number of people a manager can direct.

▶ *Unity of command.* For a given assignment, an employee should report to only one superior.

▶ *Delegation of authority.* A right to manage that is delegated, usually from above.

▶ *Responsibility.* The obligation to exercise authority properly.

Alternative forms of organizational structure, i.e., line, line/staff, matrix, are used depending on the functions to be performed, the nature of tasks involved, and the characteristics of the people employed. It should be remembered that organizations are dynamic entities and they may need to be restructured to be responsive to public needs.

CASE STUDIES

1. Reorganization of the Florida Department of Health and Rehabilitative Services

The Florida Department of Health and Rehabilitative Services (DHRS) is the state's largest agency. It spends over one billion dollars a year from revenues received from several federal programs, counties, and clients (in the form of fees). The department employs about 28,000 persons, serves over one million clients, and contracts with more than 30,000 individuals and agencies annually.

A panel of the National Academy of Public Administration (NAPA) identified the basic need for DHRS reorganization:

"The client, not the government, had the responsibility to identify and marshal available resources, trudging from office to office, waiting on many queues, filling out innumerable eligibility forms, challenging or appealing many decisions. Each citizen grappled alone with many bureaucracies to coordinate related services offered by state and local, public and private agencies.

"Repeated attempts have been made in various parts of the country to deal with this chaotic situation. It has been easier to

diagnose the problem than to solve it. In Florida, the solution—
or, rather, the problem—before 1975 consisted of nine separate
bureaucracies encompassing more than 70 separately funded programs, each designed to meet specific federal regulations and
funding requirements. Each bureaucracy operated independently with many of the same clients, providers, and community
agencies; each was subject to coordination, in the community
and state, only or principally by the departmental secretary."

To address these needs, the Florida Legislature in 1975
passed the Health and Rehabilitative Services Act. The Act
moved all program line authority to eleven integrated district
offices. This integration of a wide range of social, health, and
rehabilitative services administered by the same governmental
unit was expected to include these elements at the local level:

1. The common location of the staff of related services close
   to a large number of current and prospective clients

2. The delegation of authority to a local administrator to
   supervise and coordinate these services

3. A common intake system for new clients

4. Case management to insure that related services to an
   individual or family with multiple problems are provided, coordinated, and recorded

The NAPA panel concluded that "the Florida reorganization was the most significant current effort by any state to
consolidate the administration of social services and decen-
tralize their management. . ." But the reorganization also had
its management crises. The most serious were a breakdown in
voucher payments, the loss of accurate and current data on the
number of employees working in each classification and on the
allocations and expenditures of programs in each district.
Additional problems resulted from new and complex financial
reporting requirements; new computer systems being introduced; continuing pressures to answer complaints; and high
turnover in key management positions. It was evident that
mission attainment under reorganization would take a dedicated effort of competent HRSA managers if the legislative
intent were to be operational with the five-year time frame.

▶ Identify the problems and possible causes here.

▶ Assuming that Florida intends to continue with its
  reorganization of DHRS, what are the priorities for
  change?

▶ If you were a consultant to Florida's DHRS, what would you recommend it include in its future plans?

2. Metro's Labor Market Advisory Committee

The Metro Manpower Planning Office (MPPO) enlisted the advice of a Labor Market Advisory Council (LMAC) to develop its 1981-82 manpower plan. The MPPO wanted to find the best means of training disadvantaged citizens in specified target groups (blacks, disadvantaged youth, aged, handicapped, Spanish speaking) and locating them in meaningful employment.

The LMAC, which consisted of business, labor, and community leaders from the Metro area (the 15-county standard Metropolitan Statistical Area), was commissioned to accomplish the following within a three month period:

1. Prepare a projection of the demand for jobs in the Metro Area for the next five years.

2. Identify those employers with specific needs for various skills.

3. Evaluate the existing training programs (welding, secretarial, keypunch, auto mechanics, auto body repair, graphic arts, medical technician, and retail sales).

4. Inventory the current supply of MPPO eligible candidates for training including education level, age, and target group.

The first meeting of the LMAC was well attended and all members responded enthusiastically to the assigned mission. However, subsequent meetings attracted few members and the MPPO staff had to resort to individual contact to get the necessary information.

▶ Why do you suppose LMAC member interest dwindled?

▶ In attempting to get citizen participation, how can public managers insure their commitment to a project?

▶ If you had been in charge of developing the manpower plan for the MPPO, what role would you have assigned the LMAC?

▶ Specifically, what might the MPPO do to rejuvenate the LMAC at this point?

6

The Public Manager as Personnel Manager

Key Concepts

Merit Principles
  Job Analysis
    Affirmative Action
      Evaluation Interview
        Human Resource Development
          Performance Appraisal
            Personnel Effectiveness
              Leadership
                Motivation
                  Compensation Management
                    Job Evaluation
                      Fringe Benefits

Government serves its citizens through the skills and dedication of the people who work for it. Thus, the success of public managers depends to a large degree on the effectiveness of the people who work for them. For many managers, human resources management is the most difficult, yet rewarding, part of their jobs. This role of the public manager calls for personal knowledge about what motivates people, ingenuity, and human resources skills.

Personal expertise alone will not suffice in managing for performance effectiveness in government agencies. Regulations and laws have considerable influence on a manager's handling of people. In addition, the sheer size of government and the changing nature of its work force complicates the situation, with the result that public managers face challenges today that their predecessors did not even envision. The public sector employs more than 16 million people today. Their values, attitudes, and aspirations are different from previous generations of employees. This new breed of young, highly educated person is seeking an individual identity within a mass society. They are challenging the ingenuity of public managers to address societal problems.

PERSONNEL MANAGEMENT DEFINED

For the purposes of our discussion in this chapter we might define personnel management as *the process of supporting the accomplishment of the agency's objectives by acquiring human resources, integrating employees into the organization (agency), developing employee potential, and maintaining the workforce.*

Acquiring includes anticipating the human resource needs of an agency and employing the people necessary to staff it. Employment encompasses recruiting needed employees including filling from within, screening applicants for employment, selecting the most suitable candidates, and placing newly hired employees in appropriate job vacancies or training programs.

Integrating employees consists of making them part of the organizational team through counseling activities and interviews to learn about their backgrounds, aspirations, work experiences, and any problems in adjusting to work life.

Developing includes all activities for the education, training, appraisal, and planning of careers to prepare employees for present or future assignments and thereby enhancing their value to the agency. Training and educational activities develop skills, improve behavior, and provide information necessary for more effective performance. Performance appraisal informs employees of their progress and aids them in correcting deviations from established performance standards. Career planning combines agency needs with personal aspirations to help insure that individual talent is optimally utilized.

Maintaining involves programs of compensation and benefits to reward people's accomplishments. This activity serves to maintain an efficient and effective workforce, to retain valuable talent in government service, and to sustain and improve the favorable working environment within the agency.

This chapter discusses the concepts and techniques associated with each of these activities, including the influence of personnel and regulations, and shows how the public manager can employ them to enhance personnel effectiveness.

Personnel Regulations—The Civil Service Reform Act

The basic law governing personnel practices in the federal government is the Civil Service Reform Act, Public Law 95-454 (S. 2640). Since many states and municipalities either have patterned or will pattern their personnel systems after this Act, it is appropriate to summarize its provisions here.

The Act was designed to improve government efficiency and to balance management authority with employee protection. It became effective in 1978 and includes such major features as incentives and rewards based on performance, independent and equitable appeals process, protections against abuse of the merit system, and specific changes in federal labor relations (the latter provision will be discussed in Chapter 7).

Basic merit principles which govern all personnel practices in the federal government are included in the law. They require—

▶ recruitment from all segments of society

▶ fair and equitable treatment without regard to politics, race, color, religion, national origin, sex, marital status, age, or handicapping condition

▶ equal pay for equal work with incentives for excellent performance

▶ high standards of integrity, conduct, and concern for public interest

▶ efficient and effective use of the work force

▶ retention, correction, or separation depending on continued performance

▶ effective education and training

▶ protection of employees from arbitrary action

▶ protection of employees against reprisal for lawful disclosure of information, or whistle blowing

Prohibited practices are defined by the law. They include discriminating against an employee or applicant, using preferential treatment, or taking an improper personnel action.

New performance appraisal procedures have been instituted calling for each agency to develop and implement its own system.

Adverse actions, such as removals, suspensions for over 14 days, and reductions in pay or grade may be appealed to the *Merit Systems Protection Board* (MSPB), an independent agency that hears and decides employee appeals and orders corrective action when appropriate. The *Special Counsel* to the MSPB has authority to protect whistle blowers.

Discrimination complaints can be heard by the MSPB, but the Equal Employment Opportunity Commission (EEOC) also can be involved. In addition, the EEOC approves targets and timetables on agencies' equal employment goals and affirmative action plans.

New *grade and pay retention* provisions make it possible for employees to retain their grades for two years and to avoid taking considerable cuts in salary as a result of downgrading actions for which they are not responsible.

Supervisors and managers are required to serve a *trial period* before their appointments become final. And a *merit pay system* (for GS-13 through GS-15 employees) recognizes performance; i.e., cost efficiency; timeliness of performance; and improvements in efficiency, productivity, and quality of work or service.

A *Senior Executive Service* consisting of high level managers in the executive branch was designed to attract and keep top managers, to use their abilities productively, and to pay them according to their performance.

The Office of Personnel Management (OPM) took over the responsibilities of the Civil Service Commission including central examining and employment operations, development of personnel management policy and regulations, personnel investigations, personnel program evaluation, and executive development and training. OPM also administers the retirement and insurance programs for federal employees and exercises management leadership in affirmative action and labor relations.

ACQUIRING HUMAN RESOURCES

Public managers often become annoyed at the length of time it takes to fill a position. Planning for people needs can help reduce that time; several aspects of planning that can help include the following:[1]

► Anticipate vacancies and start recruiting well in advance.

► Know the steps that must be accomplished, including budget and ceiling approval, and stay abreast of the paperwork.

► Prepare written position description(s) and qualification requirements and understand the classification standards which are used to establish the series, title, and salary grade of each position.

► Adhere to a realistic timetable.

► Allocate the necessary time for review of applications and interviews.

Job analysis is performed to determine the criteria for successful performance so that selection methods such as exams and interviews can be valid. The analysis identifies and describes distinguishing characteristics of a job and the requirements for its performance. Agencies use observation, interviews, questionnaires, and studies to gain data for the analysis. Essentially, the process of job analysis consists of three basic elements: (1) identifying the jobs, i.e., designating the classifications needed to carry out the agency's mission; (2) determining the specific content of the job; and (3) preparing a written job description. Generally, the agency has a job analyst or personnel specialist employed who performs the analysis; thus a detailed description of the job analysis procedure is not relevant for this discussion.[2]

---

[1]United States Office of Personnel Management, *Manager's Handbook* (Washington, D.C.: Office of Personnel Management, 1979), p. 9.

[2]Those who wish for more detail on analyzing jobs can find it in two useful references: *The Dictionary of Occupational Titles*, Vol. 2, Occupational Classification edition (Washington, D.C.: Department of Labor, 1977); *Job Analysis Handbook* (Washington, D.C.: Department of Labor, 1968).

Selection methods. Whether selecting from within or from the outside, principles of open competition apply. Merit system regulations call for workforce composition that is representative of society; selection and promotion based on relative knowledge, skills and abilities; and the use of open competition to assure equal opportunity. As a direct result of the Civil Service Reform Act, agencies, on request, are now receiving delegations of authority to perform direct recruitment and examining with Office of Personnel Management oversight.

Examinations. As part of the hiring process, applicants are usually examined using one of two methods: assembled or unassembled exams. *Assembled* exams are written and/or performance tests. *Unassembled* exams generate ratings of experience, education, training, and other job-related achievements described by the applicant. Examinations can be a combination of the assembled and unassembled types. The federal government's Uniform Guidelines on Selection Procedures, applicable to public and private sector employers, mandate that any requirements established for positions being filled be necessary for successful job performance, and that any tests based on such requirements do distinguish between potentially successful and potentially unsuccessful candidates.

Hiring from outside the agency. A variety of methods is used to attract talent. These include: announcements, recruiting bulletins, consolidated job listings, or similar notices to invite interested persons to apply. Many agencies develop their own recruiting literature and they regularly visit college campuses to recruit candidates. With the current emphasis on affirmative action, agencies are exerting special efforts to locate minority and female talent. Toward this end, they take a multifaceted approach to recruiting using such sources as employee referrals; advertising campaigns; speakers at high schools, colleges and universities; labor organizations; professional groups; and special interest groups.[3]

---

[3]Special interest groups include such organizations as the Urban League, the National Association for the Advancement of Colored People, the National Organization for Women, the Golden Age Club, Senior Citizens of America, state and local vocational rehabilitation agencies, and others.

The *employment application* is essential to the examining process. It provides biographical information, employment experience data, and other essentials that help the employing agency make a more objective selection decision. In addition, employment applications designed to provide quick and systematic information help to plan the employment interview and are a source of information for personnel records if the applicant is hired.

Processing applications. Agencies usually maintain registers which include the names of qualified candidates for positions where there are anticipated vacancies. It seems most practical for the manager to screen these registers whenever there is an impending vacancy. This, of course, does not preclude the initiation of recruiting efforts, but it can save time and expense when an acceptable candidate appears on the register.

Once the applicants for a position are identified, the examining office screens them for minimum qualifications and applies qualification standards to determine who is eligible. Candidates are then ranked on their relative qualifications based on education, training, experience, and scores of evaluation instruments. Usually the individual or agency making the hiring decision will also make an evaluation of the unassembled examinations. In federal agencies, eligible applicants with veteran preference receive additional points on their ratings. Those listed as "best" among the eligible candidates are *certified* by the examining office based on *selective* and/or *quality ranking* factors. A selective factor would be the knowledge, skill, or ability to do the job which, for an auditor, for example, would be knowledge of cost accounting. A quality ranking factor would be skill, knowledge, or ability that is desirable, but not essential to the job, such as knowledge of computer programming for the auditor. Some candidates, however, are certified based on scores derived from general aptitude tests and/or education or experience.

Selection. In selecting from outside the agency, the "rule of three" applies. Under most merit systems, for each vacancy, managers may select one of the top three available candidates who have been certified. Sometimes an agency may determine that none of the "top three" referred on the certificate are acceptable, because of lack of experience, poor interview results, conflict of interest, lack of availability, unsuitability for the agency or the job, or other relevant factors. Managers must be able to substantiate such objections in case appeal or discrimination complaints are lodged.

Excepted Service jobs may be exempted from competitive service, but they do not necessarily waive exam requirements. Excepted agencies, e.g., the Tennessee Valley Authority, have their own merit systems which require applicants to demonstrate that they have the basic qualifications required to do the job.

Hiring from within. Internal selection or promotion from within the agency allows greater flexibility than hiring from the outside. Candidates are already employed, so the agency has performance information in addition to the data gathered for the initial employment. Consequently, candidates for internal selection are usually ranked as "best qualified," "well qualified," and "qualified." A maximum number of candidates who can be considered for each vacancy is established in the agency merit promotion plan, but the number may vary considerably from one agency to another. The promotion plans are often subject to negotiation when employee organizations are recognized as an appropriate bargaining agent of the employees (see Chapter 7).

Affirmative Action

The Civil Service Reform Act makes clear the obligation of all government agencies to ensure that all personnel actions are made on a nondiscriminatory basis. At all levels of government the federal Equal Employment Opportunity Commission is empowered to bring civil actions against agencies which discriminate in their personnel practices. Whenever selection procedures tend to screen out candidates of a particular minority group or sex, selection devices should be investigated. This factor admonishes all agencies to validate their selection devices and base their selection requirements on rational relevant job analysis.

In order to comply with the Act, agencies must prepare Affirmative Action plans. Affirmative action stresses *objective* employment practices. It means achieving representative bureaucracy through open employment systems that include goals and special efforts to recruit and hire, and make provisions for upward mobility of, minorities and women. (Details on such programs are covered later in this chapter under "Women and Minority Development.")

INTEGRATING EMPLOYEES INTO THE ORGANIZATION

Once employees are selected and assigned, they must be made a part of the organization. Public managers use personnel records for evaluating and controlling personnel activities, and for gaining insight into the backgrounds, capabilities, and aspirations of employees. Then, through interviews and counseling sessions, these managers can help individual employees become viable members of the working team.

Personnel Records

Records are a primary source of data for evaluating and controlling personnel activities; they are also a basis for reports and research on human resources. Personnel records provide facts for a number of uses, such as reports to regulatory agencies, (e.g., records can classify applicants and employees according to sex, race and religion for the EEOC); reports within the agency on the effectiveness of personnel activities; controls on operating problems (e.g., absenteeism) and problem situations (e.g., grievances); and surveys of wages and personnel practices. Computers have facilitated record keeping of personnel information. Human resource data banks store a vast amount of data that can be retrieved quickly and simply in the form of a variety of reports.

Interviewing/Counseling

Public managers have numerous occasions to conduct personnel interviews. Interview skills are important in selecting employees, orienting new candidates, teaching or coaching subordinates to improve their job performance, counseling people on their personal problems, or resolving disputes. An understanding of interviewing is essential to effective management, and special programs on the techniques of interviewing usually are included in supervisory training sessions. Some discussion of the counseling interview, however, is appropriate here because it is basic to integrating employees into the organization.

Employee counseling usually involves a nondirective approach, in which the interview is guided by how the interviewee sees the situation. The interviewer asks an open-ended question like, "Tell me about yourself," and listens carefully. The nondirective interview encourages expression of feelings, opinions, and ideas and permits interviewees to emphasize what they feel is relevant and important. The interviewer makes comments or asks questions to stimulate thinking and facial expression. A typical question might be, "How do you feel about your work in government?" Or a comment such as, "You seem to feel that your work is causing you stress," would be an example of a nondirective approach. This approach is most appropriate in counseling because individuals often are in the best position to solve their own problems by gaining greater insight into them. The nondirective approach helps people accept their problems and gain a better understanding of themselves—of both their strengths and weaknesses.

At one time or another all employees have problems; although many are work connected, some are not. Managers often have no choice about counseling. They cannot escape dealing with the problems that employees bring to them, even if they wish to. Therefore, the public manager's role in counseling requires a sensitivity to employees' needs and an approachable attitude that encourages employees to consult them about problems. Also, public managers should be alert for signs that employees are experiencing difficulties. Frequently, managers find that these problems are best referred to a specialist who is experienced in diagnosing a specific difficulty and in working with the employee toward recovery.

DEVELOPING EMPLOYEE POTENTIAL

In order to have employees function effectively in the organization, public managers find they must insure that proper attitudes are instilled, appropriate skills are taught, and necessary information is provided. Enlightened managers emphasize the continuous development of all people within their jurisdiction.

Human Resource Development

Human resource effectiveness depends to a large degree on developing the capabilities of employees. Rapid change in all aspects of government, from technology to social interaction, demands constant efforts to keep employees informed of new policies, techniques, and developments within the agency and the government service. Considering the varied composition of the work force, public managers face a real challenge and responsibility in developing the full potential of every employee. Various federal and state statutes require ongoing in-service, interagency, and nongovernment training programs. The Government Employees Training Act (GETA) enacted in 1958 essentially allows agencies to provide whatever training is necessary to develop the skills, knowledge, and abilities that will best qualify their employees for the performance of official duties. The Office of Personnel Management, as the training arm for the federal government, carries out the provisions of federal laws and Executive Orders on training. But the OPM also provides guidance and training services for state and local agencies primarily through the programs established under the Inter-Governmental Personnel Act of 1970.

The training/development process is depicted by Figure 6.1. The basic elements of the model include identifying training/development needs through data analysis, selecting and writing training objectives, conducting instruction, and evaluating training effectiveness. Each of these elements is discussed below.

Identifying training/development needs. Job needs data are collected by observation, interviews, surveys, and analyses of records and reports. Governmental agencies use the following methods to analyze training needs:

▶ *Analysis of management reports* that may indicate low efficiency, poor attitudes, high costs.

▶ *Analysis of personnel reports* may show problems with grievances, turnover, attendance, or communications.

▶ *Discussion with supervisors* who are closest to the problems that training can overcome may indicate deficiencies in specific employee skills.

Figure 6.1. Model of the Training/Development Process

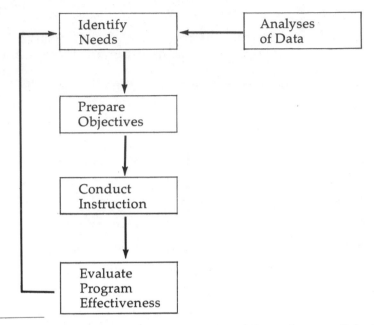

Source: Adapted from *Personnel: The Management of Human Resources*, 3rd ed. by Donald P. Crane (Belmont, Calif.: Wadsworth, 1982), p. 383.

▶ *Review of position descriptions* may be used to ascertain if employees know how to perform all necessary details of the job.

▶ *Surveys of employee attitudes* may pinpoint problem areas from the employee's view of the work environment.

▶ *Analysis of planned organizational changes* provides lead time for training. For example, if payroll will be handled by electronic data processing, payroll clerks can be retrained in keypunch operation, computer programming, and related fields.

▶ *Exit interviews* with personnel who are leaving the organization can uncover existing or potential problem areas.

A primary consideration in determining training needs is to establish whether training can correct problems. Often training is not necessary, and simply telling people what is expected and letting them know how well they are doing will have a greater impact.

Selecting and writing training objectives. Objectives provide the basis for planning a training program. They delineate the knowledge required in each subject area and guide training specialists in selecting appropriate teaching methods. Managers can then evaluate training effectiveness against these objectives. The following criteria are guideposts in defining objectives:

▶ Training objectives and agency goals must be compatible.

▶ Objectives must be realistic.

▶ Objectives must be clearly stated in writing.

▶ Results must be measurable and verifiable.

At the same time objectives are being selected, the basis for evaluating effectiveness of training should be established— criterion measures need to be determined and methods for implementing them planned. There also should be plans for developing course outlines and lesson plans, selecting and sequencing course content, developing training aids and hand-out materials, and arranging for instructors and training facilities. In many government agencies, full time training specialists are responsible for planning and implementing the programs; however, all managers should be aware of the role of the training specialists.

Conducting instruction. The training content and the manner in which it is presented are key to the reception and retention of the material by participants. Instructors must not only thoroughly understand the material they present, but also must be well-versed in the fundamentals of teaching. Technique also affects the impact of teaching. Studies have shown that instruction can be more effective when participants are involved through action-oriented techniques such as role play, case analyses, simulation exercises, in-basket exercises, projects, and group discussions. However, the lecture method can also be effective, particularly when theoretical information or a variety of details are to be imparted. In developing managers outside the classroom, public agencies have found such techniques as coaching, counseling, job rotation assignments, special projects, and assistant-to positions particularly useful.

Course content should address itself to the stated training objectives. The state of Pennsylvania, for example, designed a program that was intended to offer an integrated approach to the development of state and local personnel. Teaching methods, e.g., seminars, lectures, varied according to the type of personnel and the nature of the jurisdiction, e.g., state or city; large or small. The program combined management theory, program analysis methodology and program technologies, and issues. At the highest levels of the largest jurisdictions the focus was on system-wide issues in the areas of health services, welfare, and the administration of justice. At the more technical levels, emphasis was on state-of-the-art in substantive issues such as new technologies for solid-waste disposal.[4]

Evaluating training systems. The effectiveness of a training program is determined by measuring results against objectives. The most scientific means of accomplishing this is by selecting a control group similar to the group being trained. Both groups are administered tests before and after training. Ideally, the training group shows the greater improvement in test scores, indicating that the training was effective. However, this procedure can often be too expensive and time consuming for smaller agencies, so alternative methods are used. It is advisable to measure training results at several points: during and immediately following instruction, to determine the level of the participant's understanding of the subject; shortly after the training, one to two weeks, to examine the effect on the trainee's attitudes, behavior, and skills; and six months to a year later, to determine how much of the training has been retained and applied on the job. This type of evaluation can be accomplished in a number of ways. Performance tests and questionnaires or opinion surveys are formal methods. On an informal basis, questioning by the instructor, observations by outside consultants, and discussions with individual students can prove useful.

---

[4]Robert T. Mowitz, "Training Model for State and Local Governmental Personnel," *Public Personnel Management* (September–October 1974), p. 451.

Management and Executive Development

Training has relevance for all classifications within the agency including executives. Since government agencies at all levels stress the importance of a "succession of competent managers," the subject of executive and management development warrants some attention. The Civil Service Reform Act established the federal Senior Executive Service (SES) which serves as a model for executive development programs throughout government. The development features of SES include:

1. A climate within each agency conducive to executive growth.

2. Individual Development Plans that focus on enhancing managerial skills, correcting deficiencies identified in performance evaluations, and preparing for future assignments. The plans include these features:

   ▶ developmental assignments

   ▶ attendance at seminars and conferences

   ▶ formal education and training

3. The Federal Executive Institute—an interagency development center operated by OPM.

4. Sabbaticals for study and/or work experience outside the government.

5. Annual summary ratings of the executive's performance.

The Senior Executive Service began in 1979 as a separate personnel system for individuals in managerial, supervisory, and other policy making jobs equivalent to GS-16 through Executive Level IV. The Office of Personnel Management determines the number of SES positions in each agency and incumbents in these positions may choose to enter the SES. The number of SES positions are limited (about 8,500) so that those who choose to enter the Service must meet specific qualification requirements and those who seek Career Appointments (versus noncareer or limited terms) must compete for a position. Career Executives in the Service who perform well become eligible for rewards. Each year fifty percent of them may be given a lump sum bonus of up to 20 percent of base salary; up to 5 percent of SES executives may receive the rank of "Meritorious Executive" which carries an award of $10,000; and the "Distinguished Executive" rank has a special award of $20,000 (limited to 1 percent of SES).

Success with SES so far has been mixed. Evidence of its success is the fact that 98.5 percent of the career executives "voluntarily joined" SES; and the SES is fully operational since all agencies covered by the Act have an OPM approved (SES) system. However, according to one observer some executives have expressed concern that with removal of job protection in SES, career executives are not protected against adverse actions unrelated to job performance. This factor could inhibit their speaking up as analytically and critically as they might if they had the protection. Since these executives may span several administrations, newly elected presidents will have to use their power with civilized restraint over these career executives if SES is to succeed. Some high performing executives expressed frustration when Congress recently cut in half the number of career executives who can receive bonuses. As a final SES problem, agency discretion under the Act resulted in significant differences in the operation of the system. But despite these concerns, if OPM can actually guide and monitor SES in cooperation with the agencies, the great promise of SES can be realized, e.g., significant improvement of government operations.[5]

Performance Appraisal[6]

The Civil Service Reform Act places considerable emphasis on the evaluation of employee performance. It mandates that each agency develop its own appraisal system, suitable to the peculiar conditions of the agency. Thus, there is no "best" system, but there are certain elements that should be contained in all of them. These elements are discussed below.

Critical elements and performance standards. Any component of an employee's job that is so important that below-

---

[5]Bernard Rosen, "Uncertainty in the Senior Executive Service," *Public Administration Review* (March–April 1981), pp. 203-207.

[6]This section was adapted from United States Office of Personnel Management, *Manager's Handbook,* pp. 42-45.

standard performance for that component requires remedial action (including denial of a within-grade increase or even reduction in grade level) is a critical element. A performance standard is the explicit (measured) level of achievement (quantity, quality, timeliness) established for the duties and responsibilities of a position or positions. Performance standards should be objective, job related, and clearly communicated; and managers are encouraged to elicit employee participation in their development.

Performance appraisal discussion. Discussions of appraisal results are crucial to the success of the system. They serve to keep employees informed of their accomplishments relative to management's expectations, enable the timely correction of unacceptable performance, allow for recognition of exemplary performance, provide for documentation of performance, and avoid unpleasant surprises to employees who may have a different perception of their performance.

Unacceptable performance—appropriate action. When an employee fails to meet established standards in one or more critical areas of a position, he or she may be reassigned, reduced in grade, or removed. However, the employee must first be given an opportunity to correct the unacceptable performance. The manager's approach is the key to the success of performance appraisal. To make it work properly, the following factors are essential.

Good communication. This entails a mutual understanding of performance standards, an acceptance of all concerned of the purposes and procedures of the system, and continuous feedback on the employee's accomplishments. The appraisal process includes coaching and counseling throughout the year prior to the official appraisal interview.

Adequate training. All managers associated with the appraisal system must understand its importance and how it works, and they must know the techniques of evaluating performance and of conducting the appraisal interview.

System evaluation. To insure that the system is working as intended, continuous checks need to be made. Someone in authority can see if appraisals are actually being completed on a timely basis, and if appraisal interviews are being conducted, see that the employee understands what was supposed to have been communicated.

Investing time and effort. Job analyses, establishment of performance standards, completion of the appraisal forms, interviews, and reviews require considerable time and effort. But it is a worthwhile task for managers in terms of the improved performance and employee development that result.

Development of Women and Minorities

A special aspect of developing employee potential is the preparation of women, blacks, and other minorities for management responsibilities. Affirmative action calls for special efforts by public managers in this regard. Recognizing a critical need to expand opportunities for members of minority groups to assume leadership roles in the public service, the American Society for Public Administration (ASPA) in 1970 helped form the Conference on Minority Public Administrators (COMPA) as an affiliate. Its activities include:

- ▶ workshops on the roles, problems, and opportunities of minority managers
- ▶ seminars with public officials to discuss issues relevant to minorities, e.g., low-cost housing and health-care administration
- ▶ awards for outstanding contributions of members
- ▶ employment assistance
- ▶ peer counseling for career development
- ▶ various publications and papers presented at ASPA meetings[7]

---

[7]Rose M. Robinson, "Conferences of Minority Public Administrators," in Adam W. Herbert, ed. "Symposium on Minorities in Public Administration," *Public Administration Review*, Vol. 34 (November–December, 1974), pp. 544-555

Agencies that have reported the greatest success in developing women and minorities for management positions cite the following two practices as essential:

Career counseling can help women, especially, to work out the conflict associated with entering a world of work that formerly was the province of men. Counselors can guide them in their efforts to change their image and improve their self-esteem. Counseling becomes particularly meaningful to women who need to deal with the conflict between career and marriage.[8] (Career planning is discussed in detail in Chapter 10.)

Training is tailored to individual needs. Frequently a sponsor or mentor is designated to guide the candidate and insure a successful training experience. Courses in assertive skills are offered for women to educate them in their personal rights and teach them to stand up for their rights in such a way that others' rights are not violated. And black managerial aspirants are exposed to programs in politics and governmental management to overcome possible educational gaps in these areas.

MAINTAINING PERSONNEL EFFECTIVENESS

Stimulating improved productivity involves the application of techniques of communications, leadership, and motivation as well as financial inducements provided through compensation administration. Each of these activities include concepts for public managers' better understanding of people in their organizations. They will be dealt with from both a conceptual and practical standpoint.

Communication

Communication is the means for transmitting information, ideas, feelings, and attitudes among everyone in the organization, thereby coordinating the activities of all personnel and channeling them toward a common objective. Day-to-day dealings with employees require continual, effective communication.

---

[8]Louise Vetter, "Career Counseling for Women" in Lenore W. Harmon et al., *Counseling Women* (Monterey: Brooks/Cole, 1978), p. 89.

Effective communication depends on the solution of two entirely different problems. On one hand, communicators must transmit a message so that the words, ideas, and feelings will be received as intended. Getting *feedback* by observing the recipient's response or by having the recipient repeat the message can help alleviate the problem. Keeping the message simple and using multimedia (e.g., spoken word, memo, demonstration, mock-up) may also help insure that the message is received as transmitted. On the other hand, senders must correctly perceive the reactions and responses of the receiver to the communication. Sensitivity to the feelings and reactions of others plays a vital role here, especially when one considers the problems attendant with male-female, black-white and young-aged relationships on the job. Perhaps key to this second problem and the whole communications process for that matter, is listening. One has to listen to obtain feedback and to perceive the reactions of others.

A constant flow of information and feedback up, down, and across the organization can go a long way toward accomplishing objectives. Public agencies practice communications through a variety of formal programs. Grievance and complaint procedures encourage employees to express their concerns, questions, or job problems; provide fair hearings; and offer timely answers. Meetings with employees in an atmosphere of openness allow for exchange of information and problems, and facilitates upward communications. Finally, bulletin boards, reading racks, and newsletters are an effective means of disseminating announcements and news of an immediate nature.

Leadership

The ability of managers to get employees to work with zeal and confidence toward organizational objectives is known as leadership. Writers on this subject have identified various leadership styles which, theoretically, yield positive or negative results depending on their application.

Fiedler[9] suggests that task-oriented, authoritarian leadership is most effective in situations that are either very favorable

---

[9]Fred E. Fiedler, *A Theory of Leadership Effectiveness* (New York: McGraw-Hill, 1967).

or very unfavorable to the leader. A favorable situation is where the leader's influence is high, and relations with the work group are good, and the task is highly structured. In an unfavorable situation the leader has little influence, relations are poor, and the task is unstructured and unpredictable. Situations of intermediate favorableness are better handled through more participative, people-oriented approaches or styles.

Fiedler's situational approach was carried a step further by Victor Vroom and Philip Yetton whose research developed a normative model of leadership.[10] They found that to be effective, leaders should fit their style to the demands of the situation. They maintain that, when considering the available evidence, there is a likelihood that the participative style will increase productivity under some circumstances, but decrease it under others.

The path-goal theory of leadership is an extension of the situational approach. It attempts to define situationally the relationship between leader behavior and employee work attitudes and performance. Developed by Robert House, path-goal theory suggests that a leader functions to: (1) assure the employees' personal rewards for accomplishing work goals by clarifying the paths to their desired rewards and removing roadblocks and pitfalls to successful work performance, and (2) improve the opportunities for work satisfaction en route by showing consideration and support for the employees.[11]

Motivation

Like work, motivation is a highly complex phenomenon. There are many reasons why people work, and these reasons vary among individuals. In addition, motivation is not only generated within individuals, but also from outside factors; behavior on the job rarely stems from a single motive. Often, employees themselves are at a loss to explain their motives.

Figure 6.2 graphically portrays the basic motivation process. Human beings constantly strive to satisfy a multitude of *needs* and *desires* which vary in strength among individuals.

---

[10]Victor H. Vroom and Philip W. Yetton, *Leadership and Decision Making* (Pittsburgh: University of Pittsburgh Press, 1973).

[11]Robert J. House, "A Path-Goal Theory of Leader Effectiveness," *Administrative Science Quarterly* (September 1971), pp. 324ff.

Figure 6.2. The Basic Motivation Process

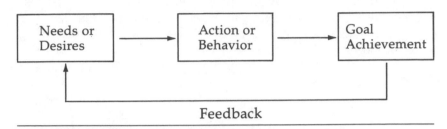

Feedback

They may, for instance, have a high need for additional income or a strong desire to be accepted by their peers. These are the activators of the process and create a restlessness within individuals which they will try to reduce or remedy. These needs and wants are generally associated with a belief that certain actions will lead to a satisfaction of needs, e.g., goal attainment. As individuals begin to work toward these goals, they receive information or cues either within themselves or from the external environment which either reassures them that their behavior is correct or dissuades them from the course of action. The result is that they may persist in their present behavior or they may modify or discontinue it altogether.

Expectancy theory is the prevailing theory of motivation today. It postulates that for a person to be motivated to perform, he or she must feel that his or her effort will lead to expected performance and the performance will result in a valued outcome.[12] For example, pay can be tied to a desired behavior such as effective performance; but it might not be enough to motivate the desired behavior unless the employee values pay highly and sees it as closely related to performance. However, if negative outcomes, such as becoming fatigued or being rejected by peers, are viewed as related to good performance, the motivation to perform will be absent. Similarly, when good workers perceive that they receive the same rewards (e.g., pay) as poor performers or that the job itself is simple and offers no inherent satisfaction from doing it well, they may conclude that being highly productive does little more than make one tired.[13]

[12]Victor H. Vroom, *Work and Motivation* (New York: John Wiley and Sons, 1967).

[13]Edward E. Lawler, III, *Motivation in Work Organizations* (Belmont, Calif.: Wadsworth, 1973), pp. 44ff.

Work environments can be designed to provide positive motivational factors and yield greater performance effectiveness. A number of city and county governments have reported success with programs to increase worker motivation. For example, Nassau County, New York has been experimenting with job redesign to increase worker productivity. And the cities of Eugene, Oregon; Simi Valley, California; and Glendale, Arizona have used job rotation programs to broaden the perspective of city employees and to expose them to possible better ways of performing their jobs. In Washington, D.C. the municipality and the sanitation workers, under a union contract provision, jointly review service problems and mutually work toward ways to solve them. All of these efforts tend to enrich jobs and stimulate personnel effectiveness. In the same respect, properly administered compensation programs can provide the stimulus for personnel effectiveness. Employees who feel they are sufficiently compensated for their efforts can be stimulated to achieve more. Compensation not only is used to attract and retain employees, but it is essential in encouraging effort through providing incentives and rewarding performance.

Compensation Management

Pay plans attempt to provide rewards commensurate with an employee's contributions, although compensation rarely accomplishes this goal in practice. Such an objective assumes that there is complete economic freedom throughout the organization to disseminate rewards; this situation never occurs because pay rewards are contingent on factors beyond the control of individual managers. Agencies cannot provide tangible remunerative benefits when budget appropriations are not adequate, despite employees' achievements for the organization. The individual manager can, however, attempt to make sure the monetary resources that are available are allocated on an equitable basis and provide an incentive for maximum employee performance.

Equity in compensation is another difficult area. Employees tend to compare their work and pay to similar classifications in other organizations both public and private. Employees tend to be satisfied with their pay when it compares favorably with that of employees whom they perceive as holding similar jobs.

Government agencies generally use the prevailing wage to establish rates within their organizations. Since the 1970 enactment of the Federal Pay Comparability Act, most government agencies have attempted to maintain comparability with pay rates in the private sector. There is considerable difficulty with the job-matching process because of the variety of pay schedules among government agencies, i.e., most have fixed rate ranges, like the federal GS schedule, that vary in the width of the ranges and in the nature of the schedule. Business professor David Lewin characterizes the problem:

> "While one objective of these plans is to reflect prevailing market wages, the fixed (i.e., static) nature of public-wage schedules may not facilitate a close matching with the range of private rates found in dynamic labor markets."[14]

Lewin and behavioral scientist Walter Fogel studied the application of the prevailing wage practices in municipalities. They conclude that "Government employers frequently pay more than necessary to attract a work force at the low- and middle-skill ranges and generally pay less than necessary to attract employees of average quality at the upper managerial and professional levels."[15] In addition to the prevailing wage practice, many states and municipalities have attempted to retain a relationship of parity between certain classifications, e.g., between police and firefighters, or between administrators and supervisors.

Job evaluation. The pay relationships among classifications can be maintained equitably through systems of job evaluation. An example of a system that is becoming increasingly popular among government agencies is the Factor Evaluation System (FES) approved by the OPM for implementation for nonsupervisory positions. Using a position description as a departure point, each job is assigned numerical points for each of nine factors. Each factor contains levels with varying point values. The total points for all factors translate into the pay

---

[14]David Lewin, "The Prevailing Wage Principle and Public Wage Decisions," in Jay M. Shafritz, ed., *A New World: Readings on Modern Public Personnel Management* (Chicago, International Personnel Management Association, 1975), p. 135.

[15]Walter Fogel and David Lewin, "Wage Determination in the Public Sector," *Industrial and Labor Relations Review* (April 1974), p. 430.

grade for the position. These same factors are used to evaluate all positions in the system:

Factor 1. *Knowledge required by the position.* This factor measures the nature and extent of information or facts which the worker must understand to do acceptable work.

Factor 2. *Supervisory controls.* This factor covers the nature and extent of direct or indirect controls exercised by the supervisor, the employee's responsibility, and the review of completed work.

Factor 3. *Guidelines.* This factor covers the nature of guidelines and the judgment needed to apply these guidelines.

Factor 4. *Complexity.* This factor covers the nature and variety of tasks, steps, processes, methods, or activities in the work performed, and the degree to which the employee must vary the work, discern interrelationships and deviations, or develop new techniques, criteria, or information.

Factor 5. *Scope and effect.* This factor covers the purpose of the assignment and the effect of work products both within and outside the organization.

Factor 6. *Personal contacts.* This factor includes face-to-face contacts and telephone and radio dialogue with persons not in the supervisory chain.

Factor 7. *Purpose of contacts.* This factor covers the range of contacts from factual exchanges of information to situations involving significant or controversial issues and differing viewpoints, goals, or objectives.

Factor 8. *Physical demands.* This factor covers the physical requirements of the work assignment. (For example, climbing, lifting, pushing, balancing, stooping, kneeling, crouching, crawling, or reaching.)

Factor 9. *Work environment.* This factor considers the risks, discomforts, or unpleasantness that may be imposed upon employees by various physical surroundings or situations.

FES provides a rational basis for assigning salary ranges to positions. Theoretically, merit plays a major role in determining how rapidly an employee progresses within a salary range. One of the most perplexing issues in personnel management is that of linking employee performance to salary administration. Van Adelsberg urges the adoption of a "pay-for-performance" approach whereby increases above a certain point, e.g., the midpoint of the range, would be justified only by superior performance. He laments that "the mania for the perpetual increase has destroyed any vestige of true 'pay-for-performance' in the public sector."[16]

Benefits

As a rule, employee benefits appear to be more generous in public agencies than among private employers. Paid leave and retirement benefits in particular are usually relatively higher in government than in private organizations.[17] There is a good reason why this phenomenon exists. Government agencies historically have heeded the admonition to set an example. In times of economic inflation, they endeavored to keep labor costs to a minimum so as not to contribute to the trend. Benefits were considered noninflationary because they did not increase employee purchasing power. Yet agencies had to compete with the private sector for talent. Added benefits made *total* compensation appear attractive to employment candidates and were considered a stabilizing influence on employment. Employees realized that benefits improved with longer service, and tended to remain in government service to accrue benefits and preserve their "investment."

Benefits represent supplements to pay that are either financial in nature, or that protect employees against financial loss. Protection-type benefits include life insurance, accident and sickness plans, and hospital-medical-surgical and major medical plans. In general, their inclusion in a benefits package is fairly standard among government agencies, but the provisions

---

[16]Henry Van Adelsberg, "Relating Performance Evaluation to Compensation of Public Sector Employees," *Public Personnel Management* (March–April 1978), p. 72.

[17]"Changes in the Compensation Structure of Federal Government and in Private Industry, 1970-72," (Washington, D.C.: U.S. Department of Labor, Bureau of Labor Statistics, undated), p. 1.

of the plans vary widely as to limits of coverage and specific provisions.

Time off with pay has become popular among government service employees. The amount and forms of leave time varies among agencies, but generally they pay employees for holidays, vacations, sick leave, and personal leave. Many agencies have experimented with various forms of flexible work hours to enable employees to arrange their schedules for greater personal convenience without interfering with efficient operations. In June 1980, the City of Los Angeles became the first city to put all its municipal employees on "flex-time." Its primary motive was to enhance productivity while reducing air pollution and saving energy. Experiments with four-day work weeks have had mixed results, although there have been numerous reports that the appeal of a longer weekend has attracted the interest of employees. The State of Oregon, for instance, polled its employees and found that 68 percent favored a 4/40 (four ten-hour days) schedule.[18]

Retirement plans are becoming more flexible, and the trend is toward less stringent age and service requirements. Vesting provisions are also becoming more liberal and many agencies permit employees to transfer benefits to other agencies if they relocate within the system.

Other benefits that are offered by some agencies are:

▶ Tuition refund plans that underwrite a portion of educational expenses for approved programs, usually courses that directly relate to present or future work.

▶ Thrift or savings plans, sometimes with matching contributions by the agency. An additional benefit can be realized when savings plans incorporate a tax sheltered annuity. Kansas City, Missouri was one of the first municipalities to institute such a benefit through a "Deferred Compensation" program. It was designed as a long term savings plan using before-tax income to supplement its regular retirement program.[19]

---

[18]Martin T. Kenny, "Public Employee Attitudes Toward the Four-Day Work Week," Public Personnel Management (March–April 1974), p. 159-161.

[19]Ralph E. Tannahill, "A Deferred Compensation Program for Kansas City, Missouri City Employees," Public Personnel Management (September–October 1973), p. 362.

▶ Suggestion systems to stimulate money-saving improvements from employees and reward them when their ideas are adopted.

A host of employee services are offered through government employers. Activities that can be supported by, and provide benefits to, employees include: employee clubs, recreation programs, athletic teams, social events, cultural activities, counseling services, credit unions, and communications programs providing employee newspapers, bulletin boards, and reading racks.

SUMMARY

Government agencies are measured by the results they achieve. These results are determined by the effectiveness of the personnel within the agencies.

Personnel effectiveness can be achieved through the integration of activities that acquire human resources, integrate employees into the organization, develop employee potential, and maintain personnel effectiveness.

Acquiring human resources involves planning the personnel needs of the agency and implementing the plans through employment programs. Employment encompasses recruiting needed employees, screening applicants for employment, selecting the most suitable candidates, and placing newly hired employees in appropriate job vacancies or training programs.

Integrating employees into the organization entails making them part of the employee group through counseling activities. Records are maintained on their experience, abilities, performance, and potential so that public managers can insure that their efforts make a positive contribution.

Developing employee potential includes activities for the education, training, and continuous development of all employees to the maximum of their capability. In this respect affirmative action programs give particular attention to the development of women and minorities.

Maintaining personnel effectiveness involves inducements and incentives to build employee confidence and stimulate improved productivity. The managerial skills related to communication, motivation, and leadership are brought to bear,

and compensation administration helps provide incentives and
rewards.

CASE STUDIES

1. The Personnel Manager

Art Reilley, a personnel specialist in his state's Department
of Transportation, was discussing personnel management with
Dorothy Daniel, the personnel manager of the state Department
of Education. Ms. Daniel was completing her explanation of
her agency's performance appraisal system.

"I think that I can fairly say that ours is the most comprehensive evaluation system in this state. Not only that—it is
accepted with enthusiasm by both the raters and the ratees.
Every six months we require a formal appraisal of all our managers by their superiors. This formal appraisal, of course, is in
addition to the daily coaching we encourage.

"Our form of appraisal has two parts, one of which concerns itself with the traits, abilities, and attributes of the person. This part helps us make decisions concerning promotions,
transfers, schooling, and the like. The second part has to do
with results—statements of objectives set and attained, projects completed, and so forth.

"After the appraisers complete the form, they must conduct
an appraisal interview, taking as long as they need to discuss
appraisal results with their employees. Each appraisal is
reviewed by the rater's immediate superiors to insure fairness
and accuracy. And here, in personnel, we analyze each form to
detect trends and determine how well each manager evaluates."

Jack Harmon, Ms. Daniel's administrative assistant, fol-
lowed the discussion with interest. When Ms. Daniel paused,
Jack made the following statement:

"Dorothy, are you sure that we require an appraisal interview? I've been working for you for three years now, and
you've never discussed my appraisals with me."

"Jack," said Ms. Daniel, "I am sure you will agree that that hasn't been needed. We work together so closely that I am sure you always know how I appraise you."

▶ What do you think of this formal performance appraisal system?

▶ Why was Jack Harmon never interviewed?

▶ What should Art Reilley recommend to his department to insure that managers conduct appraisals thoroughly?

2. The Instructor

"Okay girls, I want you to pay attention," Stan Maxwell, keypunch supervisor in the data processing unit said as he walked up to the keypunch machine. "Errors are way up, and it's about time you girls learned how to do this job right."

"Big deal," Sally muttered to Grace, as they stood at the edge of the group. "Old Stan's going to tell *us* how to do our jobs."

"I think he's drunk with power," Grace mumbled. "They send him off to some quickie training course, and now he knows more than any of us, who've been doing the job for the past ten years."

"Shut up and listen, you girls!" Stan yelled, "Now when you insert the data card. . ."

"How did a creep like Stan ever get to be supervisor, Grace?"

"Beats me, except he is a creep. That's the only kind of supervisor this outfit gets."

"Look at him fumbling with the keys—I could do better with my eyes closed," said Grace.

"Maybe you should do it with your eyes closed, Grace— you have more errors than anyone around here," said Sally.

"Sure," Grace said. "The department's got plenty of money—they can afford it."

"I'd say, if they had any sense, they'd get one of us to go for training. How'd you like that, Grace? Two weeks in Miami at government expense. But they had to send him, for crying out loud. He couldn't keypunch if he had to."

"Sally, shut up," Stan shouted. "You're not so hot on this job, you know—your error rate is way above standard."

"Sure boss, sure," Sally responded. "Grace," she muttered out of the corner of her mouth, "doesn't the union have some rule against this sort of hogwash? Do we have to listen to that guy rave?"

"I suppose so," Grace said. "Just grin and bear it."

"With luck I won't remember a thing," Sally said. "Hey, are you coming to the party tonight?"

▶ Why would employees mistrust a supervisor to this extent? What's going on behind the scenes?

▶ Would it make sense to have a keypunch operator go through the instructor training course instead of a supervisor?

▶ What other kinds of training are needed for:

a. the supervisor?

b. Sally and Grace?

7

The Public Manager as Labor Relations Manager

Key Concepts

Collective Bargaining
  Exclusive Recognition
    Unfair Labor Practices
      Strike
        Corrective Discipline
          Grievance Handling
            Mediation
              Arbitration

Public managers are key figures in effective labor relations. When a union or association first seeks recognition, the public manager plays an active role by encouraging employees to vote in a representation election, by correcting any false or misleading information, and by conveying labor relations policy and procedures to employees. The manner in which public managers treat their employees' dealings with union representatives can help produce an environment of cooperation. By keeping the union informed of plans which may affect employees and by treating union representatives with respect, the harmonious union-management relationship can be enhanced.

Often public managers represent the agency at the bargaining table either in the role of spokesperson or as an advisor to the management negotiating team—collecting and analyzing data, evaluating proposals, forming counter proposals, and observing labor strategies.

Discipline is essential to the smooth running of the agency, and the public manager has the basic responsibility for administering this essential aspect of the labor relations process. Public managers also answer grievances that may arise. Their manner of handling them determines how effectively they are resolved. But some disputes arise which cannot be resolved by the parties themselves; consequently, the public manager might have the responsibility for presenting management's side to the arbitration, fact-finding, or impasse panel.

This chapter covers all these aspects of the public manager's responsibilities in the role of labor relations manager.

PUBLIC SECTOR BARGAINING

Public employee unions and associations are not a recent phenomenon, but their rapid growth in the past decade occurred while the percentage of union membership in the private economy was declining. Most government union members have joined since 1962, the year President John F. Kennedy issued Executive Order 10988 which established the basis for collective bargaining among federal government employees. That executive action provided the impetus for the burgeoning growth of public sector unionism among federal employees. By 1978, 1.4 million employees of the federal government had enrolled in unions, as had 2.2 million state and local government workers; almost one of every five public service employees belonged to a union in 1978. Employee associations claimed an additional 2.5 million government employees as members, virtually all at the state and local levels.[1] Figure 7.1 shows the growth in membership of government unions.

One example of union growth is the American Federation of State, County and Municipal Employees (AFSCME) with more than 700,000 members. AFSCME was ranked 4th in 1978 compared to 21st thirteen years earlier and has gained 270,000 new members between 1977 and 1978.[2]

Clearly, the sanctioning of union organization by EO 10988 provided the impetus for growth of federal employee unions,

---

[1] U.S. Department of Labor, Bureau of Labor Statistics, *Directory of National Unions and Employee Associations 1979* (Washington, D.C.: U.S. Department of Labor, 1980).
[2] *Id.*, p. 61.

Figure 7.1.   Number of Government Employees in Public-Sector Unions, 1964-1978

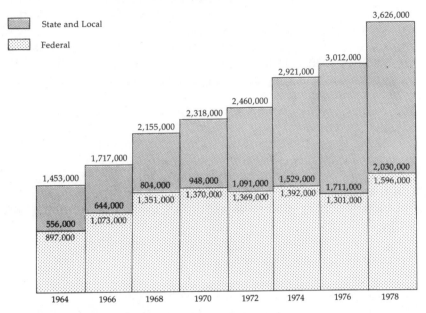

Note: At latest count, 1 in every 5 public-service employees belonged to a union, compared with 1 in 7 in 1964. An additional 2.2 million government workers belong to associations that, though not considered unions, bargain on behalf of employees. Thus, a total of 5.8 million public employees—more than one third of all employees who work for government—are in unions or in bargaining associations.

Source: U.S. Department of Labor, Bureau of Labor Statistics, *Handbook of Labor Statistics* (Washington, D.C., 1980). Figures for 1966 in *Handbook of Labor Statistics* (Washington, D.C., 1969).

and the momentum generated proved irresistible in states and municipalities. While public employees continued to flock to unions, their managers became perplexed. Why were public employees joining unions? The Civil Service system provides benefits for all federal government employees; and unions in government, legally deprived of some of the traditional sources of union power, are relatively weaker than their private sector counterparts. An analysis of findings of a survey of public employees revealed that dissatisfaction with the work situation had the greatest influence on an individual's decision to join a union.[3] From the union member's perspective, collective bargaining not only increases economic benefits, but gives individuals a sense of participation and a degree of influence over the forces that control their work environment.

Other reasons for organization of government employees are also apparent. As the economy became progressively inflationary in the past decade, the security of government employment was less appealing to workers whose earnings were not competitive with private sector earnings. Thus, they resorted to collective action to force an improvement in their economic position. Even the resort to militant actions such as strikes became acceptable in light of contemporary events, such as civil rights movements, war protests, and student uprisings. Conduct of perhaps questionable legality became accepted, and above all, achieved results where more conventional means failed.[4]

THEORETICAL ASPECTS OF COLLECTIVE BARGAINING

Collective bargaining lies at the heart of labor relations. Whenever employee-employer relationships involve unions or employee associations, collective bargaining establishes, administers, and enforces agreements between the parties. The bargaining process includes the actual negotiation of an agreement and involves interactions between agency and union representatives.

Walton and McKersie identified several subprocesses in labor negotiations.[5] Negotiations in which the gain of one party represents a loss to the other is called *distributive bargaining*. A joint problem-solving approach, working toward mutually beneficial solutions, is labeled *integrative bargaining*. Attitudes (e.g., trust and fear) and social relationships (e.g., competitiveness and cooperation) are changed and restructured during negotiations.

---

[3]Russell L. Smith and Anne H. Hopkins, "Public Employee Attitudes Toward Unions," *Industrial and Labor Relations Review* (July 1979), p. 484.

[4]Harry P. Cohany and Lucretia M. Dewey, "Union Membership Among Government Employees," *Monthly Labor Review* (July 1970), p. 18.

[5]Richard Walton and Robert McKersie, *A Behavioral Theory of Labor Negotiations* (New York: McGraw-Hill, 1965).

This behavioral theory is perhaps an oversimplification of the collective bargaining relationships as far as the public sector is concerned. In addition to managers and union representatives, other segments of the legislative and executive branches, and sometimes even citizen groups and neutrals became involved in public sector negotiations. Frequently, collective bargaining becomes an extension of politics. This process is considered multilateral because more than two distinct parties are involved and there exists no clear dichotomy between management and employee organizations. In his major study of formal bargaining relationships in 228 cities, Thomas Kochan[6] developed a theoretical model of multilateral collective bargaining. He hypothesized that multilateral bargaining is more likely to take place when certain conditions prevail, for example:

▶ There is a greater extent of internal conflict among management.

▶ There is a weak commitment of management decision makers to collective bargaining.

▶ Employee organizations use more political pressure tactics.

▶ The union has ready political access to city officials.

▶ The union is involved in city elections.

▶ There are a greater number of visible impasse pressure tactics used by the union in negotiations.

In essence, Kochan concludes, there is a close relationship between political conflicts that occur within city governments and the nature of the union-city bargaining process. Also, there is a high correlation between the political strength of unions and multilateral bargaining.

COLLECTIVE BARGAINING LAW

Executive Orders

Although Federal employees had the right to join unions as early as 1912 (Lloyd-La Follette Act) and municipal employ-

---

[6]Thomas A. Kochan, "A Theory of Multilateral Collective Bargaining in City Governments," *Industrial and Labor Relations Review* (July, 1974), pp. 525–542.

ees have bargained with an administration (Philadelphia) since 1939, the initial pervasive regulation of union-management relations appeared in the form of a series of executive orders. The first, EO 10988, was signed by President John F. Kennedy in 1962 and granted federal service employees the right to form or join labor organizations. It was amended by President Nixon's Executive Orders 11491 in 1969 and 11616 in 1971. They essentially required that agencies meet and confer in good faith on personnel policies, practices, and matters affecting working conditions with representatives of labor organizations which had been accorded "exclusive recognition." Specific matters, such as pay, budgets, mission, technology, or assignment of personnel were excluded from the meet and confer obligation.

Amendments contained in President Ford's EO 11838 in 1975 were designed to expand the scope of union-management activities. The most significant dimensions of EO 11838 focused on consolidation of bargaining units, scope, or range of bargaining negotiations, and grievance and arbitration procedures.

Civil Service Reform Act

These Executive Orders were expanded and translated into law through the Civil Service Reform Act of 1978. The Act reaffirms the basic rights of federal employees to form, to join, and to assist labor organizations (or to refrain from these activities). It explicitly prohibits strikes or similar actions that interfere with the operation of the government.

To obtain *exclusive* recognition, a labor organization (certified as the sole representative of all the employees in the unit) must first show by petition that 30 percent of the employees in the unit want an election and must have a majority of the employees who vote elect that organization. An "appropriate bargaining unit" is a grouping of employees who share a community of interest and who will promote effective labor-management dealings and efficient agency operations. The appropriate unit is determined by the Federal Labor Relations Authority. When a labor organization is certified as the exclusive bargaining representative, it is obliged to represent all employees in the unit fairly, whether they are union members or not.

The Act requires agencies to meet with the exclusive representatives of their employees and negotiate in good faith on conditions of employment—personnel policies and practices and general working conditions—with the expectation of signing a collective bargaining agreement. The law, however, reserves certain rights exclusively to management, thus excluding them from the bargaining process. These rights include: pay, mission, budget, organization, number of employees, internal security, and whether vacancies will be filled from within or from outside the agency. But the impact of these matters on employees and the procedures for implementing them are negotiated. Management has the exclusive right to promote employees, but the collective bargaining agreement may spell out how employees are to be ranked and certified.

Collective bargaining agreements must contain a simple procedure for the settlement of grievances arising under the contract. Most matters are resolved through the negotiated grievance procedure, but in adverse action cases, an employee can choose *either* the grievance procedure (if it covers the matter) or the statutory procedure (described later in this chapter under "discipline"). The Act specifies that negotiated grievance procedures must provide for binding arbitration if the steps of the grievance procedure fail to yield a satisfactory resolution.

The Act also lists unfair labor practices (ULPs) by both unions and management. For instance, the law prohibits management from—

▶ discriminating against union members

▶ refusing to negotiate in good faith

By the same token union officials may be cited for a ULP if they—

▶ cause an agency to discriminate against employees in exercising their rights

▶ call or participate in a strike

▶ take reprisal against a union member to hinder work performance

The Act is administered by the Federal Labor Relations Authority (FLRA) which determines appropriate bargaining units, oversees representation elections, resolves questions on

ULPs, and decides appeals from arbitration awards. When an agency reaches an impasse with its union, the parties may seek assistance and/or opinion from the Federal Service Impasses Panel. The Federal Mediation and Conciliation Service often steps in to mediate negotiations impasses. While the Impasses Panel is advisory and quasi judicial in nature, the FMCS serves to break impasses by attempting to bring the parties together. The two agencies complement the work of each other. The Office of Personnel Management provides policy guidance and technical advice to agencies concerning labor-management relations.

It should be obvious from the above summary of the Civil Service Reform Act that it is the most definitive regulation on labor-management relations to date. It will serve to clarify the roles and responsibilities of the parties and will help expand the rights of employees covered by collective bargaining agreements.

State Bargaining Laws

The wide variety of state collective bargaining statutes precludes any meaningful analysis within the confines of this chapter. However, state bargaining laws generally cover: (1) rights to organize and bargain collectively, (2) determination of appropriate bargaining units, (3) scope of bargaining, (4) resolution of collective bargaining impasses, (5) strike prohibitions, and (6) union security agreements.[7]

More than half the states have enacted collective bargaining legislation. Thirty-seven states have enacted comprehensive legislation covering state and/or municipal employees; ten have statutes covering teachers; ten have legislation covering firemen and/or policemen; and several others have laws covering only health care facilities, or transit authorities, or special districts. Only nine states have no legislative or executive authorization for public sector bargaining.

Legislation governs the conduct of the bargaining relationship and the issues involved. Those basic to most contracts are discussed below.

---

[7]Joan Weitzman, "Current Trends in Public Sector Labor Relations Legislation," *Journal of Collective Negotiations* (May 1976), pp. 234.

LABOR RELATIONS ISSUES

Traditionally, union bargaining demands have centered around economic issues such as wages, hours, and benefits. But more recently employee representatives have pressed for discussion of promotional and educational opportunities, standards of conduct and performance, rights of employees in disciplinary matters, and changes in civil service regulations or labor legislation. The Air Traffic Controllers' struggle for recognition by the Federal Aviation Administration is a case in point. Repeated refusal of the FAA to grant the Professional Air Traffic Controllers Organization exclusive recognition (PATCO represented 5,000 controllers nationwide) resulted in retaliatory slowdowns and sickouts. Following extended court and Labor Department hearings, PATCO was accorded exclusive recognition. As a representative of the Air Traffic Controllers, it helped to influence legislation (PL 92-297, 1972) that provided for appeal rights, and entitlement to receive second career training and/or retirement when a controller is removed from active control duties.[8]

The Right to Strike

As demonstrated by the 1981 Air Traffic Controllers dispute, the dominant issue in public sector relations is whether public employees should be allowed to strike. The question has been tested repeatedly in courts that have held that there is no constitutional right to strike. Legal decisions have consistently reasoned that public employees have a higher obligation to provide uninterrupted functioning of the government in order to insure public health, safety, and welfare. Nevertheless, the record shows numerous incidents of open defiance by public unions that engage in strikes or other forms of "job action."

Such militancy has led critics of public sector collective bargaining to argue that this practice is incompatible with merit systems. To support their position they make these points:

▶ Negotiated seniority arrangements are incompatible with qualifications, or merit, as the basis for selection or promotion.

---

[8]M. J. Fox and E. G. Lambert, "Air Traffic Controllers Struggle for Recognition and Second Careers," *Public Personnel Management* (May–June 1974), pp. 201ff.

▶ Collective economic bargaining disrupts the internal consistency of pay relationships.

▶ Union security arrangements, providing for a union or agency shop, often preclude the selection of otherwise qualified outside candidates.

Based on these arguments, critics feel that collective bargaining in government is not in the public interest.

On the other hand, the Civil Service Reform Act asserts that labor organization and collective bargaining in the civil service are in the public interest, and that its provisions are directed toward maintaining labor relations harmony.

New York City's special tripartite Board of Collective Bargaining serves as an example of an effort to maximize public interest while recognizing the importance of peaceful resolution of bargaining issues. The Board, which was created under the State's Taylor Law, is composed of neutrals and representatives of management and labor. It functions to oversee labor relations between the city and its public unions.[9] The tripartite Board is reported to be as successful a method as any in a situation where the law prohibits strikes by public (city) employees. As a result of this prohibition, public employees in New York City still feel they have no say despite the Board's existence.

Regardless of efforts to maintain harmony, unions argue that the only legitimate bargaining process includes the right to strike in the event of an impasse. They contend that it has traditionally been accorded legal status in the private sector, and that the ban on strikes in the public service creates an economic imbalance to the disadvantage of working people.

From a political standpoint, opponents of the strike in public employment contend that allowing unions this right would reverse the balance of power. But it should be noted that eight states grant public employees at least a limited right to strike. Moreover, unions have political weapons other than the strike at their disposal. They can exert political pressure through block votes and financial contributions and thereby accumulate bargaining power. Also, outside the bargaining area, they can circumvent negotiations by influencing public officials who are often sensitive to the political power of unions.

---

[9]George Bennett, "The Public Interest and Public Unions," *Public Personnel Management* (November–December 1974), p. 550.

DISCIPLINE IN THE UNIONIZED AGENCY

Most collective bargaining agreements recognize an agency's prerogative to administer discipline, and many statutes contain this right. However, under the just-cause principle usually included in the agreement, due process is required in initiating discipline. Furthermore, if an employee or union contests disciplinary action under a formal grievance procedure that includes arbitration, the burden of proof rests on management. Even where unions are not present, disciplinary action is subject to review by appeal panels or trial boards. In the federal service, the Merit Systems Protection Board handles appeals of employees on disciplinary, or adverse, action.

Too often agencies have lost arbitration or appealed cases on discipline because the manager failed to follow proper disciplinary procedures, or because the agency did not provide enough evidence to justify the measure it took. The following guidelines are offered for administering discipline, particularly where unions are involved.

Basic Concepts of Discipline

If management's philosophy is that the purpose of discipline is to correct rather than punish, positive results are more likely. In the corrective approach to discipline, managers counsel employees to determine the reasons for failure to comply with a rule, to explain the reasons for the rule, and to reach an understanding regarding expectations of the employee's future behavior. Punishment is used only as a last resort.

Counseling by itself does not constitute a disciplinary action. It should be noted, however, that under the law (as a result of the Supreme Court decision in *NLRB* v. *Weingarten*, 420 U.S. 251, 1975), in an inverview that an employee feels will result in discipline, a union representative must be called if the employee so requests. Agencies that have been successful with the corrective approach also have rules with appropriate penalties, and they consistently enforce them through a system of progressive discipline. Many personnel policy manuals and/or union-management agreements specifically mention types of discipline, and the offenses for which punishment may be invoked. Infractions that merit corrective action can be categorized as follows:

▶ unacceptable performance—failure to perform acceptably in one or more critical elements of the job

▶ personal misconduct—rule violations such as unreliability; insubordination; dishonesty or disloyalty, e.g., unauthorized releasing of classified information

▶ violation of the bargaining agreement

The list of penalties usually designates corrective action commensurate with the infraction. If the penalty the agency imposes is too harsh or does not fit the circumstances, arbitrators may modify or reverse the agency's action. Even more frequently, arbitrators reverse penalties for rule infractions because of inconsistent enforcement. Given similar circumstances, violators must be handled similarly. When one employee is reprimanded for habitual tardiness while a second employee with a comparable work record is discharged for the same violation, management is not consistently administering discipline.

Corrective Discipline

Consistent, impartial, and humane discipline is facilitated by a system of progressive discipline. Under such a system, employees are first cautioned or reinstructed through counseling for lesser offenses. Repeated or more serious derelictions result in penalties of increasing severity, such as:

▶ Oral cautions with a notation in the employee's record.

▶ Written reprimand.

▶ Short suspension—three days to one month, or lateral reassignment. (*Note:* In the federal government, there are no appeal rights to the MSPB for suspensions of 14 days or less.)

▶ Reduction in grade or withholding of merit increase.

▶ Suspension—thirty days to six months, with loss of seniority.

▶ Discharge—the most severe penalty.

This philosophy of discipline is best illustrated by the *hot stove rule,* as follows:

▶ The burn is *immediate.* There is no doubt about cause and effect.

▶ There was a *warning.* If the stove is red hot, people know what will happen if they touch it.

▶ The discipline is *consistent.* Everyone who touches the stove is burned.

▶ The discipline is *impersonal.* People are burned not because of who they are, but because they touch the stove.

Perhaps the following guidelines that the authors, as arbitrators, use in rendering decisions in discipline cases will be helpful to managers of human resources. A manager should be able to answer all of the following questions in the affirmative before administering a disciplinary action:

▶ Did the employee violate a rule?

▶ Did the employee know the rule?

▶ Was the employee properly warned, cautioned, or reinstructed?

▶ Did the employee have a fair hearing?

▶ Will the punishment be (a) consistent with past action? (b) fair and equitable in light of the circumstances? (c) administered within a reasonable time?

In the unionized agency as well as those regulated by a merit system, employees may appeal adverse actions through either a formal appeals procedure, or a grievance procedure. Grievance and appeals procedures serve to provide a fair hearing of employee complaints; they also minimize potential disputes and preserve harmony between employees and the administration.

GRIEVANCE HANDLING/DISPUTE RESOLUTION

The peaceful resolution of employee grievance and collective bargaining disputes is in the best interest of the agency and of the public welfare. Minimizing work disruption enhances the productivity of the agency.

Grievance procedure. Almost without exception, union-management agreements contain a grievance clause. The number of steps and the method of handling grievances vary from contract to contract, but generally follow the pattern described below.

Step 1. Either orally or in writing, an employee submits a grievance to the supervisor. If written, it should set forth a complete statement of the grievance, the facts on which it is based, the remedy the employee desires, and the specific provisions of the agreement which were allegedly violated.

Step 2. If the grievance is not settled at the first step, the employee can appeal. At this point, the employee, with the union representative, discusses the grievance with the department head.

Step 3. The deputy director, staff aid, or administrative assistant, with the advice of the agency personnel staff, confers with a committee of union representatives—usually the international representative and several grievance committeemen. As a general practice, all those involved in the initial steps are in subsequent hearings.

Step 4. If the grievance is not settled at the third step, a review board or an appeals committee consisting of the highest ranking officials of the agency and the union may conduct a formal hearing and attempt to settle the grievance.

Step 5. The final step in most grievance procedures is arbitration. When the parties themselves fail to resolve the grievance, they submit the issue to an impartial third party, who renders a decision that is binding on both.

Principles of handling grievances. Most grievances are resolved at the first step. Managers who adhere to the following principles have been most successful in minimizing problems arising from employee grievances:

Take every complaint seriously. Even though a grievance may appear ridiculous on the surface, it is a serious matter to the employee. Indicating to employees at the outset that their complaints have no merit, or that they are foolish even to think their problems warrant attention, can destroy whatever good relations exist between the agency and its employees. Managers must give full attention to any complaint and try to find the source of trouble, whether it is obvious or hidden. They try to determine why there is a grievance. One of the basic principles of good communications applies here: *Listen*—attentive and sincere listening allows employees to talk freely. Many grievances solve themselves when employees have the opportunity to express their problems, and it is the managers' duty to try to settle the grievance at their level. Experience shows that as a case proceeds through the grievance mechanism, the difficulties in making a settlement multiply, and the original complaint takes on a new face.

Work with union officials. When employees make a reasonable request for the presence of their union representative, the manager usually summons the representative promptly. Managers realize that union representatives can assist in solving problems and are not adversaries seeking to injure the government.

Check for accuracy. In written grievances, the managers make certain the grievance form is completely and correctly filled out. Many employees are not articulate, especially in writing. As a result, grievance statements are often unclear, illegible, incomplete, or otherwise confusing. Thus, managers carefully check written grievances to insure they are clear, complete statements of the problem and of the remedy sought; that they bear the date of initiation and the employee's signature.

Have issues clearly in mind. When handling a grievance with a union official, managers stick to the issue of the grievance. This is easier said than done, since emotions and side issues tend to be interjected into the conversation. Union representatives may attempt to confuse the issue and put managers on the defensive by introducing extraneous matters. Consequently, managers make every effort to redirect the discussion to the issue at hand.

Gather all the facts available. Unless an answer to the grievance appears obvious, managers use the time allowed by the agreement to investigate the problem, developing as much relevant data as possible, such as policy, previous settlements, facts regarding circumstances of the case, and other pertinent information. They contact sources, such as other managers, employees involved with the situation, witnesses, and when necessary, the department head. They develop information as though the case would be appealed to arbitration.

Keep within the time limits. Procrastination quickly creates disharmony. The agreement specifies the maximum amount of time at each step of the grievance procedure; special arrangements for extensions can be made by mutual consent. But as a general practice, management should reply within the time limits established by the agreement. Agencies have lost arbitration cases on the technicality of exceeding time limits.

Justify decisions. Management's answers include reasons, especially when a grievance is denied. The answer may not be acceptable, but the reasoning behind it can help promote understanding and convince the union not to appeal. Whatever the answer, managers have found it advisable to check these items before making a decision.

▶ *Precedent* — what has been done before.

▶ *Directives* and *statutes* applicable to the agency.

▶ *Reasons behind the complaint* — ask the employee why.

▶ *Consequences* of the decision.

It should be remembered that the answer to the grievance, if accepted by the union, is a binding, enforceable settlement!

Keep a complete record. Finally, the agency records all the facts, particularly if the grievance goes beyond the first step. When others, such as the department head, review board, or arbitrator, rule on the grievance, they need facts to base their decision on; the record preserves these facts for future reference.

Dispute settlement. Although job actions such as sick-outs, slowdowns, and strikes are generally prohibited by statute, executive order, agreement, or a combination of these, they do occur in the public sector. In 1979, less than 1.6 percent of all public sector employees were on strike compared to about 1.9 percent in the total economy. These stoppages resulted from union demands for recognition or security, economic issues, or other contractual matters such as contract renewal and length of agreement. Historically, government unions and employers have resolved their differences more expeditiously than private sector parties, probably because government strikes are legally prohibited and many jurisdictions have mandatory settlement procedures.[10]

Although low in percentage of working time, the impact of stoppages has serious implications for public health and safety. When the necessary services of police, firefighting, postal delivery, transportation, or garbage collection are curtailed, the public is inconvenienced or even endangered. The utilization of third-party neutrals then becomes a viable alternative to the disruption of production. Arbitration and mediation are the predominant forms of attempts to resolve union-management disputes in the public sector.

Undoubtedly, the interests of all concerned are best served when the parties themselves can arrive at a negotiated agreement. However, when impasses are reached, the voluntary or compulsory introduction of neutrals often produces an equitable settlement that might not otherwise transpire.

In mediation, an impartial third party attempts to persuade disputing union and management representatives to settle their differences. Mediation is either permitted or required by statute. The Civil Service Reform Act covers federal employees, and about half the states have mediation provisions in their laws. States utilizing mediation either furnish mediators from their staff, or arrange ad hoc mediation by private individuals. Mediators may need to instruct the parties in negotiating procedures when it is their first exposure to collective bargaining. By the same token, the parties may have to instruct the mediator in the labor relations, economics, personnel policies, and politics of the public sector when the mediator is unfamiliar with these matters.[11] Mediation is usually the dispute settlement procedure used prior to fact-finding and arbitration, because it enables the reduction of disputes and helps to clarify unresolved issues. Mediation is often acceptable to both parties because its aim is to assist the parties in reaching agreement themselves.

---

[10]U.S. Department of Labor, Bureau of Labor Statistics, "Work Stoppages in Government," 1979 (Washington, D.C.: U.S. Department of Labor, 1981), p. 1ff.

[11]Paul D. Staudohar, "Some Implications of Mediation of Bargaining Impasses in Public Employment," Public Personnel Management (July–August 1973), p. 300.

Similarly, arbitration utilizes a neutral third party. The arbitrator is generally selected by the parties themselves, and the arbitrator's function may be to find facts about the dispute and to render an advisory report, or to award a judgment that is binding on both parties. Arbitration can be voluntary, i.e., adopted at the discretion of the parties, or compulsory, i.e., automatically imposed by law when impasse is reached. The New Jersey Employer-Employee Relations Act is an example of a statute that allows disputes to be arbitrated by agreement of the parties. By having the advance consent of the parties rather than being imposed by statute, voluntary arbitration is more acceptable to the parties than compulsory arbitration.

Both "rights" and "interests" issues can be submitted to arbitration. Elkouri and Elkouri distinguish between them as follows: "Disputes as to 'rights' involve the interpretation or application of laws, agreements, or customary practices, whereas disputes as to 'interests' involve the question of what shall be the basic terms and conditions of employment."[12]

Legislated, compulsory interest arbitration is specifically authorized in almost one half of the states, for at least some employers.[13] But this approach is often viewed with disfavor and suspicion. Many believe that by placing final decision-making authority in the hands of persons not accountable to the public, interest arbitration weakens political democracy. These same people believe that there is an absence of definite criteria or standards to govern the arbitrator. The question becomes, does the "non-political" arbitrator arrive at a better decision than the "politicians" would through bargaining? The political implications of interest arbitration decisions are summarized by Raymond Horton as follows:

> "Too often observers of public sector labor relations overlook the fact that collective bargaining and arbitration decisions may be among the most significant of political decisions. Not only do they redistribute resources within government, both budget dollars and managerial authority, but they also affect the cost of government, taxes, and the quantity and quality of public ser-

---

[12]Frank Elkouri and Edna Asper Elkouri, *How Arbitration Works*, 3rd ed. (Washington, D.C.: Bureau of National Affairs, Inc., 1973), p. 47. *Note:* A supplement, *Legal Status of Federal Sector Arbitration* was published by BNA in 1980.

[13]Donald S. Wasserman, Discussant of Charles M. Rehmus, "Legislated Interest Arbitration," *Proceedings of the Twenty-Sixth Annual Winter Meeting, Industrial Relations Research Association* (Madison, Wis.: Industrial Relations Research Association, 1975), p. 315.

vices. When decisions affecting resource allocation are imposed on the body politic by arbitrators, both government officials and members of the public are deprived of responsibility and influence. Of course, it is precisely this opportunity to escape from responsibility that makes arbitration attractive to certain public officials."[14]

A case in point involves a county that reached an impasse over wages with the police bargaining unit. Although the county commissioners desired to pay increases for police officers, they were constrained by unavailability of funds. Taxpayers would have been hostile to the tax assessment necessary to increase police pay. When the arbitrator granted the desired increase, it relieved the commissioners who could place the blame on the arbitrator and not suffer at the polls.

Although there is no magic formula for the adjudication of interest disputes, certain standards do exist and must be considered by the arbitrator in rendering an award or an advisory opinion. The arbitrator is admonished to consider what the parties might have resolved had the bargaining been successfully concluded. In addition, the arbitrator must weigh such matters as the best interests of the public, economic comparisons, existing employment conditions, availability of funds, and precedent.

Henry Frazier suggests that public managers be aware, in the conduct of arbitration proceedings, that public sector arbitrators must consider not only the terms of the agreement, but the provisions of statutes and regulations that may apply to the grievance or to the interest issue under consideration. He emphasizes that the parties have the responsibility of making the arbitrator aware of the applicable legislation.[15]

The costliness in terms of time delays and money are frequent objectives voiced against arbitration. One successful effort to overcome these disadvantages is found in experiments utilizing expedited arbitration. This approach, most appropriate for discipline cases, employs preselected panels of arbitrators who agree, in advance, to conduct hearings shortly after notification, to render an award promptly (usually within 48 hours), and to accept a low level of compensation.

---

[14]Raymond D. Horton, "Arbitration, Arbitrators, and the Public Interest," *Industrial And Labor Relations Review* (July 1975), pp. 499–500.

[15]Henry B. Frazier, III, "Labor Arbitration in the Federal Service," *The George Washington Law Review* (May 1977), p. 730.

SUMMARY

Unions in the public sector have become a viable political force in recent years. Various Executive Orders have encouraged membership growth, although economic difficulties at the local level have forced union leaders to take a less aggressive posture in their demands for pay improvements.

The 1978 Civil Service Reform Act is the first pervasive legislation regulating federal labor-management relations. An increasing number of states have recognized public employee rights to bargain. More than half the states have enacted collective bargaining legislation that covers not only general working conditions, but disputes settlement methods. Despite these measures, strikes among public employees are a reality, and agencies with their unions utilize neutrals (mediators, fact finders, and arbitrators) to help settle their differences in the bargaining relationship.

Management still retains the right to discipline employees for various reasons. The authors espouse a corrective approach to discipline wherein every effort is made to redirect deviant behavior, using punishment only as a last resort. In unionized agencies, employees usually have the right to appeal disciplinary action through the grievance procedure and/or a statutory procedure.

CASE STUDIES

1. The Case of Jack Weeks

Jack Weeks, aged 58, with 18 years of satisfactory employment with the agency requested a leave of absence. On June 18, he asked his supervisor, Frank Jones, for leave from June 26–30 to travel to his son's graduation from college, and the request was granted.

Jack Weeks was one of three systems analysts who performed various functions and replaced any of the state planners who might be absent or on leave. On June 24, one of the planners was given permission to take time off due to the serious illness of his mother. On June 25, the day before Jack Weeks was to leave on his trip, Supervisor Jones asked him if he could cancel his trip and make other arrangements because the department was short of help. In reply, Jack Weeks pointed out that he had firmed up his plans, and he didn't want to disappoint his son at this late date; furthermore, the supervisor had promised the leave, and he should stick by his word. However, Supervisor Jones insisted that Weeks cancel his plans and report for work on June 26, or he would be given a disciplinary penalty. When Jack returned to work on July 1, he was given a seven day disciplinary suspension.

A grievance was filed and appealed through the steps to the merit system which reduced the penalty to a one day suspension, and ordered Jack Weeks reimbursed for all but one day's lost wages. The review board of the state merit system felt that the leave of absence had not been properly revoked.

▶ How did the outcome of this discipline case affect the relationship of Supervisor Jones with his employees?

▶ What was Jack Week's responsibility in this case?

▶ What should he have done on June 25 when his leave was cancelled?

▶ How would you have handled the situation had you been in Supervisor Jones' shoes?

▶ Do you agree with the review board's award? Why or why not?

2. Contract Negotiation in the City of Kissimmee, Florida

Under the provisions of the Florida Public Employee Relations Act, a neutral third party called a special master is selected jointly by labor and management to hear any unresolved collective bargaining issues and to render an "advisory" opinion to settle them. Following are the special master's opinions of several issues that were in dispute:

Management Rights/Prevailing Rights. The Union stated that it would be willing to accept the Management Rights clause from the expired agreement if the Prevailing Rights clause were retained. However, the City had proposed a much broader clause that excluded the Prevailing Rights provision. The City stated that it had proposed a clause that would read in essence: "All rights, privileges, and benefits shall remain in writing except as prohibited by the City Commission." The Union testified that this wording was unacceptable because "there was nothing in writing."

> *Special Master's Opinion:* These management rights existed in the previous agreement by implication; the City has merely made them explicit. Thus, the City's proposed wording of the *Management Rights* clause is accepted. By the same token, the Union's *Prevailing Rights* clause was previously accepted by the City as evidenced by its inclusion in the expired agreement. Absent a strong argument by the City for its exclusion, the Union's request that it be retained is accepted.

Work Hours. The Florida Code, Section 447.301, *Public employees' rights organization and representation,* states:

> "(2) Public employees shall have the right to . . . negotiate collectively through a certified bargaining agent with their public employer in the determination of the *terms and conditions* (emphasis added) of their employment . . ."

The City proposed to allow the City Commission to change work hours as they deem necessary, but the City explained that the Commission would hold open hearings before any change would be made. City counsel reported that a new sub-station would probably be opened in the near future which would create the need to change work hours.

The Union countered that it wanted to be assured that the hours it had negotiated would remain in effect for the duration of the Agreement.

> *Special Master's Opinion:* Universally and traditionally, hours of work have been a *basic* issue for inclusion in negotiations of the terms and conditions of employment. The Florida Code is clear in its meaning that terms and conditions be negotiated or re-negotiated as the case may be. Taking away from this basic right to negotiate hours of work would be tantamount to circumventing the Florida

Statutes. Therefore, the clause on *Work Hours* should be retained as worded in the expired Agreement.

Residency Requirement. The expired Agreement extended the residency requirement from the three mile limit to the electric utility service area (estimated to be approximately ten miles). The Union fears that the City Commission could legislate a new, more stringent requirement which would place a burden on firefighters who would be required to move back to the City. Union witness Mike McCurdy testified that because of the proximity of Disney World to the City, the cost of housing is higher in Kissimmee than in outlying areas. He also presented evidence that no other city's fire department employees have a residency requirement. An explicit exemption in the Agreement would prevail over any Commission legislation, the Union argued.

Special Master's Opinion: Why raise an issue that has little prospect of becoming a reality? No evidence was presented to indicate that the Commission had passed or intended to pass a new ordinance on residency. It is in the mutual interests of the City and the firefighters to have the Agreement remain essentially in its original form on this issue; no explicit statement regarding exemption from residency requirements should be added. The *Residency Requirement* clause should read:

"Article _____. Residency Requirements. The City agrees that the Residency Requirements for employees of the Fire Department shall continue to be the service area of the Electric Utility of the City of Kissimmee."

▶ *Management Rights/Prevailing Rights.* In a collective bargaining agreement, what is the purpose of a management rights clause? How important is it for the City to have the unencumbered right to contract out?

▶ *Work Hours.* How important is the City's prerogative to adjust work focus in this case?

▶ *Residency Requirement.* Is the residency requirement significant here?

▶ If you were city manager, would you accept the arbitrator's opinions here? Why, or why not? How might the City Commission affect the outcome of these negotiations?

8

The Public Manager as Financial Manager

Key Concepts

Budgeting
   Budget Functions
      Budget Cycles
         Budget Strategies
            Executive Budget
               Budget Reform
                  PPB—Planning-Programming-Budgeting
                  ZBB—Zero-Base Budgeting
                     Incrementalism
                        Balanced Budget
                           Program Review and Analysis

Budgeting is vital to all of the other functions of the public manager. As Wildavsky, an authority on governmental budgeting, has noted, this is where we find "the translation of financial resources into human purposes."[1] If public managers had unlimited time and resources, they would have no need for budgets. In the real world, however, resources are always scarce and the public manager never has enough time for all that the organization might do. It is in this context of scarcity

---

Note: This chapter was co-authored by Ronald B. Hoskins.
[1] Aaron Wildavsky, *The Politics of the Budgetary Process,* 3rd ed. (Boston: Little, 1979), p. 1.

that careful budgeting and financial management become essential. Given limited resources, priorities must be set, decisions must be made as to what can be done and what can be postponed or canceled. Finally, funding must be secured and allocated in the most effective and efficient manner to achieve chosen goals. Budgeting is the process by which these tasks are performed.

The process of budgeting is much the same in both business and government. For the public manager, however, the process of budgeting takes on the added dimension of politics. The manager in the public organization does not freely select goals, but chooses objectives which contribute to goals determined through the political process. For resources, the public manager must depend upon taxes and revenues established by the political system. Even the allocation of organizational resources cannot be based entirely on concerns of economy and efficiency, since budget requests are subject to the approval of political officials outside the organization.

For the public manager, budgeting and financial management are both managerial and political processes. Efficiency is an important concern, but so is responsiveness to the political system. Reconciling these two concerns is not easy, and nowhere is this more evident than in the functions related to budgeting and financial management.

FUNCTIONS OF THE BUDGET

The budget serves a variety of purposes for the public manager. In its most obvious purpose, the budget is a document that identifies planned expenditures and anticipated revenues. The budget is also an instrument by which public managers and political officials can monitor activities and expenditures. It is a tool for managerial control. Auditors scrutinize the expenditures of public organizations and report any discrepancies between agency activities and those authorized in their budgets.

From another perspective budgets have much the same purpose as contracts, although they do not necessarily have the same legal implications. A contract is basically an agreement in which persons, or organizations, promise to carry out certain activities. Other persons or organizations can then base their actions on the expectation that promised activities will be performed. Budgets become expectations both within and without the agency. Within an organization, the budget serves as a form of unofficial contract among the many units that make up the organization. It tells each unit what to expect from other units and serves as a coordinating mechanism. The personnel office, for example, can use budget information to schedule recruitment and training efforts.

The budget also serves as an important unofficial contract between different government organizations and different levels within the same organization. Contemporary government is a complex network of vertical and horizontal interdependencies among public organizations. This becomes quickly evident by looking at almost any function of government. In the area of education, for instance, local school boards, counties, municipalities, states, and the federal government all have a share of the responsibility. Each is dependent upon the actions of the others. Their budgets serve as unofficial contracts with one another, announcing their individual plans and committing their resources. Budgets, then, are vital coordinating mechanisms in both intergovernmental and interorganizational processes.

Political Aspects

The public manager must also recognize the political function served by budgets. The political process is essentially the way power is allocated in our society. It is the struggle and compromise among individuals and groups seeking to impose their preferences and values on others, and attempting to have a voice in the way resources are distributed. Since budgets are statements of resource distribution, they become scorecards of the political process. Budgets announce winners and losers in the political arena and describe the compromises which were made along the way. As Wildavsky contends, "the budget lies at the heart of the political process."[2]

From the political perspective, budgets assume several additional dimensions for the public manager, both within the agency and with regard to the broader political system. First, budgets serve as statements of management philosophy, pref-

---

[2]Ibid.

erences, and priorities. There is no better way to get to know an organization than to look at the way its resources have been allocated and to note the various levels of emphasis and support given to particular types of activities. The priorities of agency management become quite clear when price tags are attached.

Second, budgets form precedents for the way resources will probably be allocated in the future. As previously mentioned, political struggles are usually settled in compromise, and budgets become the symbols of successful compromises. Thus when it is time to prepare new budgets, it is unlikely that the participants in the process will want to reopen old conflicts which have been settled satisfactorily. Rather, the previous budget will probably be accepted as the base, and the new budget will reflect marginal adjustments. Conflicts and compromises will be a part of these adjustments, and they will become a part of the new base for future budgets.

In summary, budgets perform a variety of financial, managerial, and political purposes for the public manager. They are far more than simple statements about how the organization's bills will be paid.

THE RULES AND THE PLAYERS IN THE BUDGET GAME

John Wanat has described public budgeting as a game, that is, "a series of interactions among various participants, each of whom has goals, resources, orientations, background, and stakes that differ from those of the other participants."[3] To be effective in the budgeting process, the public manager must understand the process as well as the purpose of the game.

Budget Cycles

The appropriate place to begin a review of the process is with the budget cycle. It is a fairly consistent sequence throughout all levels of government. The process generally begins when an agency becomes aware of a need or opportunity. There are many ways this can occur. The agency may receive an unusually large number of requests from citizens seeking information or

---

[3]John Wanat, *Introduction to Budgeting* (North Scituate, Mass.: Duxbury, 1978), p. 109.

assistance; political officials may suggest that the agency initiate some new service; agency personnel may recommend expansion of current programs. In some cases, media attention will bring needs and opportunities to the attention of public organizations. Whatever the source, the cycle begins with recognition of a need or opportunity and the decision by agency management to include it in the agency's budget request.

The second stage of the budget cycle is normally the responsibility of the chief executive (e.g., mayor, governor, president). All agency requests are reviewed and coordinated into a unified plan for the executive branch. If the jurisdiction has a central budget office, it will examine agency requests against three broad criteria: (1) is the request supportive of the administration's philosophy and program goals? (2) is the recommended program the most efficient way to accomplish its objectives? (3) is the requested program of sufficiently high priority to warrant funding under a condition of limited resources? Obviously, many requests fail one or more of these criteria and are reduced or eliminated. Once the budget has been approved by the chief executive, it is presented to the legislative body (e.g., city council, legislature, or Congress).

Traditionally, legislative bodies are charged with the approval of budgets. The Constitution makes this clear at the national level directing that "No money shall be drawn from the Treasury, but in consequence of appropriations made by law." Thus legislatures assume primary responsibility for the third stage of the budget process.

At the national level, the legislative phase of the budget process is highly fragmented. Responsibilities are divided among several committees within both houses of Congress. House and Senate standing committees specialize in various program areas and perform the function of "authorizing" specific programs and organizations. They recommend to the Congress which programs should be undertaken and which should not. They also recommend funding ceilings for individual programs, but they do *not* have the authority to provide funds. This is the responsibility of the Appropriations Committees of the House and Senate and their specialized subcommittees. The Ways and Means Committee in the House and the Finance Committee in the Senate recommend tax legislation to the Congress and thereby significantly influence the level of public resources which can be considered in the appropriations process. Finally, the Budget Committees of the two houses have been charged since 1974 with the almost impossible task of setting national budget targets and keeping appropriations and revenues in some state of balance. (The concept of a "balanced budget" has a very specific meaning at the federal level, and will be discussed later in the chapter.)

Once the budget has been approved, and usually modified, by the legislature, the cycle moves into its fourth phase, that is, budget execution by the chief executive and the administrative agencies. It might be argued that this phase is not properly a part of the budget cycle since the executive branch is required to implement a budget as it was written. The executive branch, in fact, exercises considerable discretion in carrying out the programs in the budget. In reality, the execution of the budget by the executive branch may be quite different from that intended by the legislature.

The final stage in the budget cycle is the audit phase in which both the chief executive and the legislature review the accomplishments of agencies and attempt to confirm whether public funds were spent in a legal, efficient, and effective manner. Normally, within the executive branch, agencies conduct internal audits, performed by their own staffs, and report their findings to the agency head. The legislature also conducts audits, using an external auditing organization. On the federal level, such functions are conducted by the Government Accounting Office (GAO), which reports directly to the Congress. At the state level, independent audit bureaus are normally assigned this task. At the local level audits are generally performed by certified public accounting firms under contract. The results of these audits are used by both the chief executive and the legislature in judging the effectiveness and efficiency of programs, and they influence decisions on future budget cycles.

It may appear from this discussion that the budget process is conducted in an orderly, sequential manner, with each phase executed in turn. Unfortunately, it is not that simple. Instead, the public manager will be involved in different stages of several budget cycles at all times. While preparing budget requests for next year, he or she will often still be awaiting decision on the upcoming budget. Often, the public manager will be attempting to execute the present budget legally and efficiently, while hosting auditors reviewing the agency's work for the previous budget year. In the worst case, the manager may still be in the process of answering audit findings from last year's audit. This situation has been called "scrambled budget cycles" by some observers of the budgetary process.[4]

The complexity of budget cycles is further compounded by different time schedules at various levels of government. The federal government begins its fiscal year on October 1st, most states begin their budget years on July 1st, and many local governments set their fiscal years to coincide with the calendar year. As noted earlier, the growth of intergovernmental programs in such areas as education, health, social services, and transportation makes it essential that the budget efforts of the various levels of government be coordinated. The different time schedules used by the various levels of government, however, make that almost impossible, and many public managers are forced to base their budget requests on "educated guesses" of what other branches of government will do. For example, many federal projects require matching funds from the state or local government. The state budget for the year in which a specific program is to be undertaken, however, may not be passed until June, although the federal funds were approved in the previous October. If the state fails to include the required funds, the federal funds which were appropriated either connot be spent or must be approved for "carry over" to the next year through a cumbersome paperwork process. On the other hand, budgeters at the state or local level are often hesitant in, and may be legally prohibited from, asking the legislature for matching funds before the federal funds have been guaranteed.

There is no simple solution for sorting out overlapping cycles, or for dealing with the differing time schedules of various intergovernmental programs. This much should be clear, however; the budgeting process is not something the public manager does once a year. It is a key part of the continuous public management process.

Players and Strategies

Beyond budget steps and cycles, it is important that the public manager understand the roles that key players perform and the strategies they employ in the budgetary process.

[4]Robert D. Lee, Jr., and Ronald W. Johnson, *Public Budgeting Systems*, 2nd ed. (Baltimore: University Park Press, 1977), p. 56.

Public agency personnel, including the managers, are generally specialists in their particular program areas. Thus, the U.S. Environmental Protection Agency is heavily staffed with scientists, engineers, and related professionals whose training has been focused on the agency's programs; for example, lawyers who specialize in environmental regulatory law. Agriculture departments at both the state and federal levels are run by agricultural specialists, and so forth. In addition to their sphere of specialization, agency personnel tend to develop close relationships with clientele groups who are interested in the agency's activities. Agency contacts in the legislature tend to focus on those committees and subcommittees with responsibility for oversight and funding of the agency. In short, agencies are highly specialized organizations with relatively narrow views of the broader governmental system.

Agency officials tend to adopt the role of advocates in the budgetary process. It is the agency officials who, knowing their areas intimately and convinced of the merit of their causes, must plead the cases for their programs and clientele before the chief executive and the legislature. It is the public manager's responsibility to promote the importance of his or her agency's work and to make sure that members of the executive office and the legislature are aware of the needs of the agency. Moreover, the public manager does so with the full knowledge that peers in other agencies will be doing the same.

The chief executive and the central budget office play dual roles in the budgeting process. They must select a package of agency programs which will accomplish the administration's purposes, but they also have fiscal responsibilities. They must attempt to improve the overall efficiency of the executive branch and usually must cut some programs to meet fiscal ceilings set by the chief executive. Also, the chief executive and budget office recognize that agencies, as advocates, usually overstate their funding needs. Thus, the executive office must find the excesses in agency requests and eliminate them from the chief executive's budget proposals to the legislature. The detailed work in this area is normally performed by analysts in the central budget office using general policy guidance from the chief executive. Nevertheless, it is the chief executive who ultimately approves the executive budget proposal and submits it to the legislature.

The legislature encompasses several groups whose actions

do not always seem coordinated in the budget process. The standing committees with their high degree of specialization, narrow focus, and clientele contact play a part similar to the advocates role of the administrative agencies. Essentially, the standing committees merely authorize programs and need not worry about finding and appropriating the monies to support them. On the other hand, the appropriations committees, and more specifically their subcommittees in particular program areas, are concerned about fiscal matters and often become the agencies' adversaries, challenging requests in the executive's budget proposal. However, it is interesting to note how often the specialized subcommittees of the appropriations committees become advocates for the agencies once they have gone through the ritual of reducing their budget requests. As Wildavsky describes, "Tough as they may be in cutting the budgets of their agencies, appropriations committee members, once having made their decision, generally defend the agencies against further cuts on the floor."[5]

Appropriation committee members tend to view themselves as "protectors of the public purse." Once members feel this duty has been carried out, they try to prevent further reductions. Finally, the budget committees at the national level attempt to get the legislative players together by setting budget and revenue targets for the various committees. The effectiveness of these committees, however, has been limited at best.

In the typical budget process the major players tend to play according to a fairly consistent pattern, although the individual strategies may vary from agency to agency and from year to year. Generally, agencies ask for more than they expect to get and attempt to sell their programs to anyone who will listen. The chief executive and more specifically the central budget office analysts tend to make harsh cuts in agency requests, knowing that the legislature will probably restore some portion of those reductions. Finally the legislature, acting through its several committees, tends to give the agencies more than the chief executive recommended, but less than they originally asked.[6] The budget strategies are played out year after year.

---

[5]Wildavsky, *supra*, note 1, p. 50.

[6]This pattern has been tested at both the state and federal levels. See Ira Sharkansky, "Agency Requests, Gubernational Support and Budget Success in State Legislatures," *American Political Science Review*, 62 (December 1968), pp. 1220–1231; and "Four Agencies and an Appropriations Subcommittee: A Comparative Study of Budget Strategies," *Midwest Journal of Political Science*, 9 (August 1965), pp. 254–281.

THE DEVELOPMENT AND REFORM OF
THE BUDGET PROCESS

With this background on how the budget process operates, the public manager should be aware of how the process developed and of some of the reforms that have been tried to make public budgeting more rational.[7]

Before Executive Budgets

Government in this country operated without budgets as we know them for nearly a century and a half. It was not until 1921 that the federal government adopted an executive budget, and only a few cities and states had budgets before that date.

Charles Schultze has described the budgetary system that existed at the national level before 1921 in terms of four characteristics:

1. Individual agencies submitted their budget requests directly to the Congress. (Actually they were assembled by the Secretary of the Treasury, but they were sent to Congress without any modification.)

2. Congress made appropriations in minute detail using a cumbersome line-item format. The President had almost no authority to move funds among accounts.

3. Agency heads frequently made commitments that were beyond the levels of funding appropriated and then simply presented the bills to the Congress for payment.

4. During this time the primary concern of the Congress was to maintain control over the use of executive discretion in spending the government's money. The effective attainment of goals and concerns for agency efficiency were, at best, secondary in the minds of the legislators.[8]

This was a period, then, in which the emphasis was on control, and during which government was much smaller than it is

---

[7]The outline of the following section is based on the stages of budgetary reform identified in Allen Achick, "The Road to PPB: The Stages of Budget Reform," *Public Administration Review*, 26 (December 1966), pp. 243–258.

[8]Charles L. Schultze, *The Politics and Economics of Public Spending* (Washington, D.C.: The Brookings Institution, 1968), p. 8.

today, especially at the federal level. But it was also a time of widespread waste and corruption in government. No single person or organization in the process could be held accountable for what was happening, and the control mechanisms of line-item appropriations were simply ignored by many in the executive branch.

It was in this setting that a national reform movement began in America's cities in the late 19th century and spread to all other levels of government. The municipal reform movement sought to eliminate corruption and to make government more businesslike. To do this, the reforms that emerged placed greater responsibilities on the chief executives who could be held accountable. The move toward an executive budget was the result of such an effort.

Early Executive Budgets

The reformers achieved great success at the municipal and state levels, and in 1921 Congress passed the Budget and Accounting Act which formalized the executive budget process at the national level. These changes, of course, were not intended to strengthen the executive branch but rather to make it more accountable. Thus, control remained the primary orientation of the first executive budgets.

These early approaches emphasized control through a budget and appropriations process which was built on "line items" or "objects-of-expenditure." Each item or object needed by an office had to be identified and its cost specified in the budget document. Early budgets contained hundreds of line items appropriating funds in considerable detail and granting executive agencies little or no flexibility in carrying out their programs.

The focus of the first executive budgets was not on the goals or programs of an agency, but on the safeguarding of public funds. Against the background of 19th century governmental corruption and inefficiency, the centralized budget process represented significant improvement.

As line-item budgets became firmly established, the budget process was relieved somewhat of its watchdog role.[9]

---

[9]Nicholas Henry, *Public Administration and Public Affairs* (Englewood Cliffs, N.J.: Prentice-Hall, 1975), pp. 160–161.

Accounting, personnel, purchasing, and related control activities were set up, and it became possible to consider other uses for the budget process. The increasing size of government and the broadened views about its purpose which accompanied the New Deal gave further impetus to the additional possibilities of budgeting. Beginning in the mid-1930s, the orientation of budgeting began to shift away from the process of control and accountability. The so-called rational reforms had begun in the budget process.

Rational Budget Reforms

Rational budgets are those which produce the greatest amount of desired output for a given level of resources. Obviously, the control orientation which had dominated budgeting in the United States throughout the 19th century and for the first three decades of this century, was not concerned with the products of the budgetary process. This process, focused on legal control, simply could not produce rational budgets.

The grand programs of the New Deal expanded the functions of government, but the nation's resources remained limited. It was imperative, then, that the business of government become more efficient in order to achieve maximum productivity for available resources. The new focus of budgets was on performance, and increasing attention was paid to agency activity (i.e., the efficiency of the process) rather than to inputs (line-item appropriations). Budgets were seen as vehicles for managing activities and functions, and the relationship between resources and accomplishments was emphasized. Under this new management orientation, work measurement, performance standards, and other techniques of organization and management analysis came to the forefront. The federal Bureau of the Budget, no longer simply a financial staff agency, became a key managerial staff agency and moved from the Treasury Department to the new Executive Office of the President in 1939. Budgets had become instruments of management and coordination as well as mechanisms for control. At this early stage, however, the emphasis was still on "how" things were done—on efficiency and economy—and less emphasis on the purposes and programs of government.

By the late 1950s the nation's economy had flourished beyond all expectations. Thus when President John Kennedy was elected, the problem of budgeting was not so much how to save money, but how to spend it. Technology had progressed to such a level that it seemed to promise solutions to virtually all of society's problems. Even grand dreams like placing a man on the moon or eradicating poverty seemed within reach. The problem for budgeting in the 1960s, then, was to decide which of those programs would be accorded highest priority.

Program Budgeting—PPB

It was Defense Secretary Robert McNamara who provided the impetus for the next phase of budgetary evolution. In 1964 McNamara installed a new budgeting technique in the Defense Department which would focus not on agencies or activities, but on programs. This new technique, known as Planning-Programming-Budgeting (PPB), shifted the focus of budgeting from a management orientation to a planning orientation.

The process of planning-programming-budgeting is rather simple and is described by its name. In the planning step, the public manager identifies the alternative goals and courses of action available to the organization. In the programming step, the manager selects those goals or programs which seem most productive and conducts a thorough analysis, using such tools as economic analysis, operations research, and systems theory. Finally, in the budgeting step, funds are requested for those programs which promise the greatest potential product. Clearly, the focus of PPB is on planning and analysis rather than on the more traditional financial concerns normally associated with the budgeting process.

PPB was extremely successful in the Defense Department and proved quite effective in the selection of long-term weapons programs and other hardware-oriented programs. Under the particularly capable leadership of Robert McNamara, and in an agency where analytical skills were readily available, PPB seemed to offer the ultimate solution to rationalizing the budget process. Thus in 1965, President Johnson directed that the entire federal government adopt PPB in developing budget requests.

PPB was not, however, without problems. The Congress, still primarily concerned about control, insisted on maintaining the line-item format in its appropriations process and required the executive branch to decode its multiyear, multiagency program requests into separate agency budgets broken down by the familiar "objects-of-expenditure." These decoded documents, known as "crosswalks," added a substantial amount of work to the preparation of the budget. Essentially, the budget had to be prepared twice. In the PPB format, the public manager first had to prepare Program Memoranda (narrative justification of programs), Program Financial Plans (documents putting price tags on the programs), and Special Analytical Studies (detailed economic and operations analyses supporting the selection of specific programs). Then, because of Congress' insistence on a line-item format, the public manager had to develop crosswalks and the more traditional budget requests for the agency. PPB became a paperwork nightmare.

There were other problems as well. Although PPB had worked well in the Department of Defense, it was not easily adapted to such programs as foreign affairs and social services. Diplomatic and humanitarian efforts cannot be compared with the same analytical exactitude as weapons systems or dams. Further, the non-Defense agencies did not have the strong analytical orientation of the Defense Department and lacked sufficiently skilled analytical personnel to make PPB work. Finally, few agencies had the luxury of the personal leadership capabilities of Robert McNamara. Indeed, in several agencies the top management did not understand PPB and did not want it. In such an environment, PPB had little chance for success, and in 1971, the Office of Management and Budget quietly announced in its budget call to the agencies that the PPB format was no longer required.

Nevertheless, PPB has continued to be used as an internal budgeting technique in several federal agencies (including the Defense Department) and has been adopted by several state governments.

Zero-Base Budgeting—ZBB

A recent attempt to rationalize public budgeting has moved the process from the program or planning orientation of PPB back to a management orientation with greater emphasis on efficiency and performance. This is the Zero-Base Budgeting (ZBB) approach, which is currently used in some areas of the federal government and in about 20 states.

ZBB was .tried as an experiment in the Department of Agriculture in the early 1960s, but the development of ZBB as we know it today is generally attributed to Peter Pyhrr and the system he developed at Texas Instruments in 1969. It was Pyhrr's account of that system in a *Harvard Business Review* article[10] in 1971 that led Jimmy Carter, then Governor of Georgia, to install the system as Georgia's official budgeting process. In 1977, after his election to the Presidency, Carter directed that the federal government adopt the ZBB process in its preparation of the executive budget proposal. The system has worked well and it continues to be the official budgetary method of the executive branch.

Unlike PPB, the process of ZBB is not apparent from its name. In fact, the label is misleading and has led to some confusion about the process.[11] Zero-base budgeting does not begin with the assumption that all programs must be completely rejustified every year or that they must assume a zero base. Although that idea may be philosophically appealing, it would obviously result in such chaos that budgets would never be developed. Instead, ZBB assumes that the cost of an individual program or activity is actually somewhat less than its current appropriations level. In some cases, this may well mean that a program has no base at all (that it has a zero-base), but in the vast majority of cases it implies simply that most programs are currently operating above their minimum level. According to ZBB principles, in order to increase certain programs beyond their current levels an agency should be able to reduce other programs which can continue to operate on a lower level.

ZBB is a management tool, and perhaps its greatest value is in getting public managers at all levels involved in the budget process. Instead of beginning at the top with high-ranking officials dictating what programs are to be included in the budget, ZBB is an upward process in which public managers from the lowest levels up to the top are given an opportunity for input. The process begins with recommendations from those managers who will ultimately have to implement the budget adopted by Congress. This represents a new opportu-

---

[10]Peter A. Pyhrr, "Zero-Base Budgeting," *Harvard Business Review,* 49 (November–December 1970), pp. 111–121.

[11]Thomas P. Lauth, "Zero-Base Budgeting in Georgia State Government: Myth or Reality," *Public Administration Review,* 38 (September–October 1978), pp. 420–421.

nity for the public manager as budgeter, but it also represents a new level of responsibility, and increases the importance of budgeting skills for public managers.

The first step in the ZBB technique is the identification of "decision units," or the lowest levels in the organization where data can be maintained on cost and performance. Usually these are sections or branches within divisions. In the second step, each of these units develops "decision packages," identifying at least three levels of output (minimum operating level, current operating level, and one or more increased levels) and the funds required to operate at those levels. Generally, the minimum level is set at about 80 to 85 percent of the current operating level.

In the third step, the public manager is called upon to make choices. The manager evaluates the decision packages that have been submitted to him and ranks them according to a system of priorities. That rank-ordered set of decision packages is then sent to the next higher level, where groups of decision packages will be ranked together. The process continues until it reaches the highest level of the organization, where the final ranking is performed. It then becomes a relatively simple matter to choose the decision packages to be included in the budget by establishing a cutoff point determined by the amount of funding the agency expects.

Although the Zero-Base Budgeting process has not resulted in massive reductions in governmental expenditures or in the elimination of large numbers of programs, it has been successful in causing managers to ask the right kinds of questions in making their budget decisions. At the same time, it has eliminated the conflict with the political, policy-making process which PPB had occasioned. Thus, it would appear that ZBB— or some related technique—will guide the development of public budgets for some time to come.

Incrementalism and the Effect of Budget Reforms

As has been shown, the focus of the budgetary process has moved through a variety of stages from control, to management, to planning, and back to management. In each of these reform attempts, the goal has been to improve the way government spends the public's money. It might be expected, then, that successful budget reforms would have had substantial

impact on the size and shape of the budgets which were produced. This, however, has not happened.

Numerous scholars have studied the outcomes of budgets
to see what change, if any, has occurred as a result of the various
reforms. The findings of almost all of these studies show that,
regardless of the budget methods used, budgets have tended
to change only incrementally. That is, budgets tend to be very
similar from one year to the next with changes occurring only
in a narrow range at the margins.[12] (One possible explanation
for "incrementalism," suggested earlier in the discussion of the
political functions of the budget, is that budgets symbolize
compromises and that those compromises tend to be very stable
over time.)

If the size of budgets is not affected by budgeting techniques, it is fair to ask what difference does a budget method
such as ZBB make? The answer is simply that we do not know
if the reforms have accomplished their purpose. It seems logical, however, to assume that while the size of budgets continues
to change only incrementally, the content and effectiveness of
those budgets have been substantially improved. In other
words, better budget decisions are being made as a result of
PPB and ZBB, and the proof of this assertion lies in the accomplishments rather than in the size of budgets.

OTHER FISCAL RESPONSIBILITIES

The public manager's fiscal responsibilities do not end
with the submission of his budget request. On the contrary,
duties as a financial manager begin there. Indeed, how the
public manager spends the government's money may be even
more important than what is requested or received.

Woodrow Wilson and other early public administrationists
discussed the importance of political neutrality in the way public managers carry out their functions. In principle, the public
manager should execute impartially the orders and directions
of the political system. Thus a politics-administration dichotomy is visualized in which decisions are made by political
officials and executed by administrators.

---

[12]See Otto A. Davis, M.A.H. Dempster, and Aaron Wildavsky, "A Theory of the
Budgetary Process," *American Political Science Review*, 60 (September 1960), pp.
529–547.

This concept has long since been recognized as impractical. Public managers must make decisions and exercise discretion if they are to accomplish their tasks. The question becomes not whether public managers should exercise discretion in carrying out their functions, but how much discretion should be exercised. This consideration is quite apparent to public managers as they attempt to implement their organization's budgets.

Because of the length and nature of budget cycles, many conditions change between the time a budget is submitted and when it is approved. Anticipated problems do not always materialize, costs for goods and services may increase, and new problems almost always emerge. Thus the public manager is faced with the dilemma of carrying out a budget which does not satisfy current conditions or of exercising discretion and changing the way the budget is executed.

A number of means are available to the public manager for exercising budget discretion. First, the manager may choose not to spend monies allocated for a program which he or she feels is no longer warranted, or may withhold funds from one program in order to increase the funds available for a higher priority program. Withholding funds is known as "rescission" and is controlled by law in the federal government and most states. Temporarily withholding money from a program is called "deferral" and is also controlled in most systems. Second, the public manager may "reprogram" (move) funds from one program to another. Third, one may "transfer" funds within a program from one line item (for example, personnel costs) to another line item (for example, travel expenses).

Each of these discretionary techniques—rescission, deferral, reprogramming, and transfer—has been used extensively by public managers attempting to carry out responsibly the will of the political system.[13] Most government systems recognize the importance of giving public managers discretion in executing their budgets and provide specific rules for the public manager to follow in using these techniques legally. Unfortunately, many public managers abuse this privilege and fail to obtain proper approval. This practice is dangerous not only to the individual public manager who may face criminal charges,

---

[13]The various devices of executive discretion are discussed in detail in George E. Hale and Scott R. Douglass, "The Politics of Budget Execution: Financial Manipulation in State and Local Governments," *Administration and Society*, 9 (November 1977), pp. 367–378.

but on a broader level, it undercuts the political process by which citizens influence their government.

Raising the Money and Balancing Budgets

Most public managers are more concerned with budgets and expenditures than they are with the processes of taxation and raising revenue. Nonetheless, it is important for the public manager to understand the revenue side of financial management. Different levels of government have different resources and varying ways of raising funds to support their activities. These differing capabilities directly affect the work of public organizations.

It is also important that public managers have a grasp of citizen attitudes about the revenue aspects of governmental finance. Indeed, "taxation without representation" was one of the major issues leading to the American Revolution. In more recent times, the focus has been on reducing or limiting governmental spending through measures such as Proposition 13 in California. President Reagan has made such reductions and limitations a cornerstone of his Administration.

The federal government relies heavily upon the personal income tax for its revenue. At the state level, revenues are generated primarily from sales tax and state income tax. Cities and counties derive their revenues largely from the property tax and from revenue sharing from the state and federal governments. Additionally, local governments frequently borrow money by issuing bonds.

At the state and local level the amount of revenues which can be raised, or borrowed, are critical to balancing the budget, that is, to insuring that expenditures do not exceed revenues. Thus, if revenues are reduced—as they were, for example, in California under Proposition 13—expenditures must also be cut. Conversely, if citizens demand increased services and expanded programs, they must be willing to pay for them through higher taxes. The public manager at the state or local level must be continuously aware that asking for increases in his or her budget is also indirectly asking that some other services be reduced or that taxes be increased.

Since 1946, the concept of a "balanced budget" has meant something quite different at the federal level. In that year,

Congress passed the Full Employment Act, which committed the national government to assuming responsibility for the economy. No longer did the national government trust the "invisible hand" of supply and demand for the regulation of the nation's economy. Instead, the government adopted the concepts of John Maynard Keynes[14] and decided to use spending and taxing as means of either stimulating or slowing the national economy. The goals were to achieve full employment and economic growth, and to control inflation.

These goals, of course, have not been realized. We have not achieved full employment, and we have been unable to gain control of inflation. However, the Act has had a major impact upon the way the federal government "balances" its budget. Since we are now committed to full employment, we begin by assuming a level of full employment and "balance" expenditures to what revenues would be if we had full employment.

The fiscal and monetary policies of the federal government under Keynesianism are far too complicated to be addressed here, but they are extremely important to the financial and budgeting systems of public organizations. As budgeter and financial manager, the public manager must be aware of the federal government's commitment to controlling the performance of the economy and must understand the effect this has on the way budgets are developed.

Program Review and Analysis

In recent years public managers as financial managers have formally assumed the additional responsibility for program review and analysis. In reality, of course, they have always been responsible for the effectiveness and efficiency of their programs.

The formalized process of review and evaluation, however, has caused public managers to become more aware of the relationship between inputs, or the resources given to an agency, and outputs, or the performance expected of an agency. This process of program evaluation, now required of many programs receiving federal aid, clearly links resources with performance.

---

[14]John Maynard Keynes, *The General Theory of Employment, Interest and Money* (New York: Harcourt, Brace and World, 1936).

Similarly, the review and analysis process in some states has been made a formal part of the budgeting and allocations process. In the State of Georgia, for example, agency officials must report on their agencies' achievements when submitting budget requests and before receiving allotments from the Governor's budget office.

The techniques for analyzing the effectiveness of an agency's work have become quite scientific, and many larger agencies have established teams of evaluation specialists familiar with research design and the advanced analytical techniques of statistics and economics. While the public manager may not necessarily be an expert in these sophisticated techniques, it is essential to develop a basic understanding of these tools and to be able to interpret evaluation reports.

SUMMARY

The public manager's role as budgeter and financial manager is central to all other responsibilities. The budget serves many functions, both managerial and political, and becomes a symbol of the public manager's priorities and philosophy. It is as a budgeter that the public manager finalizes policy decisions and provides the resources to translate those policies and strategies into action.

CASE STUDIES

1. The Problem of the Growing Budget

Suburban City had grown rapidly since its incorporation five years ago. The current population totals 8,000 and expectations call for a 50 percent growth rate over the next 3 years. In voting to incorporate, the citizens had thought they would avoid many of Central City's problems. At the heart of these problems had been a constant tension between the cost of city services and the availability of adequate city income. As a result of its growing size, Suburban City now has its own financial difficulties.

Like many such cities, Suburban City employs a minimum of professional staff. The general philosophy is that elected officials will make all important decisions and clerks, policemen, firemen, truck drivers, and other city employees will be hired as required.

Financial pressures have now increased to the point that the city council knows that something must be done. In their wisdom, the council has made two decisions—first, to research the situation before acting and second, to assign you (their administrative assistant) to do the research. Specifically, your assignment is to investigate this type of growth-related problem, and to develop an overall approach to financial management for Suburban City.

As you undertake your task, remember the need to stick to basic considerations. Suburban City needs a basic design for financing, planning, and controlling government activities. Also, be sure to determine the types of services (costs) usually provided by such cities, and, the usual sorts of revenue sources.

2. Designing a Course in Financial Management

Capital City College was recently approached by the Association of Public Financial Managers. This group, made up of federal, state, and local financial managers, asked the College to establish a new course in Public Sector Controllership. Many current and potential government employees are pursuing degrees at City College and the Association would like to see these students take at least one course of this type. No such course is currently offered.

College officials have agreed to start the course if appropriate faculty and Association representatives can agree on content. As one of the Association's senior members, you have accepted the responsibility for preparing an initial outline for the course. Your task is to identify the primary topics to be covered. In making your choices, you also realize the importance of including a brief statement of justification with each choice.

9

The Public Manager as Controller and Evaluator

Key Concepts

Evaluation
  Control
    Performance
      Efficiency
        Effectiveness
          Adaptive-Coping Cycle
            Psychological Contract
              PERT —Program Evaluation and Review Technique
              MBO —Management by Objectives
                Ombudsman
                  Representative Bureaucracy

Evaluation and control is of major concern to higher-level managers, political officials, and tax-paying citizens. The public manager's process of evaluating his or her actions and those of subordinates is the principal concern of this chapter. The purpose of such evaluation is to facilitate more informed and better control over the public agency's future efforts. This should lead to more effective goal attainment and increasingly efficient use of all available resources.

Public managers are constantly evaluated. Higher-level managers must make decisions such as who to promote, political officials must decide which program to vote appropriations for, and taxpayers must pay the bill. While taxpayers are removed from day-to-day decision making within the public manager's operational system, they certainly make their own evaluations, draw their opinions, and make their wishes known on election day.

As public managers improve with the evaluation and control process, better information should also become available to organizational superiors, politicians, and interested citizens. These evaluation processes may be established by public managers on their own initiative, or they may be processes required by higher authority. This chapter provides a look at evaluation and control processes and some of their inherent complexities and difficulties.

THE GOAL OF PERFORMANCE

Robert C. Fried, in his public administration text *Performance in American Bureaucracy*,[1] writes from the perspective of control and evaluation, stressing the importance of "performance" in American public administration. He is concerned with public administration at all levels—local, state, and national—and with the demands and expectations of the American people. While the ability of the administrative system to perform is the author's main emphasis, he also discusses the demands and preferences of citizens and the appropriate restraints of due process. Fried notes that administrative performance has often been thought of in narrow terms, and suggests that this may be the influence of business administration. In business, firms generally have relatively simple goals because of their private nature and performance is dictated by the pressure of the market place. Administrative systems in the public sector, however, must be evaluated in broader terms. Organizations must not only be responsive to accomplishing specific goals, but they must also be responsive to the public at large. They must be more careful in the way that individuals are dealt with, and in the way that money is used, because profit is of less concern than it would be in private organizations. Fried notes that public sector performance must be good because government provides the framework for individual

---

[1]Robert C. Fried, *Performance in American Bureaucracy* (Boston: Little, Brown, 1976). 1976).

and group freedoms and opportunities. As Fried points out, Government is a protector and sometimes a threat to the individual and to the rights of groups. He feels that many books about administration stress the inputs and processes of public administration, but that greater awareness is needed of the actual output and performance of such administrative systems.

Fried sees bureaucracy as being reformed and improved by both inside and outside forces. He discusses a total of thirteen outside forces or controls on administration at the federal government level. These include the following:

▶ Congress

▶ the General Accounting Office

▶ the U.S. Office of Personnel Management

▶ the Office of Management and Budget

▶ the General Services Administration

▶ Congressional committees

▶ individual congressmen

▶ the Justice Department and federal grand juries

▶ federal and state courts

▶ state and local officials

▶ individual citizens, citizen groups, professional and business associations, public interest law firms, and clientele organizations

▶ investigative journalists, the mass media, and the specialized media

▶ the White House

Fried goes on to note that state and local agencies are generally subject to very similar kinds of surveillance. The specifics and the titles will vary from state to state and from local government to local government, but very similar types of circumstances and control mechanisms are found.

Fried identifies five internal strategies for improving administrative behavior. These include: leadership, organizational structure, goals (or changed goals), recruitment and training, and decision-making processes. For our purposes we would generally relate these five areas to the process of administration or management which is of course the focus of the public manager.

EVALUATION AND CONTROL

Control and evaluation are closely tied to the notion of feedback on organizational performance. A very simplified view of this process would involve three elements: (1) establishment of a specific set of standards for organizational performance; (2) measurement of the organization's actual performance against these standards; and (3) corrective actions to improve performance as it relates to the standard and to rectify any deviations that have occurred.

The orientation of control and evaluation is toward improving the performance of the organization. Effectiveness will obviously increase to the extent all organization members have such an orientation. Control and evaluation, like most management functions can be handled in part by a separate and specialized staff. A much better result is achieved by having all organization members, especially all involved in management, constantly aware and alert to opportunities for improving the organization's efficiency and effectiveness.

A key difficulty of control and evaluation is the potential for widespread antagonism toward controls and toward people who are attempting to administer controls. Organization members who develop this type of negative attitude toward the control and evaluation process can find a variety of successful, but devious ways to resist and not comply with the efforts of the managers above them. Some managers themselves, in fact, can become involved in the process of resistance, noncompliance, or "playing the game" as a result of what they view as overcontrol by higher level administrators. In general, the higher the degree of self regulation that is exercised by each member of the organization, the more effective the organization will be in its total goals.

Organizations have very severe difficulties, both in stating goals in specific terms and in identifying ways to measure progress toward those goals. Often organizations have multiple goals, some of which may be in conflict with others. Goal definition and measurement toward goal accomplishment then becomes a very complex balancing process. Changes can be caused both by internal change within the organization and by activities which occur in the environments surrounding the organization. The organization must adapt to both internal and external changes. Information relevant to such changes must be assembled and put to use in a positive response to such change.

Edgar Schein, in his book *Organizational Psychology*, deals with what he calls the "adaptive-coping" cycle in organizations.[2] He identifies problems and pitfalls that are critical to the maintenance of effectiveness as changes occur in the external environment. First, he focuses on the possibility that the organization may fail to see, or to understand, changes that are taking place in the world around it. Universities today, for example, are faced with a potential decline in the traditional type of student. At the same time, there is a potential for greatly increased interaction with older, nontraditional types of students through community service and continuing education programs. The community also is changing its attitude towards the universities. There is a growing expectation that universities should become involved in helping to solve community problems. A few years ago this was not generally a consideration.

A second problem or pitfall in the adaptive-coping cycle identified by Schein is the potential failure of the organization to transmit the relevant information to those parts of the organization which can act upon it or use it to the organization's advantage. He stresses the fact that information must be available not just within the organization, but to the right persons within it, if it is to be used successfully. An organization that has a research department, for example, must be sure that the information developed is made available to the appropriate managers and to various other organizational components which can act to the organization's advantage.

The third area noted by Schein is the possible failure to make the necessary changes in the organization's system of production once the organization has sensed meaningful events in the environment, obtained the appropriate information, and made it available to appropriate organizational units.

---

[2]Edgar Schein, *Organizational Psychology* (Englewood Cliffs, N.J.: Prentice-Hall, 1965), pp. 96-106.

Given these conditions, changes must be made if the desired effects are to be achieved. Important components of this process are to inform both managers and employees in the organization of the nature and need for the change that is desired and to seek understanding and acceptance of necessary changes.

A fourth potential problem for the organization is to fail to consider the impact of change on other parts of the organization. An organization is very much an interdependent body, and its various parts provide inputs and outputs that influence other component parts.

A fifth potential problem is a possible failure to export the new service, information, or product back into the outside environment. If the organization, for example, wishes to recruit employees with new kinds of skills, it must convey its interest in new kinds of applicants to the job market. If a local government wishes to make changes in certain aspects of its garbage collection department, it might be much easier to accomplish this by informing citizens and requesting their understanding and/or help as the changes are implemented.

A sixth and final pitfall cited by Schein is the failure to obtain feedback on the success or lack of success of the changes introduced. The adaptive-coping cycle is a continuing process. The organization cannot identify a problem, attempt to rectify it, then assume that everything is working well. Continuous feedback is necessary to determine the success of changes that are made, to determine whether further change is necessary and, if so, of what type and to what degree.

Schein also discusses four conditions which are important to an organization's dealing successfully with the six problem areas listed. First, he emphasizes the importance of the organization's recruitment, selection, and training processes. He stresses the necessity for an organization to concentrate on hiring employees through a systematic process which makes the individuals feel that they are in fact wanted by the organization, that they are provided with meaningful activity on the job, and that they are encouraged through training involvement and other activities to make some kind of personal commitment to the goals of the organization.

Second is the utilization of employees and the psychological contract between the organization and each of its members. This psychological contract relates to expectations of the organization toward the member and the member's expectations with regard to the organization. Schein places great importance upon the psychological contract as well as the contract that exists between the organization and its members with regard to such things as pay and fringe benefits.

A third area is the potential problem of group and inter-group relations within the organization. The organization is not in a position to choose whether or not to allow informal groups—they will inevitably exist. Managers must understand and relate to groups in such a manner that they do not become "anti-management" in their attitudes and behavior.

A fourth area is that of leadership as a function of the organization rather than a trait of a particular individual. Leadership roles must be distributed among members of the organization and not automatically given to the single individual who happens to hold a position at the top of the formal hierarchy. Leadership, like membership, is something that is diffused throughout an effective organization, and something that each individual member should be encouraged to exercise in a positive and creative fashion.

Schein's central point through all of the items discussed is to argue for an approach to organizational effectiveness which is based on such factors as effective communication, flexible organizational procedures, creativity, and encouragement of psychological commitment on the part of organizational members. Each of the above four factors are important aspects of an organization.

TECHNIQUES OF EVALUATION AND CONTROL IN LARGE ORGANIZATIONS

In the previous chapter, financially oriented control devices, such as planning, programming, budgeting systems, and zero-based budgeting were discussed. There are other control-oriented mechanisms which are not geared to the financial management or budgeting process. Two of the most well known are management by objectives (MBO) and program evaluation and review technique (PERT). Both of these are designed for use in large-scale organizations. Both are designed to focus on the objectives of the organization, with a view toward coordinating the activities of component parts toward the accomplishment of objectives.

Figure 9.1.   A Simplified PERT Chart

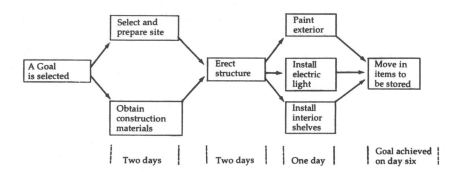

Note: PERT links specific events/activities with specific points in time. The simplified chart represents the construction of a storage shed in a public park. An actual application of PERT would be more complex than this example because the goal involved would be more complicated.

PERT

Program evaluation and review technique is illustrated by Figure 9.1.

As the reader can see, the basic thrust is on the amount of time required for various subtasks within a larger task setting. If the subtasks are accomplished in proper sequence and with proper timing, then larger goals premised upon the subtasks will also be accomplished within a given time frame. This technique was used extensively by The National Aeronautics and Space Administration in its Apollo program which resulted in sending men to the moon and back on several occasions. Large-scale goals, organizations, and tasks require some kind of coordinating mechanism; some way of bringing together the efforts of people and units if the total organization is to achieve a reasonable degree of total productivity. PERT has been used in such efforts as producing large-scale weapons systems for the military, in military operations themselves, and in various other activities where many people and many dollars are involved.

MBO

Management by objectives has been a somewhat controversial approach to management which has been discussed pro
and con for several years now. The discussion has also involved
some variation in the definition applied to MBO by various
management writers. Some have claimed that MBO is simply
a new group of words which have the same basic definition as
management itself. Others have focused on the process of
enhancing employee commitment and participation in the
organization as being a primary goal of MBO. Others have
attributed planning and planning processes as being the central
and most important keys in the MBO process. Still others have
considered the process of evaluation and control itself as being
the central focus of an effective MBO program.

One source of information on MBO and its application in
government is George L. Morrisey's *Management by Objectives
and Results in the Public Sector*.[3] According to Morrisey, management methodology can generally be placed on a continuum
between two extremes. At one extreme is management on the
basis of activity or reaction, and at the other is management on
the basis of objectives and results. Morrisey feels that government is all too often managed on the basis of activity and
reactions. The activity- or reaction-oriented manager simply
counts the number of widgets that are processed or judges the
flurry of activity when a visiting dignitary arrives as being an
indication of productive effort. The manager who has the objective and results orientation, however, is more geared to results
achieved and the plans for action required to achieve such
results. Basically, planning is a central key to the difference in
these two approaches. Morrisey recognizes, of course, that neither extreme will exist in its purest form. He also recognizes
that in any management situation, some of both will exist. His
goal, however, is to urge the manager to move in the direction
of managing by objectives and results, rather than by reacting
to problems and emergencies. A forward-looking orientation
prevents many of these situations from ever occuring. Proper
planning also provides for and facilitates the handling of such
situations that do occur.

---

[3]George L. Morrisey, *Management by Objectives and Results in the Public Sector* (Reading, Mass.: Addison-Wesley, 1976).

Management by objectives and results is seen as a total approach to management, not just as an approach to control and evaluation. In addition to controlling and evaluating, public managers are seen to have four other primary functions. These include: planning (determining what work must be done); organizing (classifying and dividing work in the manageable units); staffing (obtaining personnel to do the work); and directing, or leading (bringing about the human activity which is necessary to accomplish objectives.) These, of course, are capped off by the process of controlling or of insuring that effective accomplishment does in fact take place.

Morrisey depicts the MBO process as going from the general to the specific. It begins with roles and missions, and works through key result areas, indicators, objectives, action plans, and finally, controls. Morrisey sees the management process as focusing more and more specifically on things to be done and verifying that those are in fact done. He sees the process as basically very simple, commonsensical, logical, and as a way to arrange and to practice the proven principles and techniques of management.

Jong S. Jung gives a different emphasis to the MBO processes, defining management by objectives as "a process whereby organizational goals and objectives are set through the participation of organizational members in terms of results expected."[4]

The basic idea is that of participative management. Goal setting processes are seen as the key factor and Jung stresses individual participation, self-management, and decentralization within the organization. Strong communication and feedback processes are considered critical to an integrated approach to management.

One of the founding fathers of MBO, George S. Odiorne, has described the basic elements of MBO by identifying the following five items:

▶ Goal setting—each administrator works with his or her superior in a mutual agreement as to what kinds of results are expected.

▶ Budgeting—to the extent possible, objectives are

---

[4]Jong S. Jung, "Management by Objectives in the Public Sector," *Public Administration Review* (January–February 1976), pp. 1–45.

related to necessary resources and budgets related to tasks and responsibility.

▶ Autonomy—individuals are left alone to the extent possible once goals and resources are agreed upon.

▶ Feedback—the individual manager is provided with information on his performance, and on what corrective action is needed, or what shortcomings exist.

▶ Payoffs—rewards are provided for accomplishment, and the renumeration of managers is based upon incentives to improve their own performance, rather than on political affiliations or on some other factor, such as personality.[5]

Perhaps the most significant thing about all of the techniques, or approaches, to large-scale management is not so much the specific accomplishments of each method but simply the focus on the system itself. In many respects, these and many other management techniques are like successive waves: each has its moment of triumph, but will be superseded by later techniques. The important lesson for the manager to learn and to remember is the analysis of the management process, particularly in the consideration of control and evaluation. In addition to control and evaluation with respect to goals and programs, it is necessary for the manager to be constantly aware of the need to control and evaluate the management process itself, whether it be a process of management by objectives or some other kind of system. It is desirable to achieve goals and objectives effectively, but the process itself must be made increasingly effective. In this context, MBO, PERT, PPB, and other techniques certainly demonstrate the complexity of the management process, help to identify those points at which improvement is necessary, and help to understand the difficulties in obtaining such improvements.

MONITORING PUBLIC MANAGERS' PERFORMANCE FROM "OUTSIDE"

In a discussion of public managers, and their efforts to control and evaluate, the perspectives of "outsiders" with

---

[5]George S. Odiorne, "MBO in State Government," *Public Administration Review* (January–February 1976), pp. 28-32.

regard to public managers and their organizations connot be overlooked. Earlier in this chapter, Robert Fried's list of thirteen outside forces or controls was described. Much has been written about each of these, both individually and in various combinations. While space prohibits a lengthy discussion here, a few key points need to be emphasized.

Legislative Controls

Joseph Harris, a political scientist noted for his work in this area, has observed, "Control of administration is one of the most important functions of legislative bodies in all modern democracies."[6] He emphasizes the highly administrative nature of our modern state and the importance of legislative preeminence.

According to Harris, the purpose of legislative controls are:

▶ to determine whether laws are being implemented in a faithful, effective, and economical manner

▶ to determine whether legislated programs are achieving the desired results

▶ to determine whether legislative policies are administered in the public interest and to encourage administrative diligence

▶ to discover administrative abuse, arbitrariness, or judgmental errors

▶ to review internal management systems, procedures, and controls of agencies to see if they are adequate

▶ to hold public managers accountable for their use of resources provided by the legislative body

While some of the above purposes are unique to legislative control, there is also a generic quality to each of them. High level public managers, the judiciary, and citizens in general, desire the same results. The legislature's means for seeking these results is somewhat more unique.

Harris goes into these means at great length. Since the

---

[6]Joseph P. Harris, *Congressional Control of Administration* (Washington: The Brookings Institution, 1964).

public manager is directly involved, at least some of the major types of legislative control must be identified. These would generally apply at the state and local levels of government, even though Harris is concerned only with the federal. In the category of formal means of control, the author includes:

▶ the passage of laws

▶ the appropriations process

▶ legislative investigations

▶ oversight responsibility assigned to appropriate committee(s)

▶ advice and consent on (Presidential) nominations

▶ legislative veto voiding executive actions

Informal means of control discussed by Harris include such things as suggestions, advice, inspections, and instructions which flow from legislators and/or legislative committees to both political and career agency managers. It is not essential to dwell on the legislative view in a discussion of control and evaluation by public managers. The reader might pause, however, and ask a question which troubles author Harris—how can the legislative body exercise appropriate controls without weakening the authority of the Chief Executive and of public managers and without otherwise hindering or impeding administration?

One control mechanism used more in other countries than in the United States is the *ombudsman*.[7] This approach is more commonly associated with the Scandinavian countries, although the Soviet Union, Japan, and other countries have also tried it. The key element in the ombudsman idea is to provide an impartial and politically independent investigator. This investigator has the power to investigate on his own initiative or to respond to appeals and complaints brought to his attention by outsiders. He or she is empowered to investigate administrative activities in a direct, although informal, and speedy manner. Frequently the ombudsman is an officer of the

---

[7]See Walter Gellhorn, *When Americans Complain* (Cambridge: Harvard University Press, 1966). Also helpful is Stanley V. Anderson, ed., *Ombudsmen for American Government* (Englewood Cliffs, N.J.: Prentice-Hall, 1968).

legislative branch rather than the executive branch. He or she generally has no power to reverse decisions, but attempts to secure remedial action through publicity and through interaction with various administrative and political officials.

The ombudsman approach has been tried primarily at the local government level in the United States, although some state level bureaucracies also have ombudsmen. The federal government generally does not use this approach, although a few agencies use it to some degree internally. Some would say that congressmen and senators, in part, function as federal ombudsmen in their work with constituents on individual needs and problems. Politically appointed heads of agencies might also function to some degree in this role, although generally they would be hearing from more formalized groups, such as lobby or interest groups. Individual citizens might interact with them also, but they would be more likely to contact their legislator.

Another idea for controlling the bureaucracy which has received a fair amount of attention is to make it as representative as possible of the society at large. This idea suggests that society's bureaucracies should be a reflection of the society itself. This would produce organizations which reflect the cultures and needs of all groups within the society.

Lewis Mainzer cites four elements of the case for representative civil service agencies.[8] (1) Everyone in the society should have a chance at the best job he can manage without being excluded on the basis of race, class, or other such factor. (2) Bureaucrats make policy and are influenced in their policymaking activity by the nature of their social background and such backgrounds should be reflected throughout the bureaucracy. (3) Social, economic, and ethnic backgrounds affect the ways that people treat each other and, since these backgrounds are spread throughout the society, they should also be spread throughout the bureaucracy. (4) The psychological identification of the population with its bureaucracy requires that such bureaucracy be representative if government by consent of the governed is in fact to be the case.

---

[8]Lewis C. Mainzer, *Political Bureaucracy* (Glenview, Ill.:Scott, Foresman, 1973), pp. 129-130.

DIFFICULTIES IN THE EVALUATION
AND CONTROL PROCESS

In a symposium on evaluation in the *Public Administration Review,* Joseph S. Wholey and other members of the Urban Institute provide an excellent overview of the process and problems of program management at the federal level.[9] They note that while evaluation has been fairly firmly established since the 1960s, there is little evidence to show that evaluation has had much impact on policies and programs. They identified several reasons for this:

▶ Evaluations are generally not planned to support the decision-making process.

▶ The timing, format, and precision of evaluation studies are not geared to user needs.

▶ Evaluation findings are not adequately communicated to decision makers.

▶ Different evaluations of the same program often are done in ways that preclude their joint, or comparative, use.

▶ Evaluation fails to provide an accumulating, increasingly accurate body of knowledge.

▶ Evaluation studies often address unanswerable questions and produce inconclusive results.[10]

The authors go on to note that these are generally the reasons found for ineffective programs. Upon further analysis, however, they feel that these can really be reduced to three basic propositions which are root causes of the above items. These three propositions are:

1. *Lack of definition*—this is essentially a failure to address the goal definition process accurately at the beginning of a program. The expected or desired output is not defined in a manner that sufficiently enables measurement.

---

[9]Orville F. Poland, ed., "Program Evaluation," *Public Administration Review* (July–August 1974), pp. 299-338.
[10]*Id.,* pp. 301.

2. *Lack of clear logic* — the cause and effect process is not adequately examined and faulty assumptions are made about the application of resources and the outcomes of such application in relation to the long-term impact. Often in this process, this linkage is not sufficiently specified or understood to permit its testing.

3. *Lack of management* — failures in understanding, motivation, authority, and various other dimensions of management can result in a failure to act on evaluation measurements.

The authors point out other problems, such as how to define "improved mental health" or "adequate quality of life." They emphasize the difficulty in trying to propose a solution to a problem that is really undefined and note that it is even harder to evaluate the success of such a proposed solution. Coupled with this is a general lack of any overall guide for program evaluation. There is generally no framework, and the assumptions in the evaluation processes are often too different and too diverse to adequately link program activities with outcomes.

One central problem in evaluation is finding a proper yardstick or standard. In his analysis, policy expert Yehezkel Dror identifies seven main standards that can be used for appraising quality:

1. How does the achieved result compare with previous efforts? How different is the current output from last year?

2. How does current outcome compare with that of similar organizations?

3. Does the achieved quality satisfy client demands? Are students' parents pleased with the school?

4. How does the achieved result compare to accepted professional standards? Does the college pay scale meet the American Association of University Professors recommendations?

5. Does the current quality and volume of output assure survival? Are minimum standards being met? For example, is the college's accreditation safe?

6. How does current quality compare with that originally planned for?

7. How does the quality achieved compare with the optimum possible? What is the best possible result?[11]

Political scientist Thomas R. Dye sees governmental agencies as generally doing a poor job of policy and program evaluation.[12] Dye is especially concerned with impact of agency programs and activities, and he considers agencies ill-suited for evaluating their own success or failure. Several reasons are provided to support this argument.

▶ Many governmental activities are viewed as primarily symbolic in value. Impact on target groups may be less important, especially to political policy makers, than making such groups aware that government "cares."

▶ Agencies have a natural bias toward "proving" that their programs are producing positive results.

▶ Agencies are not eager to find things "not working out" when they have made major financial, psychological, or other investment in current programs and policies.

▶ Demands of day-to-day activities will usually take priority over study and evaluation efforts (Gresham's Law applied to public management). Serious efforts to study agency impact could also interfere with ongoing activities. Experiments in alternative methods of delivering human service programs, for example, could deprive clients of rights provided to them under existing laws.

▶ Evaluation and impact studies are expensive undertakings. Most agencies prefer to use personnel, funds, facilities, and other resources to meet ongoing program needs.

▶ The purposes of governmental programs are often seen differently by different people, especially political lead-

---

[11]Yehezkel Dror, *Public Policymaking Reexamined* (Scranton: Chandler, 1968), pp. 28-29.
 [12]Thomas R. Dye, *Policy Analysis: What Governments Do, Why They Do It, and What Difference It Makes* (University, Ala.: University of Alabama Press, 1976), p. 97.

ers. For example, should a program strive to serve as many people as possible, or should it strive for high-quality service to a limited audience?[13]

Aaron Wildavsky has suggested that the idea of organizations evaluating themselves may be, to some extent, contradictory.[14] While he admits that an ideal organization should be self-evaluating, the evaluation process, he points out, is geared to the discovery of better programs, better decisions, and better methods. Organizations, on the other hand, tend to value stability and are designed to develop and generate commitment to existing means and goals. Wildavsky questions whether a self-evaluating organization can even exist, let alone become a prevailing form of administration. The organization must convince its members to work toward goals and objectives through processes and techniques that are taught. To be self-evaluating, however, it must convince its members to live with constant change and to seek and desire change. This, Wildavsky notes, will be extremely difficult at best.

One of Wildavsky's conclusions is that evaluation must generally remain as one of many elements in organizational structures. He does note, however, that evaluation is not presently being overemphasized. He suggests that we are far from achieving an adequate joining of knowledge and power in most organizations.

POINTS FOR THE PUBLIC MANAGER TO CONSIDER

In many respects, control from the public manager's point of view is a "carrot or stick" proposition. The manager has organizational rewards and sanctions which can be used to encourage or to discourage organization members' actions. Sociologist Amitai Etzioni, in *Modern Organizations*, identifies three methods of control.

1. Control can be based on coercion or physical means (as might be used in a hospital or prison).

2. Control can be based on material rewards such as money which allows recipients to purchase other desired goods and services.

---

[13]*Id.*, pp. 97-98.
[14]Aaron Wildavsky, "The Self-Evaluating Organization," *Public Administration Review* (September–October 1972), pp. 509-520.

3. Control can be based on symbolic or normative means. Included in this category are prestige and esteem, love and acceptance, and internalization of the goals and purposes of the organization.[15]

The general movement in management theory and practice toward greater participation by members in organizational policy and decision making is based in part on the belief that the third means mentioned above is the most effective. As organization members become more involved and committed to group goals, it is believed that they contribute more and need less control. This result is, no doubt, linked to organization members' perception that the organization is likewise involved and committed to helping members achieve their own goals.

Management scholar William Newman has provided useful insights in his book *Constructive Control:Design and Use of Control Systems.*[16] Newman notes the failure of many managers to pay adequate attention to organizational evaluation and control. He believes this may be due, in part, to the punitive and degrading connotations frequently associated with control. Newman sees the need to focus our attitudes and expectations on four significant points:

1. Control is a normal, pervasive, and positive force in the managerial process. Purposeful activity cannot be successful if no control is exercised.

2. Control can be effective only if it is a guide to behavior. The goal is to secure certain actions.

3. Control must be oriented toward the future. It must be geared to respond to both a changing environment and to goals that are possibly subject to change.

4. All human endeavors require control. All organizations have limited resources, and all are concerned with achieving their goals, whatever they may be.[17]

Managerial control is seen by Newman as "the series of steps a manager takes to assure that actual performance con-

---

[15]Amitai Etzioni, *Modern Organizations* (Englewood Cliffs, N.J.: Prentice-Hall, 1964), pp. 59-61.
[16]William Newman, *Constructive Control: Design and Use of Control Systems* (Englewood Cliffs, N.J.: Prentice-Hall, 1975).
[17]*Id.*, pp. 3-5

forms as nearly as practical to plan."[18] Three basic types of control are recognized.

1. "Steering control" is oriented toward corrective actions before results are known. Course corrections made by navigators are of this type.

2. "Yes-no" control is a check-point approach, requiring approval before the process continues. The hiring, or employment, process works this way with applicants going through such steps as application form, testing, interview, and physical examination. Each step is a yes-no decision point controlling organizational entry.

3. "Post-action" control focuses on examination of completed results. Here the goal is to compare results obtained with those desired and to make corrections to improve future results. Employee performance appraisals or health inspections of operating restaurants would fall in this category.

Almost all organizations are seen by Newman as using a variety of all three types of controls. Usually a balance of independent and interdependent control processes are required. Control, like other public management activities, is a complex and dynamic process.

SUMMARY

Control and evaluation are important and complex dimensions of public management. The goal of "performance" must be a central concern of every proficient public manager. Both efficiency and effectiveness must be taken into account. Techniques such as PERT and MBO must be considered when applicable. The public manager must also understand, and be sensitive to, outside forces of an evaluative and control nature.

---

[18]*Ibid.*

CASE STUDIES

1. Evaluating the Academy

The State of Tranquility has been a national leader in its efforts to train, develop, and "professionalize" its highway patrol force. A State Police Academy has long been in existence and over the last 15 to 20 years it has become a major state agency. A substantial amount of "mandatory" training is now required of all state officers. The Academy also makes a number of training courses available to local police departments throughout the state.

The size and budget of the Academy have become sufficiently large that the agency has considerable public visibility. A number of persons seeking political office have suggested that the state could save a lot of money by cutting back the Academy budget. Part of their argument is that less training would be required if the "right" applicants were hired in the first place.

Governor Smith is aware of the growing controversy over state police training expenditures, but is not sure what action to take. The Governor's only concern is to do the "right thing," especially since her term will soon be over, and she has no further interest in elective office.

As her Executive Assistant, the Governor has asked you to develop an evaluation plan to assess the efficiency and effectiveness of the State Police Academy. Identify, prioritize, and explain the key criteria you will include in your proposal. Assess the strengths and weaknesses of your plan.

2. Time to Get Tough?

As the City Manager of Exurbia you have become increasingly perplexed over your difficulties in "controlling" the various city departments. With a current work force of several hundred, located in nine different departments, you know that personal control of everything and everyone is impossible. At the same time, it seems that the department heads prefer not to exercise strong control. They also seem reluctant to give you all the information you need in working with the City Council.

For example, a number of complaints about garbage collection and police actions have come to you from council members, even though the respective department heads had the information several days earlier. The department heads seem totally unwilling to give you any negative information about their departments. They also appear to be more concerned about being "one of the boys" in their department than about being the manager—and a member of your team.

At this point you've decided the time has come to "lay down the law" to the department heads. You want to be firm, but at the same time tactful, and your goal is to secure their cooperation. You do know, however, that one result could be conflict.

How can you best approach the department heads in order to achieve cooperative effort? Outline your proposed presentation and analyze the alternative reactions you may get. Also, consider the possibility that your control problems may be the result of your own management style. What kinds of behavior on your part might be contributing to your current problems?

10

The Public Manager as a Professional

Key Concepts

Profession Criteria
  Professional
    Professionalism
      Ethics
        Morality
          Career Planning
            Personal Values
              Individual Development Planning
                Certification

The public manager has one of the most challenging jobs in existence. The high stakes and constant demands of managing public organizations require dedicated, competent people who are committed to the public welfare. Dynamism and complexity characterize the political and managerial environments of the public manager and a "bureaucratic syndrome" is no longer viable; professionalism in public management is the order of the day.

Government's impact on health care, education, transportation, and environmental improvement illustrates the intricacies of public management and its importance to the citizenry. The authors believe that the quality of public managers is the key to effective public service, and for this reason espouse a "professional" perspective to public management. Professionalism is an attitude that causes public managers to attach the highest priority to continuous self-development, to have a career orientation, and to exhibit distinctive competence in each of their managerial roles.

THE PROFESSIONAL PERSPECTIVE

Public Management—A Profession?

The term "profession" was originally defined by sociologists in terms so strict that only a few occupations, such as medicine and law, qualified as professions. In recent years, models of professionalism have incorporated a wide variety of occupations, including public management. Both the traditional and contemporary viewpoints will be discussed to determine where public management fits.

Traditional Criteria for Professions

Sociologist William Goode's criteria reflect the traditional criteria used by most writers. He suggests that professions essentially possess these four characteristics:

1. Lengthy training in a body of generalized and systematic knowledge. People become professional only after completing a rigorous program of courses that make them expert in a specialized field. Medicine, law, engineering, and education, among others, require a specialized degree and certification or licensing before a person can begin practicing in one of these fields.

2. An orientation toward service. Professionals adhere to the belief that their work contributes significantly to the public welfare. They devote themselves to the client's interests more than to commercial profit. In this respect professions maintain public respect by "weeding out" those who do not adhere to the high moral and technical precepts of the order.

3. A high degree of internal control. Professions are self-policing in that they encourage high standards of performance; they promulgate "codes of conduct" that delineate standards; and they exercise substantial peer control over their colleagues.

4. Freedom from lay control and judgment. Professionals are virtually autonomous in exercising the special competence required. Because persons outside the profession are not equipped with the detailed knowledge of the field, they are rarely in a position to judge the quality of a professional's services.[1]

These criteria present an ideal model of a profession which writer Richard Schott[2] argues does not include public management. He claims that there is not a systematic, scientific theory or body of knowledge that comprises public management education. The thrust of the educational process seems to have been away from the science of administration and toward its political aspects. In addition, he points out that few middle- or upper-level public officials have had formal training in the field. Furthermore, what constitutes "proper" training has still not been resolved; a diversity of approaches in public administration stems from a disagreement over whether political science or public management should be the focus. Finally, he cites the fact that the American Society for Public Administration (ASPA) membership includes a very small proportion of public managers and is not as representative of the practitioner membership as the American Medical Association is for physicians or the American Bar Association is for lawyers. Also, there is no peer control over the quality of work performed by its practitioners. Rather, performance reviews conducted by superiors in large bureaucratic organizations are the basis for assessing the performance of public managers. Thus, a strict application of traditional indices of a profession would exclude public management. While Schott believes that public management is not a profession, other writers point to professional aspects of public management.

---

[1]William J. Goode, "Encroachment, Charlatanism, and the Emerging Profession," *American Sociological Review* (December 1960), pp. 902–914; "The Theoretical Finds of Professionalization" in Amitai Etzioni, ed., *Semi-Professions and their Organization* (New York: Free Press, 1969), p. 277; "Community Within a Community: The Professions," *American Sociological Review* (April 1957), pp. 194–195.

[2]Richard L. Schott, "Public Administration as a Profession: Problem and Prospects," *Public Administration Review* (May–June 1976), pp. 254 ff.

Profession, Professional, and Professionalism

Perhaps at this point we should clarify the concepts of profession, professional and professionalism. As previously discussed, a *profession* is characterized by specific criteria, and occupations can be construed as professions to the degree that they meet or approach these criteria. Medicine, law, the clergy, university teaching, dentistry, architecture, and some fields of engineering are generally accepted as professions because they meet all the stated criteria.[3] Similarly, police, firefighters, and military occupations are beginning to be viewed as professions as they meet more of the criteria of a profession. A *professional*, then, is one who is a member of an occupational profession. But a public manager, without being a member of a profession, per se, can exhibit the qualities of a professional. Public managers can adopt a professional perspective which is broad and flexible enough to enable them to maintain a diversity of interests, yet firm and understandable enough to provide some sense of direction, purpose, and unity to the field.[4] The analogy of the medical profession might serve to illustrate this point. Medicine is a profession, but it is also an assortment of professions and specializations. It is science, art, theory, practice, study, and application all rolled into one, and yet not based on a single discipline. Medical doctors must know something of chemistry and biology, but they are neither chemists nor biologists; they must know something of a number of fields and of their application in specific ways.

The academic and intellectual home of public administration, or public management, has historically been the field of political science. To the extent that the public manager deals with public purposes as a governmental employee in a political environment, he or she should know something of that field. To the extent that the task is to perform managerial duties within a formal organization, the public manager needs to know something of the fields of general management, law, sociology, psychology, and economics. Public managers would also benefit from an understanding of decision sciences that

[3]Harold Wilensky, "The Professionalization of Everyone?", *American Journal of Sociology* (September 1964), pp. 138–139.

[4]Dwight Waldo, "Scope of the Theory of Public Administration," in James C. Charlesworth, ed., *Theory and Practice of Public Administration: Political and Social Sciences* (Philadelphia: American Academy of Political and Social Science, 1968), pp. 9 ff.

draw upon mathematics, systems analysis, and information systems. In essence, public management is an eclectic field where practitioners synthesize knowledge from a number of fields and apply it in performing their managerial tasks.

Professionalism is a socialization process. As an individual adopts a professional perspective and approximates the characteristics of a professional, he or she is undergoing professionalism. This process is discussed in detail in a later section of this chapter.

Professionalism and Politics

Professionalism is viewed as diametrically opposed to politics. "Professionalism," Mosher wrote, "rests upon specialized knowledge, science, a rationality. These are correct ways of solving problems and doing things. Politics is seen as constituting negotiations, elections, votes, compromises—all carried on by subject-matter amateurs. Politics is to the professions as ambiguity is to truth, expediency to rightness, heresy to true belief."[5]

This aversion of professionals to politics becomes a problem when public management is one's primary or secondary profession because politics are an integral part of the public manager's environment. Consequently, professional public managers find that an understanding of the political environment in which they operate is essential to their effectiveness.

The Process of Professionalism

A variety of factors are now emerging in American society which influence the professionalization of public managers. The field of public management has become a career occupation and specialized education is considered essential for practitioners. Professional organizations in the general area of administration, such as the American Society for Public Administration, and in more specific areas, such as the International Personnel Management Association and the International City Management Association, emphasize standards of

---

[5]Frederick Mosher, *Democracy and the Public Service* (New York: Oxford University Press, 1968), p. 109.

conduct and recognition of excellence in job performance. (See Appendix 3 for a list of associations for public managers.) Accreditation and licensing of practitioners is gaining acceptance in the field, and codes of ethics along with mechanisms for their enforcement are becoming evident. These are the steps in the process of professionalism described earlier in this chapter.[6]

The preponderance of traditional professions in government is an obvious influence on the professionalism of public managers. Research supports the conclusion that a new breed of manager is emerging—the administrator-professional who was hired for technical or professional skills and later moved into administrative positions. One study found that a significant number of federal supervisors are in professional occupations.[7] Another revealed that many federal executives hold professional degrees.[8]

An analysis by the former U.S. Civil Service Commission (now Office of Personnel Management) of federal executive positions in grades GS 16 to 18 indicated that 68 percent of the occupations represented require professional training; thus their incumbents are professionals in the traditional sense.[9] The presence of these professionals in government organizations and their association with other managers is bound to influence those outside the traditional professions to strive for professionalism. It is the authors' belief that as more individual public managers subscribe to standards of professionalism, public management as an occupation will reach a degree of professionalization.

Standards of Professionalism

The Professional Standards and Ethics Committee of the American Society for Public Administration is developing professional standards for public managers. Each of the areas

[6]Wilensky, *supra*, note 3.
[7]John J. Corson and L. Shale Paul, *Men Near the Top* (Baltimore: Johns Hopkins Press, 1966), pp. 97–102.
[8]Lloyd Warner, et al., *The American Federal Executive* (New Haven: Yale University Press, 1963), pp. 107 ff.
[9]U.S. Civil Service Commission, *Executive Manpower in the Federal Service: March 1973* (Washington, D.C.: U.S. Government Printing Office, 1973), p. 8.

around which standards will be developed are discussed below with particular attention to their application toward professionalizing public managers.

1. *Knowledge and skills.* Specialized training in the field of public management would considerably enhance the professional standing of the field. Toward this end, the National Association of Schools of Public Affairs and Administration in 1974 adopted *Guidelines and Standards for Professional Masters Degree Programs in Public Affairs/Public Administration* for the purpose of fostering a professional focus and approach to Public Management and to build the necessary competencies in public managers to enable them to perform with excellence. The guidelines consist of a matrix of professional competencies that include components of (a) knowledge, (b) skills, (c) values, and (d) behavior. A qualified public manager should be able to apply each of these components to the following subject-matter areas: (a) the political, social, and economic context of administration, (b) quantitative and nonquantitative analytical tools, (c) individual group/organizational dynamics, (d) policy analysis and administrative/management processes. The content and application of each component to each subject matter area is specified in the guidelines. NASPAA hopes that the application of the standards will consistently and uniformly establish highly relevant training for public management practitioners.[10]

Those occupations that claim professional standing place high value on educational credentials. For example, the International City Management Association reports that among city managers aged 29 and under, 92 percent hold a bachelor's degree and 39 percent have a Master of Public Administration degree.[11] Military officers are selected for a hierarchy of professional schools during their careers: career courses and update around the fifth year of service, command and staff colleges at

---

[10]*Guidelines and Standards for Professional Masters Degree Programs in Public Affairs/ Public Administration: A Report of the Standards Committee of the National Association of Schools of Public Affairs and Administration,* prepared with the Assistance of Ernest A. Englebert (Washington, D.C.: NASPAA, April 1974) pp. 11 ff.
[11]International City Management Association, *Municipal Yearbook: 1964* (Chicago: ICMA, 1964) pp. 498 ff.

mid-career, and senior service colleges near their eighteenth year of service.[12]

2. *Performance and behavior*. When public managers adopt a professional perspective, they strive to perform their functions with distinctive competence. They display excellence in their behavior. But how can individual performance be assessed? Unfortunately, government performance is invariably measured in terms of inputs (tax dollars spent, number of clients interviewed, and so on) rather than on results achieved. Until valid measures of manager performance can be found and behaviors identified that yield effectiveness, assessment efforts will be difficult.

3. *Personal development and achievement of potential*. The individual public manager must assume full responsibility for his or her professional development. Continuous self-development is essential to a successful public service career. This area for professional standards has special meaning for each public manager; a later section of this chapter is devoted to detailed discussion of the activities for individual professional development.

4. *Relationships to law and political processes*. The political environment of the public manager where the realities of the situation involve "expediencies" that are not always completely rational was discussed in Chapter 2. Standards for public management in these areas might be built around a manager's effectiveness in combining the professional with the political aspects of the job in carrying out legislated programs.

5. *Commitment to the needs of the public service*. One of the basic criteria of a profession is a service orientation. The notion that professionalism is good for the public because high quality management invariably produces better service is a well established precept. It is idealistic to assume that all public managers will be dedicated to serving the public interest, but that attitude is essential to building and maintaining professionalism.

---

[12]Colonel William J. Taylor, Jr., "Military Professionals in Changing Times," *Public Administration Review* (November–December 1977), p. 635.

6. *Responsiveness, responsibility, and accountability.* How readily does a manager respond to public needs? And how timely is the response? Commensurate with the authority vested in the manager's office is an obligation, or responsibility, to exercise that authority for the good of the organization and of the public. Public managers are held accountable for the results of their actions both by higher authority within the organization and by their constituencies, e.g., other agencies and the public. Managers who are considered professional have to gain the respect of both the public and of higher authority by being responsive to the public's needs, responsible for their actions, and willing to be judged for their performance.

7. *Ethics, conflicts of interest, public disclosure, and confidentiality.* As a result of the Civil Service Reform Act a list of specific competencies were developed for managers who comprised the feeder group for the Senior Executive Service. These competencies are listed in Figure 10.1 and they might serve as a guide for the development of any professional manager who wishes to grow professionally.

Figure 10.1.   Management and Executive Competencies

I. *Management Processes* (Competencies relating to the structures, activities, and procedures through which work is accomplished in an organization)

1. Know agency organization, responsibilities, and role
2. Know and accept the role of manager
3. Know and accept the role of the executive
4. Be able to set objectives and evaluate their accomplishment
5. Be able to make timely decisions and use appropriate decision-making aids
6. Be able to establish priorities among alternatives
7. Be able to develop and implement action plans for the accomplishment of program goals
8. Be able to develop long-range program goals
9. Be able to organize resources and structure to accomplish program goals
10. Be able to effectively delegate
11. Be able to set individual performance standards and appraise performance
12. Be able to interact with noncareer managers/executives/staff persons

13. Be able to utilize the basic management support systems in personnel, budget, research and development, EDP/ information systems, and procurement
14. Be able to apply agency personnel policies in key areas such as LMR and EEO
15. Be able to plan for the adaptation of the organization to a changing environment

II. *Personal / Interpersonal* (Competencies relating to working with and through people)

16. Be able to assess own strengths and limitations
17. Be able to speak clearly and concisely
18. Be able to write clearly and concisely
19. Be able to coach and counsel subordinates
20. Be able to give and receive feedback constructively
21. Be able to deal with diverse views and ambiguity
22. Be able to recognize and overcome blocks to communication
23. Be able to use various leadership styles
24. Be able to create an organizational climate which results in a motivated workforce
25. Be able to negotiate on a wide variety of issues

III. *Environment* (Competencies relating to the interaction between the organization and the broader arena within which it operates)

26. Understand relevant social and political forces
27. Be familiar with relevant technological developments
28. Understand general economic conditions and issues
29. Be able to consider agency policy/programs within the context of broad national priorities
30. Understand the relationships among the workings of Congress, the Office of the President, the executive departments and agencies, and the courts
31. Understand the relationships between career executives and political executives
32. Understand the purposes and structure of government as an institution in our democratic society
33. Recognize the special responsibilities of the public trust
34. Be familiar with the responsibilities of state and local governments

---

Source: Office of Personnel Management (mimeo)

THE ETHICS OF PUBLIC MANAGEMENT

The Watergate affair emphasized to public managers the need to maintain a standard of conduct that is above reproach. Their every action is subject to public scrutiny. Since managers interact with people within their own agencies as well as with managers in other agencies, the probability of criticism from both their constituency and their peers is high. To insure against this eventuality, public servants must accept higher standards of personal conduct than other people because the public is extremely demanding in this respect.

Norman Poirier, former president of the Federal Bar Association, cites the example of the legal officer in government. He emphasizes that this lawyer assumes a public trust for his or her agency, its employees, and the government at large and is responsible to the publics that the agency serves. Poirier elaborates as follows:

> "the client of the federally employed lawyer, using the term in the sense of where lies his immediate professional obligation and responsibility, is the agency where he is employed including those charged with its administration insofar as they are engaged in the conduct of the public business. The relationship is a confidential one, an attribute of the lawyers' profession which accompanies him in his government service. . . ."[13]

Perhaps the same can be said of any public manager. Any deviation from ethical conduct is likely to arouse the suspicions of others and might lead to an erosion of the public's image of government and a deterioration of its credibility.

Public Image and Credibility

Shortly after the Watergate hearings, Frank P. Sherwood, Director of the Washington Public Affairs Center of the University of Southern California lamented that "The present shockingly low level of confidence in all levels of government can be cancerous; distrust is no friend of a vital and participative democratic system."[14] A Harris Poll at the time showed 60

---

[13]C. Norman Poirier, "The Federal Government Lawyer and Professional Ethics," *American Bar Association Journal* (December 1974), p. 1542.
[14]Frank P. Sherwood, "Professional Ethics," *Public Management* (June 1975), p. 13.

percent of the American people believing that the chief objective of politicians was to make money. Loss of citizen credibility in government did not stem from Watergate alone and it was not confined necessarily to the Nixon years. Withholding of information, clandestine operations, conflicts of interest, misuse of funds, among others, are unprofessional acts and have created a public skepticism of government. Citizens often feel that public officials are more concerned with their own advancement and the interests of their own organization than with the interests of their clientele.

Fortunately, abuses by public managers are limited to a very few. Nevertheless, this lack of complete morality has been sufficiently visible, as in the Watergate case and in more recent incidents involving several U.S. senators and representatives, to create a crisis in confidence in public management. Although these examples are negative (and for the most part did *not* involve career public managers), they serve to illustrate the consequences of less-than-ethical conduct by public officials.

Setting the Moral Tone

Perhaps one of the highest responsibilities of the public manager is that of setting the moral tone for the organization. By the manager's example, the ethics and morals of all subordinate managers can be established. In his classic work, *The Functions of the Executive,* Chester Barnard underscored the public manager's responsibility in establishing morality in his or her organization.

Barnard explained that executive managerial responsibility requires compliance with a complex code of morals as well as the setting of a code for others to follow. In this sense the manager secures, creates, and inspires "morale" in an organization. And it logically follows that the loyal employee will subordinate his or her individual interests to the overall good of the organization.[15]

Senator Sam Ervin as Chairman of the Senate's Select Committee on Presidential Campaign Activities in the 93rd Congress went a step further by emphasizing that public managers

---

[15]Chester I. Barnard, *The Functions of the Executive* (Cambridge, Mass.: Harvard University Press, 1938), p. 279.

must be characterized by the abiding conviction that public office is a public trust, not to be abused for private gain, and that they must be imbued with a high degree of moral integrity.[16]

The evidence strongly suggests that the manager's own value system guides his or her actions in setting the moral tone for the organization. An "ethic of managerial action" might evolve from a consistent system of values that stresses "right" action. One writer advocates, "what is needed is an ethic of managerial action which satisfies the expectations of the individual, the organization and the public. To the extent that employees are encouraged to identify with . . . big government and to abdicate personal concepts of responsibility, such an ethic should compel people to confront their values and take responsibility for the consequences of their behavior."[17]

Guidelines for Moral Conduct

Codes of ethics often delineate the standards of acceptable behavior of managers. An example of such a code is displayed in Figure 10.2, The Code of Ethics of the International City Management Association. It was modified in 1972 to underscore efforts to improve the image of local government. The Association enforces the Code through the Executive Board on advice of the Committee on Professional Conduct. Although sanctions are limited to admonition, private or public censure, or expulsion from membership, the ethics process reportedly is working well.

In an effort to stimulate professional thought and discussion on the ethical aspects of public administration, the National Academy of Public Administration published in 1974 a set of ethical guidelines for administrators.[18] And Congress issued a Code for Government Service in June of 1980 (PL 96-303) to provide guidelines for the ethical conduct of federal public managers. (See Figure 10.3.)

---

[16]James L. Kirkpatrick, "The Codification of Honor," *Nation's Business* (February 1975), p. 12.

[17]James S. Bowman, "Management Ethics in Business and Government," *Business Horizons* (October 1976), p. 54.

[18]George A. Graham, "Ethical Guidelines for Public Administrators: Observations on Rules of the Game," *Public Administration Review*, Vol. 34 (January–February 1974), pp. 90–92.

Figure 10.2. City Management Code of Ethics

THE PURPOSE of the International City Management Association is to increase the proficiency of city managers, county managers, and other municipal administrators and to strengthen the quality of urban government through professional management. To further these objectives, certain ethical principles shall govern the conduct of every member of the International City Management Association, who shall:

1 Be dedicated to the concepts of effective and democratic local government by responsible elected officials and believe that professional general management is essential to the achievement of this objective.

2 Affirm the dignity and worth of the services rendered by government and maintain a constructive, creative, and practical attitude toward urban affairs and a deep sense of social responsibility as a trusted public servant.

3 Be dedicated to the highest ideals of honor and integrity in all public and personal relationships in order that the member may merit the respect and confidence of the elected officials, of other officials and employees, and of the public.

4 Recognize that the chief function of local government at all times is to serve the best interests of all of the people.

5 Submit policy proposals to elected officials, provide them with facts and advice on matters of policy as a basis for making decisions and setting community goals, and uphold and implement municipal policies adopted by elected officials.

6 Recognize that elected representatives of the people are entitled to the credit for the establishment of municipal policies; responsibility for policy execution rests with the members.

7 Refrain from participation in the election of the members of the employing legislative body, and from all partisan political activities which would impair performance as a professional administrator.

8 Make it a duty continually to improve the member's professional ability and to develop the competence of associates in the use of management techniques.

9 Keep the community informed on municipal affairs; encourage communication between the citizens and all municipal officers; emphasize friendly and courteous service to the public; and seek to improve the quality and image of public service.

10 Resist any encroachment on professional responsibilities, believing the member should be free to carry out official policies without interference, and handle each problem without discrimination on the basis of principle and justice.

11 Handle all matters of personnel on the basis of merit so that fairness and impartiality govern a member's decisions, pertaining to appointments, pay adjustments, promotions, and discipline.

12 Seek no favor; believe that personal aggrandizement or profit secured by confidential information or by misuse of public time is dishonest.

International
City
Management
Association

This Code was originally adopted in 1924 by the members of the International City Management Association and has since been amended in 1938, 1952, 1969, 1972, and 1976.

Note: Reprinted with permission of International City Management Association.

Figure 10.3.   Code of Ethics for Government Service

ANY PERSON IN GOVERNMENT SERVICE SHOULD

I. Put loyalty to the highest moral principles and to country above loyalty to persons, party, or Government department.

II. Uphold the Constitution, laws, and regulations of the United States and of all governments therein and never be a party to their evasion.

III. Give a full day's labor for a full day's pay; giving earnest effort and best thought to the performance of duties.

IV. Seek to find and employ more efficient and economical ways of getting tasks accomplished.

V. Never discriminate unfairly by the dispensing of special favors or privileges to anyone, whether for remuneration or not; and never accept, for himself or herself or for family members, favors or benefits under circumstances which might be construed by reasonable persons as influencing the performance of governmental duties.

VI. Make no private promises of any kind binding upon the duties of any office, since a Government employee has no private word which can be binding on public duty.

VII. Engage in no business with the Government, either directly or indirectly, which is inconsistent with the conscientious performance of governmental duties.

VIII. Never use any information gained confidentially in the performance of governmental duties as a means of making private profit.

IX. Expose corruption wherever discovered.

X. Uphold these principles, ever conscious that public office is a public trust.

Authority of Public Law 96-303, unanimously passed by the Congress of the United States on June 27, 1980, and signed into law by the President on July 3, 1980.

According to some observers, codes can be overly strict. As David A. Burkhalter, City Manager of Charlotte, North Carolina, stated, "I know one governmental agency, for example, that I have been out with, talking about some of the problems we have, they are absolutely forbidden to let anybody buy them a sandwich—even a sandwich. If a person can be bought off for a sandwich, he must be in pretty bad shape."[19] Former President Carter's stringent rules of ethical conduct for high level appointees were viewed in some circles as a detriment to attracting highly talented prospects. Carter's code barred, for one year, policy-making appointees from representing anyone for pay before their former department or agency. It also required these appointees to divest themselves of holdings likely to be affected by their official acts. Some of the Cabinet appointees might have to give up a lifetime of wealth accumulation, a high price to pay for a short stint in service to one's country.

As tight as some codes are, they may not be enough. Often they do not induce the kinds of behavior the public desires of its officeholders. Most of the Watergate offenders were lawyers. This profession has one of the most stringent sets of behavior requirements, but they were not a sufficient deterrent to the actions of the Watergate actors, including the President.[20]

Openness, according to writer Harlan Cleveland, would augment ethical codes by removing the veil of secrecy surrounding the decisions of public managers. He elaborates:

"Openness, then, is the buzzword of modernization. In its firmament the duties are the public hearing, the news conference, the investigative reporter, *Meet the Press,* and *Face the Nation* and *Issues and Answers* and *The Advocates.* Its devils are also familiar: smoke-filled rooms, secret plans, hidden or edited tapes.

"In consequence, compared to a generation of even a decade ago, most public officials are more inclined now to ask themselves, before acting, how their actions would look on the *front page* of the *Washington Post* or on the evening newscast."[21]

This type of openness, Cleveland reports, has given rise to Sunshine laws in many states and in the U.S. Senate. The

---

[19]David A. Burkhalter, interviewed in "A Post Watergate Code of Ethics," *Public Management* (June 1975), p. 10.

[20]Sherwood, *supra,* note 14.

[21]Harlan Cleveland, "How Do You Get Everybody in the Act and Still Get Some Action?", *Public Management* (June 1975), p. 4.

Hawaii law, for example, makes it a crime for public officials to hold any type of private meeting without first notifying and inviting the public and the press. Other writers say that this approach is excessive. They claim that Sunshine laws carry with them the connotation that people in government are suspect and that citizens ought to take positive measures to see that their wishes are properly executed. According to this view, Sunshine laws arouse public suspicion and create doubts that public managers are responding correctly to their responsibilities.[22]

Nevertheless, public managers are in positions of public trust where every action is publicly observed. Thus, their ability to inspire respect and confidence depends on the manner in which they fulfill their public trust. Thus, as John Patriarche, City Manager of East Lansing, Michigan contends, the manager "must deal fairly and equally with all segments of the community. He or she must be open and honest and be a person of his word, recognizing that a verbal commitment is just as sacred as a written contract."[23]

Although there is no single regulator of a public manager's conscience, one's own system of ethical values combined with codes and laws should provide the basis for "right" action.

Some argue that *commonly accepted* practice is a proper guide for public managers. If the private actions of public managers would stand up publicly, then they are probably correct. However, in Vice President Spiro Agnew's case what had been a commonly accepted practice in Maryland on kickbacks from contractors was not an appropriate guide.

Regulatory boards are a means of overseeing the activities of public managers. The Governor of California Jerry Brown took an unprecedented step to remove control of the state regulatory boards from the special interests they were created to regulate. In what may become a model for the rest of the nation, Governor Brown appointed "lobbyists for the people"—lay members—to a majority of posts on regulatory boards under the Department of Consumer Affairs. These new members were nonprofessionals in the fields they would supervise and many have been highly critical of the protectionist influences that

---

[22]Burkhalter, *supra*, note 19, p. 8.
[23]John M. Patriarche, "Ethical Questions Which Administrators Face," *Public Management* (June 1975), p. 19.

dominated the boards. Governor Brown emphasized that he used this measure to insure that the occupations and professions serve people, not just themselves. He said in an interview on the subject, "The concept of public members reflects the idea whose time has come, that lay control and public participation is a vital ingredient of our democratic process."[24]

THE PROCESS OF PROFESSIONALISM

The previous discussion on ethics serves to underscore the significance of high moral conduct in public management. It is an essential foundation for developing professionalism. A prerequisite for professionalism is continuous self-development to stay abreast of new developments in the field and to upgrade managerial and technical skills. This section is designed to stimulate the public manager's thinking about career planning and to provide some ideas for professional self-development.

Career Planning

One of the attributes of a profession is that it is viewed as spanning a lifetime. Thus, professional managers perceive their work in terms of a career. Elmer Staats, former head of the federal General Accounting Office, emphasizes that an individual's career direction is a blend of the person's aspirations and the organization's needs. And the degree of "success" of a person's career is based on his or her own assessment and *self*-development—not someone else's.[25] Individual managers can and do exercise some control over their destinies by planning their careers. Many public agencies have career paths or ladders through which an individual advances, but even without this formal mechanism the public manager can prepare a plan for his or her own career progression. Unfortunately, so many of us spend our lives working *at* something that we fail to take the time to plan to work *toward* something. The following section presents a strategy for planning a professional career—a "kit of tools" for working toward future career goals.

---

[24]"Brown Places 60 on California Regulatory Boards As Lobbyists for People Instead of Special Interests," *New York Times* (February 7, 1977), p. A-1.

[25]Elmer Staats, "Career Planning and Development: What Way Is Up?" *Public Administration Review* (January–February 1977), pp. 73–76.

A Strategy for Professional Career Planning

The authors teach a graduate course in career planning to students enrolled in a Master of Public Administration program. As a term project, students are required to prepare a comprehensive and personal career plan; the elements of such a plan, which are displayed in Figure 10.4, are explained in the following discussion.

Personal values system. Milton Rokeach defines values as "multi-faceted standards that guide conduct in a variety of ways."[26] Although some values are generic to society, in general, or to a particular time (e.g., patriotism during World War II), value systems are highly individualistic. Thus, it becomes necessary for each person to establish his or her own particular set of values. Numerous exercises, tests and related psychological instruments are available for exploring and identifying one's values.

(An abundance of "career awareness" information is available. A sampling of sources is listed in Appendix 2.)

Setting personal objectives. Career objectives are stated as short-term, typically one year, or long-range aspirations, looking ahead five or more years. The importance of a thorough exploration of one's values becomes evident at this point. For example, the individual who values a family relationship, but who seeks high pay through an office that requires extensive travel, may want to reassess the trade-offs. Many public managers who are disillusioned with their present situation state a job change as being their prime objective. Professionals in public service find that they must update their skills periodically to avoid obsolescence. Hence, conflicts and decisions regarding what a person is presently doing and what he or she wants to do are essential first steps in setting personal objectives.

Next, the objective-setting process requires quantifying the objectives including a measure of their attainment. Properly developed objectives are reduced to writing. The importance

---

[26]Milton Rokeach, *The Nature of Human Values* (New York: Free Press, 1973), p. 13. See also Maury Smith, *A Practical Guide to Value Clarification* (La Jolla: University Associates, 1977) and Sidney Simon, *Meeting Yourself Halfway* (Niles, Ill.: Argus Communications, 1974).

Figure 10.4. Professional Career-Planning Model

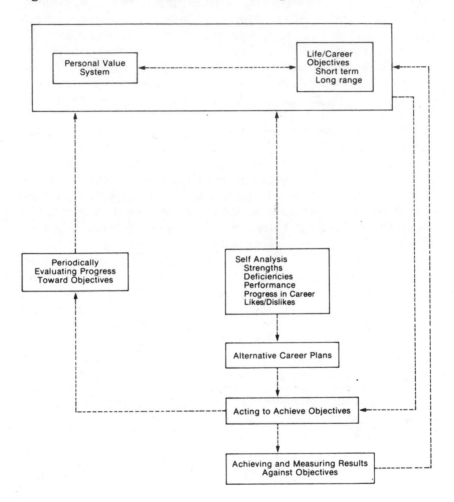

Source: Donald P. Crane, *Personnel: The Management of Human Resources,* 3rd ed. (Boston: Kent Publishing Company, 1982), p. 523. © 1982 by Wadsworth Publishing Company, Inc. Reprinted by permission of Kent Publishing Company, a Division of Wadsworth, Inc., 20 Providence Street, Boston, Mass. 02116.

of *written* objectives cannot be overemphasized. By expressing them in writing, one becomes committed to their attainment; individuals with written objectives have a harder time rationalizing a failure to accomplish and are more inclined to make an effort to insure their fulfillment. In recognition of the dynamic nature of public service, managers are well-advised to develop alternative objectives and to anticipate contingency plans to meet them.

Individual development planning. Personal objectives are put into action through the individual development plan. The students, or public managers, analyze their own strengths that will help them meet objectives and they identify shortcomings that might be drawbacks to achieving the objectives. Then they specify what actions they can take to overcome their shortcomings and preserve their strengths. It is recommended that they develop a set of contingency plans. Too often, in developing career plans, individuals chart only one path because they assume their present employers will move them up a career ladder based on "superior" performance. On the other hand, they may become resigned to being locked into a particular career path. A contingency planning model for career development outlined by Professors Reif and Newstrom describes four phases that help the individual set and eventually attain career objectives. These phases are: (1) conducting a rigorous analysis of self, career opportunities and career obstacles; (2) setting career objectives; (3) developing realistic plans; and (4) reviewing progress toward their achievement.[27] The career planning scheme in Figure 10.3 parallels this model.

Finally, there are myriad possible activities that individuals can engage in to enhance their professionalism and improve the chances of attaining their objectives. Representative of such development activities are the following:

1. *Reading programs.* Regular reading of current articles in management journals, both public and private, will help the public manager in keeping aware of emerging concepts, practices and techniques in management. In addition, journals and current literature of a technical nature contain information pertinent to one's specialty field, e.g., information sciences,

---

[27]William E. Rief and John W. Newstrom, "Career Development by Objectives," *Business Horizons* (October 1974), pp. 5–10.

accounting, personnel, and so on. A perusal of magazines that provide news and general information helps insure that the public manager is up-to-date on current events. Enlightened managers read consistently in all of these areas. Appendix 2 at the end of this text includes an annotated listing of sources of information for the public manager. There are sufficient entries to enable the manager to tailor a reading list to his or her needs.

2. *Membership in professional associations.* Professional associations offer current literature in the field, seminars for professional development, meetings and conventions for affiliation with peers or other agencies, and a host of career-related services. The American Society for Public Administration and the International City Managers Association are broader management-related associations. But there are also professional associations for specific occupational classifications, such as the International Personnel Management Association, the Association for Systems Management, the American Society of Mechanical Engineers. Appendix 3 at the end of this text includes a list of associations appropriate to public management.

3. *In-service training.* Most government agencies offer either independently, or in conjunction with others, specialized and general management training programs. The 1958 Government Employees Training Act requires federal agencies to provide training to employees, and the 1970 Intergovernmental Personnel Act (IPA) enables federal agencies to open programs to state and local employees. In addition, IPA and the Public Service Careers Program of the U.S. Department of Labor provide grants of training funds to agencies. Consequently, public managers can sharpen their managerial and technical skills through internal or external government–sponsored programs.

4. *Professional certification.* Professional advanced degree programs in public management, e.g., Master of Governmental Administration and Master of Public Administration, are available in numerous universities throughout the country. Increasing numbers of government jobs are requiring these advanced degrees. Similarly, many states and municipalities are encouraging certification of public managers for the purpose of maintaining their professional competence. The state of Georgia Certified Public Manager Program is a case in point. Experienced public managers can qualify for certification by com-

pleting a series of core courses in management in state government; attending professionally relevant elective seminars with at least sixty instructional hours; and successfully completing a comprehensive Certification Examination.

5. *Networking.* This is the function of establishing a personal support system, or network, of individuals a public manager recognizes as having some unique ability or talent he or she might need in the future. Generally, a network includes people from different professions in different organizations, and from scattered locations. It can prove to be an extremely valuable resource in professional development activity.

6. *"Guided" experience.* Coaching, counseling, special projects, and job rotational assignments provided by someone in higher authority can offer meaningful growth opportunities for those who aspire to be upwardly mobile. Authors Hennig and Jardim offer this advice to women, but it applies equally to any manager, "try to pick a winner whichever way you go, a winner who can become a godfather, a rabbi, a sponsor, a patron—who will invest in you, help you, teach you, and speak up for you. If you're right, you'll move with him. If you're wrong—disengage and try to leave him behind. But find another."[28] Perhaps this is easier said than done but the guided experience provided by such a mentor has proven invaluable in numerous public careers.

7. *Programs outside the agency.* Seminars, workshops, and special courses are offered through colleges and universities as well as the federal Office of Personnel Management. In response to the Civil Service Reform Act the OPM offers public managers in all sectors of government a catalog of courses and seminars to develop a wide variety of competencies.

SUMMARY

Professionalism is an attitude that imbues the public manager with a desire to excel and to attach the biggest priority to continuous self-development. Although public management is not a profession in the traditional sense, its practitioners achieve professionalism by (1) striving to upgrade their cre-

---

[28]Margaret Hennig and Anne Jardim, *The Managerial Woman* (Garden City: Anchor/Doubleday, 1977), p. 41.

dentials on a continuous basis; (2) working to perform competently; (3) being committed to serving the public's needs; (4) remaining responsive to public and organizational needs and being accountable for their own actions; and (5) exhibiting the highest order of moral conduct.

The maintenance of public confidence in government mandates that public managers subscribe to a code of morality that can withstand public scrutiny. The public manager as a professional sets the moral tone for his or her organization through example and insistence or adherence to a rigid ethical code by everyone in the agency.

Since a profession is viewed as spanning a lifetime, career planning plays a vital role in professionalism. Selection of, and development within, a career is the individual responsibility of the public manager. Toward this end, a suggested strategy for professional career planning would include: an analysis of one's personal values which become the basis for setting career objectives; delineating short- and long-term career aspirations; performing a self-analysis and developing plans to attain the objectives; and engaging in personal development activities that will enhance career advancement opportunities.

CASE STUDIES

1. Dade County Public Safety Division: A Professional Police Force

Metropolitan Dade County and the Florida Police Benevolent Association (PBA), the collective bargaining representative of the police, had reached an impasse in their negotiations. The Association was demanding a ten percent across-the-board pay increase; and the County, claiming unavailability of funds, proposed a zero increase. A Special Master was selected by the parties to hear both sides of the issue and propose a settlement. One of the considerations in this case was the "professional" caliber of the Public Safety Division. Excerpts from the Special Master's Report are presented below.

On the issues of the high caliber of Public Safety Division employees and the fine reputation of the Department, there was unanimous and enthusiastically positive feeling by the County and the PBA. One expert witness testified that the PSD was one of the "best in the country." He substantiated his claim by stating, "Book after book and article after article attests to the professionalism, the excellence, the innovativeness and creativity of this police department. It is a superior agency." The witness also said that the two most authoritative publications on police, *Task Force Report: The Police,* by the President's Commission on Law Enforcement and Administration of Justice, and the National Advisory Commission's *Report on Criminal Justice Standards and Goals* consistently cite the excellent performance of the Dade County PSD. In addition, he noted that PSD is continually called upon to perform services for other communities.

The supervisor of training for the PSD testified that $7,212 is spent to train each recruit. He described what is reputed to be the most comprehensive and innovative police training program in the country.

County officials and PSD employees praising themselves might appear immodest. Yet the Department's reputation justifies its pride. I checked with Federal regulatory and grant agencies in the law enforcement area. They confirmed that Dade County's PSD has a national reputation for being one of the best. Its selectivity—only 5 out of 100 are invited to attend the Academy, the comprehensive and innovative training, insistence on continuous upgrading of credentials—average educational level approaches three years of college and one requirement for promotion to sergeant is a Master's degree in criminal justice—and a code of ethics that is even incorporated into the [collective bargaining] agreement help make PSD a *professional* organization.

Dade County should be proud of the caliber of its Police Department and the reputation it has earned. The administration should continue to expend its resources financially and otherwise, to maintain the level of professionalism it has worked so diligently to achieve.

▶ Should Dade County be willing to pay a premium for a "professional" police force?

▶ If you were a County Commissioner, how would you respond to the Special Master's opinion?

▶ As director of labor relations for the County, how could you counter the Association's arguments for the raise without disagreeing the PSD was "the best"?

▶ How might the professional attributes of PSD affect the performance of the individual police officer?

2. An Ethical Dilemma

The Cranville County Commission had authorized the construction of a $30 million stadium and sports arena in the central part of the county. Commissioner James Konklin heads the Development Committee which accepts bids and contracts with builders. It is the county's policy to accept the low bid unless the bidder is found to be "undesirable or less than qualified." The low bid on the stadium project was from an established local contractor, Thomson Construction, whose President, Harold Thomson, is the brother-in-law of Commissioner Konklin.

When he opened the bids, Konklin was not surprised to see one from Thomson, but he really did not expect it to be the lowest. At this point, Konklin was in a quandary. He knew that Harold's company was highly respected and capable, but he *is* a close relative. "Everyone knows he's a close relative," he thought as he tapped his pencil nervously. "If the *Evening Herald* ran the story, those editors would crucify me!" he muttered to himself. "Yet," he wondered, "how can I legitimately award the bid to someone else when Harold is the lowest bidder?"

▶ In your opinion, would Commissioner Konklin's acceptance of Thomson Construction's bid be unethical? corrupt?

▶ What are the ethical considerations here?

▶ What would be the drawbacks to Commissioner Konklin's accepting the bid rather than rejecting it?

▶ What should Commissioner Konklin do in this case?

11

Prospects for the Public Manager:
Outlook for the Future

Key Concepts

Managing Change
  Anticipatory Democracy
    Cutback Management
      Semi-Bureaucracies
        Representative Democracy
          Professional Education
            Career Programs
              Revenue Sharing

One of the Midwest offices of the Employment Security Commission had a history of low performance—personnel turnover was high, morale was low, and placements were fewer and of shorter duration than the norm. The newly-appointed office manager vowed to turn the situation around and within a year, her office had the highest productivity in the country. So dramatic was the change that the General Accounting Office decided to visit the office to determine what had caused the improvement. They discovered a simple "innovation" had been the key. As an incentive to improved performance, the office manager had offered each interviewer an extra day off—with pay—for every three placements who remained on the job 90 days. Concluding that this practice was a conflict of policy and a potentially harmful precedent, GAO ordered the

office manager to discontinue it. Within two months the office
had settled back to its former state of mediocrity.

   This simple example emphasizes some of the changes that
lie ahead in public management. Essentially there is a necessity
to *manage* public agencies. More and more public managers
will *influence* policy rather than merely implement it. Our
ambitious office manager attempted to do this by introducing
an incentive program. Bold and innovative measures will have
to be taken to address the social issues that face our country—
in this case the local Employment Security Commission was
confronting unemployment. Public managers will be accountable for their actions both to their constituents—the public—
and to their organizations. They will face the dilemma of producing results at a reasonable cost within the confines of the
bureaucratic system. This dilemma can be illustrated by the
reply which a citizen gave when asked by his county government to express a preference regarding solid waste collection
services. County citizens were asked to return a questionnaire
which had been enclosed with the quarterly statement of service charges. Would citizens prefer to have solid waste collection continued on a twice-weekly basis with an increase in
service charge (to meet rising operating costs), or on a once-a-
week basis at the same rate? "Neither option is acceptable",
the citizen replied. "County government should strive to continue the present frequency of collections while maintaining
the existing fee structure." In short, the citizen was telling his
government that ways should be found to be more productive
in essential service delivery. This will call for a higher degree
of professionalism among public managers. But as government
grows to meet the increasing demands of society, the viability
of the bureaucratic model as an organizational form will be
seriously challenged.

IMPORTANCE OF THE FUTURE TO PUBLIC MANAGERS

   Throughout this text the need for planning in public management has been emphasized. Effective planning requires
predicting future problems and their relation to current
resources, and then developing programs to solve those problems. The future cannot be determined with certainty; but an
understanding of the more, or less, desirable alternatives that
lie ahead can be acquired. In this manner future-minded man-

agers can think ahead, anticipate obstructions to their plans, and effect the necessary changes that will allow their organizations to accomplish its objectives.

Managing change will be the key to the effective performance of future public managers. Growing technology and the expansion of new knowledge will make it imperative for public organizations to adapt to change. As new and more complex social issues demand public solutions, the public manager will be challenged to influence policies and create the necessary changes. Frederick C. Mosher pointed out a decade ago that the role of government has changed:

> "Government has ceased to be merely the keeper of the peace, the arbiter of disputes, and the provider of common and mundane services. For better or worse, government has directly and indirectly become a principal innovator, a major determiner of social and economic priorities, the guide as well as the guardian of social values, the capitalist and entrepreneur or subsidizer and guarantor of most new enterprises of great scale."[1]

Thus, the public manager will change current trends as necessary and work toward a more desirable future.

THE PUBLIC ENVIRONMENT OF THE FUTURE

As discussed in Chapter 2, the public environment—the needs, wants, and desires of society—provides the inputs of a system that responds through specific programs. These programs, or outputs deprive some groups while benefitting others. Consequently, competing interests continue to apply pressure on the system to meet their demands. As this country enters the final decades of the twentieth century, several social issues emerge as forebearers of future demands.

Societal Trends and Directions

On the domestic front is the problem of rapidly depleting nonrenewable resources. Future government policies will have to focus on means to conserve metals, water, and petroleum. Comprehensive energy development programs are needed

---

[1]Frederick C. Mosher, "The Public Service in the Temporary Society," *Public Administration Review*, Vol. 31 (January–February 1971), pp. 48–49.

today to insure future supplies of fuel for manufacturing, transportation, and environmental controls. If America is to retain its leadership position in world affairs, it must find remedial measures to counter the dwindling supply of petroleum. Other demands will originate with citizens' groups dismayed by the misuse and destruction of natural resources.

The resulting scarcities will cause the public to demand improved accountability, honesty, integrity, and greater productivity as well as to have less tolerance of inefficiency in the public service. The public is becoming increasingly concerned about environmental pollution, the destruction of wildlife, health hazards created by pesticides, and the decline of recreational areas. Future public policy decisions will have to give cognizance to these concerns.

As hospital and medical costs accelerate, Americans insist on greater involvement by government to insure adequate health care delivery. Efforts to improve service may produce a "dehumanizing" effect as patients are processed through diagnostic and therapeutic centers on a production basis. Emphasis will be on accuracy of diagnosis and propriety of treatment which may insult the dignity of individuals who feel they are being treated more as a case than as a person. Managers must be mindful of the need to protect human dignity in all areas of service delivery no matter how great the demand for increased productivity.

As cities face the problem of crime, they must also be able to deal successfully with police forces that are unionized. Can the public manager refuse demands by police and thereby precipitate a strike? Will the citizens realize that the discontinuance of police protection is a consequence of the public manager's disinclination to increase the tax burden in order to meet salary demands? The public manager is caught in the cross fire between the public which insists on a balanced budget and police protection and public safety employees who demand higher wages and more benefits. Current trends in public employee collective bargaining strongly suggest that the public manager of the future will have to be a sensitive "people" manager as well as a shrewd negotiator.

But America is not isolated from world problems. The problem of human hunger is perhaps one of the major global issues involving this country. Grain production and distribution is an example. In 1961, the worldwide grain reserves were sufficient for 95 days. In 1972 to 1973, the reserves dwindled to 70 days and today there are only sufficient supplies to feed the world for 30 days. Poverty and starvation will continue to be demands imposed on our political environment.

Consequences of Citizens' Demands

Future demands by society on the political system will have some interesting implications for government and for the public manager. Alvin Toffler of *Future Shock* fame prophesizes that the public environment must have the foresight to antici- pate problems and opportunities and it must involve the citi- zens in the decision-making process.[2] He maintains that "anticipatory democracy"—a process for reaching decisions that determine our future—can help us regain control over tomorrow. He contends that a lack of future consciousness causes crisis management. He also decries the lack of citizen participation, citing the fact that the government has grown so large and complicated that people feel powerless—they com- plain of being "planned upon." This is because they are literally frozen out of the decision process; they are seldom consulted about their own future.

Anticipatory democracy appears to be a trend for the future in government. Some of its various forms might include:

▶ City or statewide organizations that bring citizens together to help set long-range goals.

▶ Congressional reform; for example, a recent proposal of a "foresight provision" in the U.S. House of Represen- tatives requires that most standing committees engage in futures research and long-range analysis; also, antic- ipatory democratic organizations such as Alternatives for Washington or Iowa 2000 involve citizens in future planning.

▶ Community Action Programs; for example, there are about 900 neighborhood-based planning programs aimed at combating poverty.

---

[2]Alvin Toffler, "What is Anticipatory?," *The Futurist* (October 1975), p. 224–226.

▶ Referenda that let politicians know how the public feels on specific future issues.

▶ Citizen Advisory panels that advise on the long-range effects of new technologies.

THE PUBLIC MANAGEMENT ENVIRONMENT
OF THE FUTURE

Government organizations of the future will be characterized as "big" in size; bureaucratic, but representative; more responsive to public needs; and decentralized. Each of these characteristics represents a trend which is described below.

Size

Bigness is a fact of government life that cannot be overlooked. As citizen groups push their demands—energy conservation, consumer protection, quality of life—and legislatures champion particular causes—occupational safety and health, pension reform, truth in lending—the government responds. All of this translates into more and bigger government.

According to the U.S. Department of Commerce, employment in the public sector will be 19.8 million by 1990. (See Figure 11.1.) The trend is toward an increased proportion of state and local employees as a consequence of increased revenue sharing to augment the policy of decentralizing administrative decisions. The rationale behind this policy is that as our large population increases—from 208 million in 1970 to 260 million in 1990—state and local managers are in a much better position to tailor programs to the particular needs of their proportionately smaller constituencies. However, it is expected the *legislation* will continue to be more centralized in Congress. These two trends probably will produce an appropriate mixture of diversity and uniformity in American government.

However, the vastness of government will lead to new challenges for the public manager. Citizen group actions, such as California's Proposition 13, are likely to predominate during the coming decade. These pressures should manifest themselves in cost-effective programs. Even now, public managers are facing cutbacks in management brought about by tax and

Figure 11.1.   Composition of Government Employment—1990 Estimate

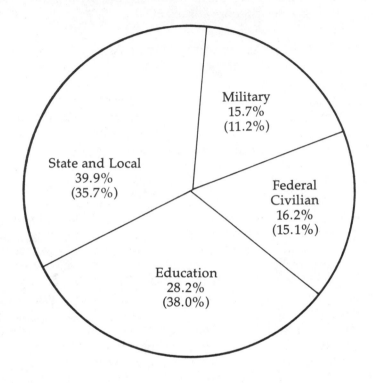

Military
15.7%
(11.2%)

State and Local
39.9%
(35.7%)

Federal
Civilian
16.2%
(15.1%)

Education
28.2%
(38.0%)

Note: 1980 percentages are included in parentheses
Source: U.S. Department of Commerce

expenditure limitations. In the future, major city and state governments will have to cope with financial constraints, and even crises, stemming from inflation, federal aid slowdowns, tax and spending limits, and declining citizen confidence. The response to these pressures may involve reorganizations, including termination of personnel; the elimination of low-prestige programs; functional transfers and redefinition of functions and/or priorities; interlocal contracting of services; and possibly even tax caps. The need to combine social justice with efficiency will not be an easy matter.

Harvard's Richard A. Musgrave suggests several options to demands for fiscal austerity of the type envisaged by Proposition 13:[3]

▶ Remove hidden increases in tax rates through "truth in taxation laws," such as enacted in Florida.

▶ Establish a clear nexus between public services and their cost by linking expenditure decisions to tax provisions.

▶ Use budgeting for efficient project selection.

▶ Review old programs and discontinue inappropriate ones.

▶ Improve the equity of property tax by effectively equalized assessment.

Bureaucracy

"Bureaucracy will continue to be a central if not an expanding factor in our society over the next several decades," insists Joseph Coates of the Office of Technology Assessment, U.S. Congress. He substantiates his claim with the reasoning that bureaucracy incorporates expertise which is essential in a society that relies on technology and knowledge. Further, he asserts, bureaucracies are agencies for management and control and they will be sustained because our society consists of complex networks that require sophisticated management.[4]

Although the bureaucratic model facilitates specialization, expertise, and control, it draws criticism for encouraging a mechanistic approach that stifles individual initiative, it is fraught with inefficiencies, and it tends to produce less-than-desired results. Semi-bureaucracies, management scholars Bennis and Slater[5] propose, can overcome these deficiencies without relinquishing management's prerogative to establish

[3]Richard A. Musgrave, "The Tax Revolt," *Social Science Quarterly* (March 1979), pp. 702–703.

[4]Joseph P. Coates, "Why Think About the Future: Some Administrative-Political Perspectives," *Public Administration Review* (September–October 1976), p. 582.

[5]Warren G. Bennis and Philip E. Slater, *The Temporary Society* (New York: Harper and Row, 1968), p. 4.

overall policy. Their model calls for full and free communication throughout the organization, conflict management by consensus, rather than coercion; and influence based on technical competence rather than prerogatives of power.

The managerial system developed by The Metropolitan Atlanta Rapid Transit Authority provides an interesting example of a variation on the hierarchical model. MARTA is charged with responsibility for building, developing and later maintaining a rapid transportation system for the Atlanta metropolitan area. During each of the phases of the agency's mission, significantly different tasks are to be performed, and different kinds of specialized skills and talents are required. Personnel needs and organizational relationships are expected to change substantially during the early life of the agency. In order to facilitate transitions from one phase of operations to another, an organic management system was attempted which focused on problem solving, emphasized the temporary nature of organizational arrangements, and sought to avoid the inflexibility of hierarchical structures.[6]

REPRESENTATIVE DEMOCRACY

Compatible with the semi-bureaucratic model is the notion that public institutions should be representative of their constituencies; that is, the national, ethnic, cultural, and religious composition of the community should be reflected in the employee population of the agency. Ethnic minorities, youth, women, and the elderly have campaigned for "equal rights" in employment and their demands will have largely been met within a decade, but new interests will arise to demand attention. Legal requirements, claims of special interest and power groups, technical needs of specialists, and other considerations will have to be weighed by public policy makers. Writer Dwight Waldo contends that as tomorrow's public managers endeavor to reach decisions and formulate action plans, "they will have to balance out many more fact and value premises than they do today."[7]

---

[6]Robert T. Golembiewski and Alan Kiepper, "MARTA: Toward an Effective Open Giant," *Public Administration Review*, Vol. 36 (January–February 1976), pp. 46–60.
[7]Dwight Waldo, ed., "A Symposium: Organizations for the Future," *Public Administration Review* (July–August 1973), p. 302.

Performance

Public managers are already focusing their attention on making government more productive and this should continue to be a major concern in the future. Public servants at all levels will continue to dedicate themselves to achieving results. In the future, managers should see a greater emphasis on rewards for accomplishment of expected results. Contributions to the organization can be explicitly described and used as evaluative criteria in performance appraisals. These "performance contracts" will attempt to reduce the manager's expected accomplishments to explicit statements of job-related behavior which, it is hoped, will be translated into meaningful contributions.

THE NATURE OF TOMORROW'S PUBLIC MANAGER

The public manager of the future will have to be not only a "jack-of-all-trades," but a master of them as well. We have described the public manager as acting in the roles of planner, organizer, controller, statesman/politician; being skilled in leadership, communication, delegation, decision making, and diplomacy; performing in a professional manner within a political environment. This may appear an imponderable task, yet the public manager is expected to demonstrate distinctive competence in each of these roles continuously.

The agenda for tomorrow calls for public leaders at all levels of government to *manage* their organizations. Our country's president, especially, must provide strong managerial impetus for effective government. Dwight Ink emphasizes, "our government is too complex, the political environment too hostile, and the problems too serious for the federal government to become effective without [it]."[8]

PROFESSIONAL EDUCATION

The trend toward improved and continuing professional education will help equip public managers with the requisite

---

[8]Dwight A. Ink, "The President as Manager," *Public Administration Review* (September–October 1976), p. 510.

knowledge and skills. The increasing demand for such educational programs has prompted more and more American colleges and universities to offer degree programs in Public Administration. These curricula blend practical as well as theoretical subject material. Schools that teach public administration, warns political scientist Don Price, "cannot be content to teach only the systematic thought that is the stuff of the scholarly disciplines, but also must develop in their students a taste for action, a willingness to accept responsibility and a concern for the accomplishment of humane and public purposes."[9] Whether this education should be oriented toward political science or managerial in nature remains in dispute among academicians. However, it is the authors' view that public managers' education should equip them with management concepts and skills that are taught from a public standpoint and are complemented with thorough preparation in political science.

There is general agreement that the public manager's education should be a continuing concern. In order to keep abreast of changing developments in public management and to develop specialized skills, the public manager will find it necessary to enroll in advanced academic programs and professionally sponsored seminars and workshops.

Graduate work, especially for mid-career managers, equips candidates with updated skills and gives them some coaching in the complexities of the governing process. However, graduate work cannot teach the principles which a manager must apply at work. Here, "guided" experience is the best teacher. Such activities as work internships, private/public sector cross training, and planned on-the-job experiences will enhance the professional development of public managers.

The Career Public Manager

Career programs in public management seem to be encouraging a capacity for generalization combined with management specialties. These programs are taking professional specialists

---

[9]Don K. Price, "1984 and Beyond: Social Engineering or Political Values?," in Frederick C. Mosher, ed., *American Public Administration: Past, Present, Future* (University, Alabama: University of Alabama Press, 1975), p. 234.

and relating their knowledge to broader interests and to the general purposes of government and society, rather than to a narrower perspective. This pattern of career development puts high premiums, of both money and prestige, on the manager going beyond his or her specialty to a concern for the comprehensive policies of the government as a whole. To continue to attract the best talent to top leadership jobs, government agencies will need to give closer attention to the intrinsic rewards for performance at executive levels.

As life expectancy continues to be extended and mandatory retirement age increases, public managers will have greater interest in long-term and post-career considerations. They and their employees will need to plan for longer years of retirement and the attendant monetary problem. They may even explore the viability of multiple careers and/or part-time or shared-time work following retirement.

CONCLUSION

Public agencies can and must be managed in the most effective manner possible. By applying basic management principles to the running of their organizations, public managers can be more effective in accomplishing the missions of their agencies. Those who are served by government will continue to demand responsiveness to their needs and excellence in delivery of services. Public pressure on government agencies will continue unabated while resources to implement programs will become more scarce. This "cutback" management underscores the critical nature of the public manager's job.

In this book the authors have attempted to present the concepts which are key to managing a public agency, as well as the current issues which may influence public managers' performance. The authors contend that successful managers will apply these concepts and management principles, and that they will not only implement public policy with effective programs, but will shape policies by anticipating the needs of their clientele.

The integrative purpose of this book has been to describe the various roles of the public manager and the interrelationship of these roles. The public manager was described as functioning within a political environment, thus making it essential that he or she have reasonable sophistication in policy matters.

But within this political context, it has become increasingly important to give attention to matters of administration and management. These are most directly relevant to the day-to-day roles of public managers.

Appendix 1

Questions and Exercises by Chapter

CHAPTER 1

Review Questions

1. Write a succinct definition of "public management."
2. How have the concepts and definitions of public administration/management changed over the years?
3. Identify five public manager positions and comment on the similarities and differences in the jobs.
4. What makes the job of the public manager different?
5. Who should study public management? Why?

Discussion Questions

1. How do you feel the public manager's job differs today from 100 years ago?
2. Distinguish between the "science" and the "art" of public management.
3. Of what use is the classification of managerial activities or roles (planning, organizing, etc.)?
4. Should every public manager be able to perform all of the roles identified in this chapter? What determines the degree of expertise needed in various roles?
5. What changes will face public managers over the next 10 to 20 years?

Learning Exercises

1. *(Field Assignment)* Select any three public managers. Each must have a different assignment and each should serve in a different agency and/or function of government. From a discussion with each manager, list his or her duties (in detail) and compare the lists for each of the managers. Explain why some of the duties are common to all three managers, and other duties are unique to one of the managers.

2. *(Library Assignment)* Locate descriptions of three different public management jobs. Write a brief synopsis for each of the jobs and write a short paragraph explaining how one might aspire to each of the positions.

CHAPTER 2

Review Questions

1. Outline and explain the "political system" approach to American government.

2. Identify several of the "values" that are associated with Americans and the "American way of life."

3. Discuss the nature and role of "values" in public management. Explain the significance of values to practicing public managers.

4. Enumerate and discuss several functions that government must perform in every society.

5. Why are "government" and "politics" such frequent topics for discussion?

Discussion Questions

1. Is it true that America is a nation of rapid social change? What evidence can you cite to support your position? What are the likely directions of future changes?

2. Discuss the processes and problems of our political system's response to social unrest.

3. How can the public manager stay in touch with the important elements of his or her public environment?

4. What changes could be made in the American political system to improve upon it? Be sure to clarify your goal(s) as you respond.

5. Discuss the interactions that take place between the "political system" and other American "systems," such as business, religion, and labor. What other "systems" can you include?

Learning Exercises

1. *(Field Assignment)* Visit a local political party headquarters and find out how that party is organized to raise funds and muster voter support for its candidates. Prepare a chart of the local organization and describe how each element or member of the organization functions to carry out its intended purpose.

2. *(Library Assignment)* Through library research, describe how each of the following contributors to political thought have influenced present-day politics. Cite at least one example of an application of each contributor's influence on today's political scene.

Thomas Jefferson
Woodrow Wilson
John Locke
John Stuart Mill
Henry David Thoreau
Alexis De Tocqueville

CHAPTER 3

Review Questions

1. Describe five criteria for the evaluation of a public organization's effectiveness.

2. What function do goals and objectives serve in the managing of an organization?

3. Discuss the various roles of the public manager in the management environment.

4. How does the management environment relate to the political environment?

5. In what ways does contingency theory integrate the various components of the management environment?

Discussion Questions

1. Choose any public organization and describe how each element of the Weber model has been implemented in this organization.

2. How can the informal organization contribute to the overall effectiveness of the formal organization?

3. Cite at least three examples of the (positive or negative) impact of politics on an organization.

4. Describe a training program that would develop human, technical, and conceptual skills in a public manager. What specific subjects would you include?

5. Is it possible to measure objectively the outputs (programs and services) of the management system? If so, how? If not, why?

Learning Exercises

1. *(Field Assignment)* Visit any government agency and interview one of its managers to determine how his or her agency (or unit) evaluates the efficiency and the effectiveness of its programs and services.

2. *(Library Assignment)* Assume you were hired as a consultant to Central City to set up the "ideal" city organization. Central City has a population of 400,000 with a projected annual growth rate of 10 percent. It is a commercial center with higher than average per capita income. The city council has informed you that the major problems of the city include: high crime rate, unemployment, a declining tax base, and business apathy toward the inner city. Develop an organization chart and describe the structure you will recommend. Discuss how the various elements of the structure will interact to carry out their functions.

CHAPTER 4

Review Questions

1. Give a definition for policy.

2. Outline and explain the policy process as described in this chapter.

3. Identify the primary actors in the policy process.

4. Discuss the public manager's role in the policy-making process.

5. Explain the relationship between policy and values, and give several examples of American values, or policy preferences.

Discussion Questions

1. Compare the public-policy process with policy making in a large private corporation.

2. Would it be possible to train public managers to be better policy makers? How would you go about it?

3. How is the public manager's involvement in policy making today different from 100 years ago?

4. Identify a public official whom you consider to be a good policy maker. Explain your choice.

Learning Exercises

1. *(Field Assignment)* Select a specific governmental or organizational policy (national or state law, local ordinance, business or government agency rule or decision, fraternity requirement) and ascertain through interviews with involved persons how this policy came into existence. Prepare a critical analysis of the process which took place. Include your assessment of the "quality" of the particular policy.

2. *(Library Assignment)* Carry out a policy study as above, but use newspaper accounts as your primary information source. Prepare a critical analysis, not of the policy itself, but of the coverages provided by the press. How objective and how complete is the information?

CHAPTER 5

Review Questions

1. What are the basic purposes of planning in public agencies?

2. Discuss the differences and similarities between a matrix or project form of organization and the typical line/staff structure.

3. How are authority, responsibility and accountability related?

4. Under what circumstance is group decision making more desirable than individual decision making? When would a manager make a decision alone instead of allowing the group to participate?

5. Describe the steps in the planning process.

Discussion Questions

1. Consider the problem of racially integrating a given school system. Recommend a solution by going through each step of the rational problem-solving approach as described in this chapter.

2. The text claimed that public managers are more than implementers of public policy. In what respects are they *more* than implementers and how do they arrive at these roles?

3. Staff organizations have often been criticized as being "overhead" and of no useful purpose. How would you recommend that staff organizations operate to avoid this criticism?

4. In large bureaucratic organizations, policies tend to be ignored or misinterpreted as they pass from one level to another. What can public agencies do to insure consistent and effective application of policies?

5. Compare and contrast the rational approach to decision making versus the alternatives: disjointed incrementalism and mixed scanning. What are the implications of each for today's public manager?

Learning Exercises

1. *(Field Assignment)* Secure a copy of an organization chart of any public agency. Through interview, observation, or other first-hand knowledge describe how the organization functions in accordance with the chart. Discuss where organizational functioning deviates, either formally or informally, from the chart and cite reasons why this might occur.

2. *(Library Assignment)* Obtain from a textbook, journal article, or directly from an agency a copy of a plan. Discuss the process used to develop the plan, the elements of the plan, and the results of its implementation.

CHAPTER 6

Review Questions

1. Describe the various activities involved in personnel management.

2. Discuss the various methods for examining applicants for employment.

3. What is meant by "personnel (human resource) effectiveness"? How can it be achieved?

4. Discuss various means for identifying training needs.

5. In what ways can compensation be geared to performance?

Discussion Questions

1. Discuss how tests can be used to discriminate against a particular group of people.

2. What types of fringe benefits do you feel will have the greatest appeal to young public managers in the future?

3. Promotion from within is a policy that has been espoused in public agencies since the introduction of merit systems. Occasionally, however, outsiders are hired, even for high level administrative positions. Discuss the merits and shortcomings of hiring from the open market in lieu of promoting from within.

4. Are student opinions a good measure of a training program's effectiveness? Why, or why not? What other methods might be useful in evaluating training programs, specifically those for public managers?

5. How can a public organization develop women for high level assignments? What can the organization do to insure that upwardly mobile women are successful as managers? What problems should be anticipated in developing women for management?

Learning Exercises

1. (Field Assignment) Obtain a written copy of the compensation program offered by your agency (or any government agency). A description of the program might be included in a personnel manual, employer handbook, special compensation/benefits booklet, or agency directives. Perform a detailed analysis of the program and recommend changes you feel are appropriate. In your analysis you might want to consider the following:

   a. Are wages and salaries competitive with rates for similar work in government service in the area?

   b. Are there benefits to cover: loss of pay due to illness or injury? protection against mental and physical impairment? long term security?

   c. Is the program understood by the employees covered by it?

2. *(Library Assignment)* Either from the library or from a local EEOC office obtain the most current guidelines for establishing an Affirmative Action program. Develop an outline for implementing an Affirmative Action program for your agency (or a hypothetical agency) that would be in compliance with EEO regulations.

CHAPTER 7

Review Questions

1. Discuss the arguments, pros, and cons of public employees' right to strike.

2. Describe the basic public employee collective bargaining provisions of the Civil Service Reform Act.

3. Discuss the principles for handling employee grievances.

4. Describe the guidelines to insure "just cause" in employee discipline.

5. What are the various roles of the public manager in labor relations?

Discussion Questions

1. Various proposals have been advanced in the Senate and House of Representatives for major public labor relations legislation that would give all public employees the right to organize. Discuss at least two alternative proposals and assess the possibility of the enactment of each.

2. Why do you suppose public unions have grown at such a rapid rate in the past two decades?

3. Jerry Wurf (President of AFSCME) was quoted as lamenting: "The day when unions can deal with problems by *force majeure* is over. The business of sitting at the bargaining table and saying that we'll cut off the water if you don't come through, that day is gone." If this statement expresses the attitude of organized labor, what strategy can it use to advance the welfare of public workers?

4. Organized labor has traditionally viewed seniority clauses as sacred. Seniority's purpose has been to add objectivity to selection, placement, and promotion of employees. How, then, can a seniority system be justified to Equal Employment Opportunity officers who produce statistical evidence that the preponderance of minority employees are recent hires? How can existing seniority systems be adjusted to accommodate minority employees?

5. Opponents of third-party neutrals in the collective bargaining process argue that arbitrators and mediators interfere with free and open negotiations. What are the advantages and disadvantages of utilizing neutrals in the bargaining process?

Learning Exercises

1. *(Field Assignment)* Obtain a copy of a collective bargaining agreement between a union and any government agency (federal, state, or local). List the issues addressed in the agreement. Discuss the specific rights granted to management and to the union. Is there a provision for dispute resolution in the agreement? If so, describe the procedure contained in the agreement.

2. *(Library Assignment)* Consult a Federal Information Center, a public or school library, or a catalogue of U.S. Government Publications and list the titles of at least ten publications that would be useful to a person engaged in collective bargaining. Discuss the particular relevance to collective bargaining of each publication you list.

CHAPTER 8

Review Questions

1. What are the functions of public budgets?
2. Explain the concept of "scrambled" budget cycles.
3. Describe the stages of budgetary reform in the United States.
4. What is the role of the public manager in the budget game.
5. Describe the different funding sources used by federal, state, and local governments.

Discussion Questions

1. Discuss the political aspects of public budgets.
2. Explain the steps in the ZBB process and describe the role of the public manager in setting budget priorities.
3. What is the effect of the growth of intergovernmental programs on financing government? How do budget cycles affect the public manager involved in such programs?

4. What are the budget implications of the Full Employment Act of 1946?

5. Explain why you feel policy analysis is or is not a legitimate function of budgeting.

Learning Exercises

1. *(Field Assignment)* Arrange an interview with a central budget office examiner and an agency budget officer from the same government jurisdiction. Ask them to discuss their respective roles in the budgetary process. Write an essay in which you discuss the differences and similarities in their perspectives on public budget making.

2. *(Library Assignment)* Obtain copies of federal, state, and local government budget documents. Examine those documents with respect to: (1) the kinds of information presented in each, (2) the format of the data presentations, and (3) the quality of the information offered in support of the appropriation requests.

CHAPTER 9

Review Questions

1. Discuss the significance of control and evaluation for today's public manager.

2. Explain what is meant by PERT and illustrate with an example.

3. List, and comment on, several of the "standards" that Dror presents for appraising program quality or performance.

4. What is meant by the terms "ombudsman" and "representative bureaucracy"?

5. Identify and explain three reasons why evaluation efforts have had a limited impact on public programs.

Discussion Questions

1. Should/does control and evaluation in public agencies differ from such in business and industry? Explain.

2. What are the advantages and disadvantages of encouraging greater citizen participation in the evaluation process?

3. Why should the public manager want to have his or her personal performance evaluated? Might there also be reasons for not wanting one's performance evaluated?

4. Identify and discuss the central issues involved in evaluating governmental services such as police and fire protection.

5. Compare the process and problems of organizational control and evaluation with the performance evaluation of individuals.

Learning Exercises

1. *(Field Assignment)* Prepare a list of ten questions that you feel will produce useful information about control and evaluation in public agencies. Visit at least one agency manager and one elected official, and obtain their responses to your questions. Analyze your data from the following perspectives:

   a. How important is control and evaluation to each respondent? To what extent does each person have well thought-out and consistent views?

   b. Can you identify and explain differences in the two official responses?

2. *(Library Assignment)* Locate and critique a written description of either an evaluation report or an organization control plan.

CHAPTER 10

Review Questions

1. Describe the traditional criteria for a profession.

2. Discuss the process of professionalism.

3. What guidelines are available to judge the moral conduct of a public manager?

4. Should the professional development of public managers be the individual's responsibility? Why, or why not?

5. Describe each element in the professional career planning model.

Discussion Questions

1. At what point does a public manager's conduct become unethical?

2. In this chapter we described several areas for the development of standards of professionalism. Develop a specific standard for at least two of these areas.

3. Assume the governor of your state commissioned you to prepare a training program that would develop professionalism in public managers. What subjects would you include? How would you teach the course? How would you determine the effectiveness of the training?

4. Prepare at least two career objectives of your own and share them with the class.

5. In what respects is public management a profession? In what respects is it not? How can public management be made more professional?

Learning Exercises

1. *(Field Assignment)* Interview a public manager who directs activities of one of the professions (medicine, law, engineering, architecture, higher education). Determine what standards are used to assess professional performance and write a short paper on how any or all of these standards could be applied, in general, to public managers' performance.

2. *(Library Assignment)* Develop a Code of Ethics for teachers of public administration.

CHAPTER 11

Review Questions

1. Characterize public managers as they are likely to be in the future.

2. Discuss at least three emerging trends in public sector labor relations.

3. Why is it important for public managers to be concerned with the future?

4. What changes in society are likely to affect the future of public management?

5. How will the bureaucratic form of organization likely develop in the future?

Discussion Questions

1. Assuming a knowledge of the future is important to us, what are the various ways we can get information about the future?

2. How can public managers be "anticipatory" when societal change is so rapid and uncertain?

3. The longer into the future we attempt to predict events, the less accurate our predictions are likely to be. Why is this so? And what can we (as forecasters) do to enhance the accuracy of our predictions?

4. "By 1990 there is expected to be a preponderance of a new breed of employees in government service. They are young, well educated, and tend to challenge the authority of management." Assuming this statement is correct, how can public managers make "new breed" employees viable contributors to their agencies?

5. What measures can public managers take to restore public confidence in government in general, and in a particular agency or department?

Learning Exercises

1. *(Field Assignment)* Ask three public managers what they feel will be the three most significant developments in government affecting their jobs in the next decade. Attempt to gain a concensus by reporting divergent opinions to each of the three managers. Write up your findings.

2. *(Library Assignment)* Locate at least three articles written in or after 1978 on the future of public management. Compare the views expressed in these articles with those presented in this chapter and write a report on the points of agreement and disagreement.

Appendix 2

Recommendations for Further Reading

A. BOOKS AND ARTICLES BY CHAPTER

Chapter 1

Buchele, Robert B. *The Management of Business and Public Organizations*. New York: McGraw-Hill, 1977. A book written on the premise that "management is management" whether it be in government or business. The author draws some distinctions, but, similarities are his emphasis.

Gortner, Harold F. *Administration in the Public Sector*, 2nd ed. New York: John Wiley and Sons, 1981. One of the few public administration texts that views public management, rather than public policy, as the center of public administration.

Mosher, Frederick C., ed. *American Public Administration: Past, Present, Future*. University, Alabama: University of Alabama Press, 1975. An important collection of papers on the history of public management in the United States. These writings were initially prepared for the 1974 National Meeting of the National Association of Schools of Public Affairs and Administration.

Nigro, Felix A. and Lloyd G. Nigro. *Modern Public Administration*, 5th ed. New York: Harper and Row, 1980. An important traditional work which the reader will find useful. Each edition of this very successful book has improved its quality and completeness.

Waldo, Dwight. *The Enterprise of Public Administration*. Novato, Calif.: Chandler and Sharp, 1980. A leading scholar reflects on his forty-year involvement with public administration.

Murray, Michael A. "Comparing Public and Private Management: An Exploratory Essay." *Public Administration Review* (July-August 1973). A useful statement of increasing similarities in public and private management.

Mintzberg, Henry. "The Manager's Job: Folklore and Fact." *Harvard Business Review* (July 1975). One author's view, based on his research, of what managers do.

Rogers, David. "Managing in the Public and Private Sectors: Similarities and Differences." *Management Review* (May 1981). A useful essay focusing on five central elements to develop a comparative analysis.

Waldo, Dwight. "Public Administration," in *International Encyclopedia of the Social Sciences.* New York: Crowell, Collier, and MacMillan, 1968. An outstanding scholar in the field provides a basic statement of definition and delineation.

Wilson, Woodrow. "The Study of Administration." *Political Science Quarterly* (June 1887). Generally regarded as the first American statement on public administration. Wilson's article has been the subject of several interpretations.

Chapter 2

Dye, Thomas R., and L. Harmon Zeigler. *The Irony of Democracy: An Uncommon Introduction to American Politics,* 4th ed. North Scituate, Massachusetts: Duxbury, 1978. An explanation of politics in America using an elitist approach. The authors' goal is to offer an alternative to the pluralist tradition. Their purpose is not to be anti-establishment but to encourage the reader to view the political system from an analytical perspective.

Elazar, Daniel J. *American Federalism: A View from the States,* 2nd ed. New York: Crowell, 1972. An analysis of federalism with emphasis upon the interests and values of states and regions. Builds upon earlier works by Morton Grodzins.

Lasswell, Harold. *Politics: Who Gets What, When, How.* New York: McGraw-Hill, 1936. A classic work on American politics. Very useful as an introduction or as a refresher.

Prewitt, Kenneth, and Sidney Verba. *Principles of American Government,* 3rd ed. New York: Harper and Row, 1980. A relatively brief treatment of the American political system. The authors draw from recent empirical research to present a descriptive analysis of politics in America.

Skidmore, Max J. *American Political Thought.* New York: St. Martin's, 1978. A brief and useful discussion of the evolution of political thinking in America.

Beer, Samuel. "Federalism, Nationalism, and Democracy in America." *American Political Science Review* (March 1978). A look at some of the dynamics of government and new directions that are emerging. The authors concentrate on evolutionary changes among and between the various levels of American government.

Cronin, Thomas E. "The Swelling of the Presidency." *Saturday Review of the Society* (January 20, 1973). The office of the President is examined and some central concerns are considered. Much of the discussion has general applicability to the role of chief executives, including governors and mayors.

Riggs, Fred. "The Ecology and Context of Public Administration: A Comparative Perspective." *Public Administration Review* (March-April 1980). A cross-national scholar emphasizes the importance of understanding many countries and cultures if we are to better understand our own.

Walker, Jack L. "A Critique of the Elitist Theory of Democracy." *American Political Science Review* (June 1966). A comparative analysis of both elitism and pluralism. The author considers both in relation to classical democratic theory.

Wilson, James Q. "The Bureaucracy Problem." *The Public Interest* (Winter 1967). An examination of bureaucracy's role within the governmental system and some of the effects of agencies upon political processes.

Chapter 3

Hummel, Ralph P. *The Bureaucratic Experience*. New York: St. Martin's, 1977. Provides a clear framework for organizing ideas about bureaucracy and our dealings with it.

Jackson, John H., and Cyril P. Morgan. *Organization Theory*. Englewood Cliffs, N.J.: Prentice-Hall, 1978. Authors take a macro perspective in presenting organization, "imperatives" for managers in understanding organizations, and organizational continuity.

Mescon, Michael H., Michael Albert, and Franklin Kedouri. *Management*. New York: Harper and Row, 1981. This basic text on management integrates the most widely accepted contributions of all major approaches to the subject. It communicates a fundamental understanding of formal organizations while stressing a contingency or situational view of management.

Morgan, David R. *Managing Urban America*. North Scituate, Mass.: Duxbury, 1979. The author describes what is involved in managing the modern city. Though academic in nature, the book does include substantial illustrative material to show how the world of urban managers really works.

Medeiros, James A., and David F. Schmitt. *Public Bureaucracy*. North Scituate, Mass.: Duxbury, 1977. The authors address several issues that provide the focus of the book: What approaches and techniques will enable public bureaucracy to meet contemporary pressure? What values and goals should government agencies pursue in meeting today's challenges?

Balk, Walter L., ed. "Symposium on Productivity in Government." *Public Administration Review*" (January–February 1978), pp. 1–51. Fourteen articles summarize concerns, problems, practices, and controversies on government productivity (U.S.) in the past five years.

Coulter, Philip B. "Organizational Effectiveness in the Public Sector: The Example of Municipal Fire Protection." *Administrative Science Quarterly* (March 1979), pp. 65–81. A study of three models of organizational effectiveness: behavioral-attitudinal, processual, and goal attainment. Results suggest that productivity, which binds an organization's internal processes and its societal impact, is the critical goal in the goal attainment model.

Ink, Dwight A. "The President As Manager." *Public Administration Review* (September–October 1976), pp. 508–515. Looks at the president's role as manager of the executive branch and considers whether this role has a future.

Lou, Alan W., Arthur R. Newman, and Laurie A. Broedling. "The Nature of Managerial Work in the Public Sector." *Public Administration Review* (September–October 1980), pp. 513–520. Authors researched major role functions and characteristics (complexity and content) of public versus private sector jobs and concluded that they are similar.

Myer, Marshall W., and N. Craig Brown. "The Process of Bureaucratization." *American Journal of Sociology* (September 1977), pp. 364–385. Explores formalization of personnel procedures in 229 city, county, and state finance agencies. Concludes that whereas origins and the environment account for the extent of formal personnel procedures, formalization in turn gives rise to multiplier hierarchies and hierarchy to decentralized decision making. The effects of origins are due to greater openness to environmental pressures at the time of formation than later on.

Chapter 4

Benveniste, Guy. *The Politics of Expertise*. Berkeley: Glendessary, 1972. Examines why and how administrators, or experts, are deeply involved in the making of policy.

Dror, Yehezkel. *Public Policymaking Reexamined*. Scranton, Penn.: Chandler, 1968. Argues that there is a significant gap between what is known about how policy can best be made and the ways in which it is actually made. Outlines recommendations for the development of policy science.

Dye, Thomas R. *Policy Analysis: What Governments Do, Why They Do It, and What Difference It Makes.* University, Alabama: University of Alabama Press, 1976. An attempt to describe and explain the courses and consequences of governmental activity.

Lindblom, Charles E. *The Policy Making Process,* 2nd ed. Englewood Cliffs, N.J.: Prentice-Hall, 1980. Provides a useful overview of the policy making process.

Rourke, Francis E. *Bureaucracy, Politics, and Public Policy,* 2nd ed. Boston: Little, Brown, 1976. Concentrates on the role and significance of administrators and administrative organizations in the policy process.

Easterbrook, Gregg. "The Spruce Goose of Outer Space." *The Washington Monthly* (April 1980). An interesting case study comparing Howard Hughes' Spruce Goose and NASA's Columbia.

Lambright, W. Henry. "Preparing Public Managers for the Technological Issues of the 1980's." *Public Administration Review* (July–August 1981). A review of selected scientific and technological challenges that will confront public managers over the next decade.

Lindblom, Charles E. "Still Muddling, Not Yet Through." *Public Administration Review* (November–December 1979). A leading thinker evaluates incrementalism and the use of knowledge and analysis in policy making.

Meltner, Arnold J. "Bureaucratic Policy Analysts." *Policy Analysis* (Winter 1975). This article examines bureaucratic policy analysts, their motivation, relations with clients, and methods for working on problems of public policy.

Nadel, Mark V. "The Hidden Dimension of Public Policy: Private Governments and the Policy Making Process." *Journal of Politics* (February 1975). This article looks at the nation of private governments such as corporations, as being public policy makers.

Chapter 5

Bricker, William and Donald M. Cope. *The Planning Process.* Cambridge, Massachusetts: Winthrop, 1977. This short paperback is designed to develop a manager's planning skills. The information given is very basic, covering principles of planning and how to apply them, setting objectives and goals, strategy and timing, and implementation.

Drucker, Mark L., ed. *Urban Decision Making: A Guide to Information Sources.* Detroit: Gale Research Co., 1981. An annotated bibliography of books, articles, monographs, case studies, and reports.

This body of literature was developed over the past decade to support the graduate professional education of urban decisionmakers.

Morgan, David R. *Managing Urban America: The Politics and Administration of America's Cities.* North Scituate, Mass.: Duxbury, 1979. The author discusses what is involved in managing the modern city and how cities are administered. There are sections on forms of city government, urban policy making, decision making, and decision analysis.

Beckman, Norman, ed. "A Symposium: Policy Analysis in Government: Alternatives to 'Muddling Through'." *Public Administration Review* (May–June 1977), pp. 221–263. Examines the state-of-the-art of policy analysis and the practice in major governmental institutions.

Bower, Joseph L. "Effective Public Management." *Harvard Business Review* (March–April 1977), pp. 131–139. The main contention of this article is that public management is not just different in degree from corporate management, but different in quality. The differences have important implications for public managers as they view their jobs.

Davis, Louis E. "Evolving Alternative Organization Design: Their Sociotechnical Bases." *Human Relations* (March 1977), pp. 261–273. The implicit assumptions underlying dominant or classical organization designs. Attributes commonly shared by these new designs are presented.

McGowan, Robert P. and Stephen Loveless. "Strategies for Information Management: The Administrator's Perspective." *Public Administration Review* (May–June 1981), pp. 331–339. Using the results of interviews with state agency administrators, the authors discuss methods that have been adopted for controlling the flow of information from internal and external sources.

Viteritti, Joseph P. and Daniel G. Carponncy. "Information, Organization and Control: A Study of System Application." *Public Administration Review* (March–April 1981), pp. 253–260. Article describes the implementation and application of a management reporting system at the central headquarters of the New York City public schools.

Chapter 6

Crouch, Winston W., ed. *Local Government Personnel Administration.* Washington, D.C.: International City Management Association, 1976. A variety of contributing authors present a thorough treatment of all aspects of local government personnel administration—from historical development to manpower planning, from work force structuring to recruitment and staffing, from the selection process to employee training and development, from compensation and labor relations to motivation and personnel unit management.

Miner, Mary Green, and John B. Miner. *Employee Selection Within the Law.* Washington, D.C.: The Bureau of National Affairs, Inc., 1978. A guidebook for personnel practitioners on the increasingly uncertain area of employee selection, under the requirements of equal employment opportunity legislation. Covers legal aspects of selection, influence of professional industrial psychology on selection techniques, and personnel practice itself.

Shafritz, Jay M., et al. *Personnel Management in Government: Politics and Process,* 2nd ed. New York: Dekker, 1981. An introductory textbook on public personnel management that takes a "what-is-it" approach for practitioners of public personnel management. It emphasizes the political ramifications of the process.

Stahl, O. Glenn. *Public Personnel Administration,* 8th ed. New York: Harper and Row, 1981. The classic text in the field, it brings together in one place the principal doctrines and ideas gleaned from both experience and research in the field. The concentration is on principle and reasoning with due attention to current practice and problems.

United States Office of Personnel Management. *Manager's Handbook.* Washington, D.C.: Office of Personnel Management, 1979. This handbook is designed to outline for the public manager what he or she can and cannot do in the area of personnel management. It is a composite of questions, suggestions, and recommendations to aid the manager in making personnel decisions.

Golembiewski, Robert T. and Carl W. Proehl, Jr. "Public Sector Applications of Flexible Workhours: A Review of Available Experience." *Public Administration Review* (January–February 1980), pp. 72–85. A comprehensive review of the available F-T (flexible workhours) literature and the various applications and their effects on government agencies.

Heisel, W. Donald. "The Personnel Revolution: An Optimist's View." *Public Personnel Management* (July–August 1976), pp. 234–238. Author argues that government has reached a turning point where systems designed to keep patronage out can be subordinated for an emphasis for making practical, measurable contributions to the goals of government. Personnel management has the responsibility for supporting the accomplishment of these goals through improved personnel policies, programs, and systems.

Lawler, Edward E. "Performance Appraisal and Merit Pay." *Civil Service Journal* (April–June 1979), pp. 13–18. The article explains the rationale for tying pay to performance and discusses the mechanics of making it work.

Nalbandian, John. "Performance Appraisal: If Only People Were Not Involved." *Public Administration Review* (May–June 1981), pp. 392–396. Article describes modern techniques of evaluation which attempt to minimize abuses of both the appraisal function and the employees being evaluated.

Scott, Joseph B. "Practical Aspects of Fair Employment Litigation." *Public Personnel Management* (November–December 1977), pp. 398–406. Article discusses lawsuits that challenge employment practices that are alleged to be fair in form but are discriminatory in operation, from the standpoint of the public employer.

Chapter 7

Goodman, Donald P., Thomas Rinaldo, and Eric W. Lawson, Jr. *Collective Bargaining in the Public Sector.* Niagara University, N.Y.: Niagara University Press, 1980. A case-by-case overview of the current status of the Taylor Law in New York State.

Jascourt, Hugh D., ed. *Government Labor Relations: Trends and Information for the Future.* Oak Park, Ill.: Public Employment Relations Research Institute/Moore, 1979. A compendium of significant legal decisions and significant literature on federal, state, and municipal labor relations.

Levine, Marvin J., and Eugene C. Hagburg. *Public Sector Labor Relations.* New York: West, 1979. A text on public labor relations which covers historical overview, legal framework, and administrative practices. It contains a "new" model depicting the types of relationships that are found between labor and management.

Spero, Sterling, and John M. Capazzola. *The Urban Community and Its Unionized Bureaucracies.* New York: Dunellen, 1973. This work covers the issues, practices, processes and methods of collective bargaining and its attendant pressure politics in local government labor relations.

Dunne, Thomas G. and Karel Swanson. "Public Sector Labor Relations." *Public Management* (June 1977), pp. 2–8. Describes the International City Management Association Executive Board's position on government personnel policy. Article contends that the present practice of waiting for and responding to employee demands is no longer adequate. Rather, authors say, management must establish its own goals for the negotiation process and develop a plan for achieving them.

Hayford, Stephen L. and Richard Pegretter. "Grievance Adjudication for Public Employees: A Comparison of Rights Arbitration and Civil Service Appeals Procedures." *The Arbitration Journal* (September 1980), pp. 22–29. Public sector contract grievance mechanisms are similar to those in the private sector, but civil service appeal systems evidence some significant variance from negotiated grievance procedures. Authors suggest that modest changes in civil service appeal systems could result in greater due process for public employees who are not covered by negotiated grievance procedures.

Ingrassia, Anthony F. "Reflections on the New Labor Law." *Labor Law Journal* (September 1979), pp. 539–545. Author reviews the Civil Service Reform Act and articulates his understanding of what is intended in some of the more important provisions in the new labor law.

Kochan, Thomas A. "The Politics of Interest Arbitration." *The Arbitration Journal* (March 1978), pp. 5–9. An account of the events leading up to the passage of an amendment to the New York State Public Employees Fair Employment Act (commonly known as the Taylor Law) extending compulsory interest arbitration for police officers and firefighters. Author describes the positions of the unions and the relevant management organizations.

Martin, James E. "Federal Union-Management Relations: A Longitudinal Study. *Public Administration Review* (September–October 1980), pp. 434–442. Six Federal agencies' union-management relationships were studied and areas found to be potential for cooperation were cited as: joint meetings, union involvement in decision-making, handling of union-management interactions, and the operation of grievance procedures.

Schramm, Leroy H. "The Job Rights of Strikers in the Public Sector." *Industrial and Labor Relations Review* (April 1978), pp. 322–335. Through an examination of state statutes and related court readings, this study concludes that strikers in the public sector can often be replaced, and sometimes summarily dismissed, even under laws providing the right to strike, unless those laws include Section 7 and Civil Service or tenure rights.

Chapter 8

Berman, Larry. *The Office of Management and Budget and the Presidency 1921–1979*. Princeton, N.J.: Princeton University Press, 1979. This book tells the story of the development of the Office of Management and Budget and provides insights into the political and managerial aspects of budgeting.

Kramer, Fred A., ed. *Contemporary Approaches to Public Budgeting.* Cambridge, Mass.: Winthrop, 1979. A useful collection of thirteen diverse articles.

Lee, Robert D. and Ronald W. Johnson. *Public Budgeting Systems,* 2nd ed. Baltimore: University Park, 1977. This introductory text is an excellent source of information on the historical development of public budgeting, the major budgeting systems, and the roles of the various institutions participating in the budget process.

Pyhrr, Peter A. *Zero-Base Budgeting.* New York: John Wiley and Sons, 1973. This is a readable description of the process of zero-base budgeting, written by the man who is credited with developing the first permanent ZBB systems in government.

Wildavsky, Aaron. *The Politics of the Budgetary Process,* 3rd ed. Boston: Little, Brown, 1979. This standard work examines the political aspects of the budgetary process and emphasizes the roles and strategies adopted by various participants.

Cornia, Gary C., and Charles L. Usher. "The Institutionalization of Incrementalism in Municipal Budgeting." *Southern Review of Public Administration* (Spring, 1981). A research report on the extent to which incrementalism has been incorporated in budgeting processes of large American cities.

Pyhrr, Peter A. "The Zero-Base Approach to Government Budgeting." *Public Administration Review* (January–February 1977). This is a discussion of ZBB written by the man who designed the budget process currently used in the federal government.

Schick, Allen. "The Road to PPB: The Stages of Budget Reform." *Public Administration Review* (December 1966). This article outlines the major stages of rational budget reforms and provides an excellent foundation for understanding current budget approaches.

—"A Death in the Bureaucracy: The Demise of Federal PPB." *Public Administration Review* (March–April 1973). The author suggests that PPB failed in the federal government because it challenged the traditional political system and because it was unable to penetrate the budget process.

Wildavsky, Aaron. "Rescuing Policy Analysis from PPBS." *Public Administration Review* (March–April 1969). The role of policy analysis in the budgetary process is discussed.

Chapter 9

Hatry, Harry, et al. *Program Analysis for State and Local Governments.* Washington: The Urban Institute, 1976. The authors present a systematic approach to the appraisal of the likely costs and effects of current and future governmental programs.

Morrisey, George L. *Management by Objectives and Results in the Public Sector*. Reading, Mass.: Addison-Wesley, 1976. A "how to" book prepared for managers and trainers in government. Examples are drawn from the public sector and emphasis is placed on middle and first-line management.

Newman, William H. *Constructive Control: Design and Use of Control Systems*. Englewood Cliffs, N.J.: Prentice-Hall, 1975. A future-oriented view of managerial control is presented. Improved control seen as the key to improving the effectiveness of both public and private organizations.

Rivlin, Alice M. *Systematic Thinking for Social Action*. Washington: The Brookings Institution, 1971. Analyzes PPBS as a common-sense approach to decision-making. Health, education, and, social service examples are drawn from the author's personal experience.

Weiss, Carol H. *Evaluation Research*. Englewood Cliffs, N.J.: Prentice-Hall, 1972. A systematic examination of research methods as applied to the evaluation of social programs. The author is concerned with "real-life" issues in action-oriented evaluation efforts.

Kondrasuk, Jack N. "Studies in MBO Effectiveness." *Academy of Management Review* (July 1981). The author reviews 185 earlier studies dealing with MBO in various organizations.

Legge, Jerome S., Jr. "Evaluating Title XX Programs: Problems and Prospects." *Southern Review of Public Administration* (September 1978). Problems that impede successful evaluation are analyzed and some recommendations are offered.

Lynn, Laurence E., Jr. and John M. Seidl. " 'Bottom-line' Management for Public Agencies." *Harvard Business Review* (January–February 1977). The authors discuss the management system they helped to install in two Federal departments.

Poland, Orville F., ed. "Program Evaluation: A Symposium." *Public Administration Review* (July–August 1974). A group of articles that explore a variety of issues in assessing public programs.

Wildavsky, Aaron. "The Self-Evaluating Organization." *Public Administration Review* (September–October 1972). Organization and evaluation are found to be terms that contradict one another to some extent.

Chapter 10

Bolles, Richard N. *The Three Boxes of Life and How to Get Out of Them*. Berkeley, California: Ten Speed, 1978. Offers ideas about school, work and retirement—what could be right with them, and how the reader might do something about that in his/her own life . . . now.

Bowie, Norman E., ed. *Ethical Issues in Government*. Philadelphia: Temple University Press, 1981. A collection of essays on ethical issues written specifically for this volume by nationally known philosophers.

Jelinek, Mariann. *Career Management for the Individual and the Organization*. Chicago: St. Clair, 1979. Deals with managing careers from the perspectives of the individual and the organization. Offers advice to those involved with managing their own careers or those of others.

McGregor, Douglas. *The Professional Manager*. New York: McGraw-Hill, 1967. Author takes the position that emotional reactions of management practitioners interfere with their perception of reality. Thus, managers must recognize and come to terms with their emotional and human side.

Miewald, Robert D. *Public Administration: A Critical Perspective*. New York: McGraw-Hill, 1978. Presents, in a lively discussion, a single point of view about public administration and the direction in which our society is moving.

Bowman, James S. "Managerial Ethics in Business and Government." *Business Horizons* (October 1976), pp. 48–54. Surveys reveal that business people and government officials are concerned with questions on business ethics and morality and are ready to translate that concern into action.

Dills, William R., Wallace B. S. Crowston, and Edwin J. Elton. "Strategies for Self-Education." *Harvard Business Review* (November–December 1965), pp. 119–130. To counteract the threat of personal obsolescence, managers must take the initiative for their own development (education) for present and future opportunities.

Foster, Gregory D. "Law, Morality, and the Public Servant." *Public Administration Review* (January–February 1981), pp. 29–34. In a democratic society, government is supposed to serve the people. As we look to the future, we may suppose that government will be called upon to assume even more responsibility for the provision of services, and in general, for helping society cope with an increasingly demanding environment. For the public servant, this will dictate decisions that are both more responsible and more responsive.

Malek, Frederic V. "The Development of Public Executives—Neglect and Reform." *Public Administration Review* (May–June 1974), pp. 230–233. The government needs to build effective means to prepare public managers for their critical roles. Programs need to prepare people for public service, provide expanded facilities for management development, offer incentives for improved executive performance, and generally increase managerial capabilities.

Schott, Richard L. "Public Administration as a Profession: Problems and Prospects." *Public Administration Review* (May–June 1976), pp. 253–259. Despite claims that the practice of public administration is or can become a professional activity, this article argues that it lacks the hallmarks of a true profession and has little chance of becoming one.

Chapter 11

Kerr, Clark, and Jerome M. Rosow. *Work In America: The Decade Ahead.* New York: D. Van Nostrand, 1979. Focuses on the future workforce and provides practical insight into new and better ways to advance productivity and the quality of working life.

Mosher, Frederick C., ed. *American Public Administration: Past, Present, Future.* Tuscaloosa, Alabama: University of Alabama Press, 1975. A compilation of writings on public administration with several essays on forecasted developments in the field.

Rosow, Jerome M. *Productivity: Prospects for Growth.* New York: D. Van Nostrand, 1981. This series of writings represents an original effort by the Work in America Institute to examine the prospects for U.S. productivity growth from the perspective of a variety of experts.

Schafritz, Jay M., and Albert C. Hyde, eds. *Classics of Public Administration.* Oak Grove, Illinois: Moore, 1978. Authors have collected what they consider to be "classics" in public management. They are arranged chronologically with the writings from the 1970s reflecting emerging patterns.

Wren, Daniel A. *The Evolution of Management Thought,* rev. ed. New York: Ronald, 1979. Brings together into one source the whats, whos, whys, and hows of the evolution of management thinking over a wide span of years. It discusses the history of management as a prologue to the future.

Groszyk, Walter S., and Thomas J. Madden. "Managing Without Immunity: The Challenge for State and Local Government Officials in the 1980's." *Public Administration Review* (March–April 1981), pp. 268–278. Recent court decisions have exposed government officials to a liability they had once thought remote. The article examines future implications of court actions on public managers.

Levine, Charles H., ed. "Organizational Decline and Cutback Management: A Symposium." *Public Administration Review*
(July–August, 1978), pp. 315–357. Various articles discuss the
question of organizational decline as a policy issue that involves
strategic choices and long-range planning. There are several
articles on short-term tactical responses to the needs to make
cutbacks, i.e., sunset legislation, deregulation, and cutback
leadership.
Stern, James L. "Public Sector Bargaining in 1985." *Labor Law Journal*
(May 1977), pp. 264–275. Article examines public sector bargaining questions which are critical today and speculates about how
they will change in the coming decade.
Toffler, Alvin. "The American Future Is Being Bubbled Away." *The
Futurist* (April 1976), pp. 97–107. The U.S. Government is allowing the future to be preempted by big corporations and foreign
nations. Toffler urges the government to use futurists to develop
the long-range options open to the American people, so that they
can share in deciding what their future shall be. Article is based
on his testimony before a Senate Committee.
Sherwood, Frank P. "The American Public Executive in the Third
Century." *Public Administration Review* (September–October
1976), pp. 586–591. Author hopes to see in the years ahead continued and growing interest in the process of executive leadership in the governments of the nation. Greater attention at both
the political and career levels should have its consequence for the
quality of governmental performance.

B. SELECTED BOOKS IN PUBLIC MANAGEMENT/ ADMINISTRATION

Aaron, Benjamin, Joseph R. Grodin, James L. Stern, eds. *Public-Sector
Bargaining* (Industrial Relations Research Association Series).
Washington, D.C.: The Bureau of National Affairs, Inc., 1979.
Allensworth, Don. *Public Administration: The Execution of Public Pol-
icy*. Philadelphia: Lippincott, 1973.
Altshuler, Alan A., and Norman C. Thomas, ed. *The Politics of the
Federal Bureaucracy*, 2nd ed. New York: Harper & Row, 1977.
Beckman, Norman, and Harold Handerson, ed. *New Directions in
Public Administration: The Federal View*. Reston, Va.: The Bureau-
crat, 1975.
Berkley, George E. *The Craft of Public Administration*, 2nd ed. Boston:
Allyn and Bacon, 1978.
Bernstein, Samuel J., and Patrick O'Hara. *Public Administration:
Organizations, People, and Public Policy*. New York: Harper and
Row, 1979.

Bozeman, Barry. *Public Management and Policy Analysis.* New York: St. Martin's, 1979.

Buchele, Robert B. *The Management of Business and Public Organizations.* New York: McGraw-Hill, 1977.

Buechner, John C., and Eugene J. Koprowski. *Public Administration,* 2nd ed. Belmont, Calif.: Dickenson, 1968.

Caiden, Gerald E. *The Dynamics of Public Administration: Guidelines to Current Transformations in Theory and Practice.* Hinsdale, Ill.: Dryden, 1971.

Davis, James W. *An Introduction to Public Administration: Politics, Policy and Bureaucracy.* New York: Free Press, 1974.

Dimock, Marshall Edward, and Gladys Ogden. *Public Administration,* 4th ed. Hinsdale, Ill.: Dryden, 1969.

Fried, Robert C. *Performance in American Bureaucracy.* Canada: Little, Brown, 1976.

Golembiewski, Robert T., Frank Gibson, and Geoffrey Y. Cornog, ed. *Public Administration, Readings in Institutions, Processes, Behavior, Policy,* 3rd ed. Chicago: Rand McNally, 1976.

Gordon, George J. *Public Administration in America.* New York: St. Martin's, 1978.

Gortner, Harold F. *Administration in the Public Sector.* New York: John Wiley & Sons, 1977.

Hawley, Claude E., and Rugh G. Weintraub, eds. *Administrative Questions and Political Answers.* Princeton: Van Nostrand, 1966.

Henry, Nicholas. *Public Administration and Public Affairs.* Englewood Cliffs, N.J.: Prentice-Hall, 1975.

Kramer, Fred A. *Dynamics of Public Bureaucracy: An Introduction to Public Administration.* Cambridge, Mass.: Winthrop, 1977.

——, ed. *Perspectives on Public Bureaucracy,* 2nd ed. Cambridge, Mass.: Winthrop, 1977.

Lane, Frederick S., ed. *Current Issues in Public Administration.* New York: St. Martin's, 1978.

Lorch, Robert S. *Public Administration.* St. Paul: West, 1978.

Lutrin, Carl E., and Allen K. Settle. *American Public Administration: Concepts & Cases,* 2nd ed. Palo Alto: Mayfield, 1980.

Marini, Frank, ed. *Toward a New Public Administration.* Scranton: Chandler, 1971.

McCurdy, Howard E. *Public Administration: A Synthesis.* Menlo Park: Cummings, 1977.

McKinney, Jerome B., and Lawrence C. Howard. *Public Administration: Balancing Power and Accountability.* Oak Park, Ill.: Moore, 1979.

Medeiros, James A., and David E. Schmitt. *Public Bureaucracy: Values and Perspectives.* North Scituate, Mass.: Duxbury, 1977.

Miewald, Robert D. *Public Administration: A Critical Perspective.* New York: McGraw-Hill, 1978.

Morrow, William L. *Public Administration: Politics and the Political System*. New York: Random House, 1975.

Mosher, Frederick C., ed. *American Public Administration: Past, Present, Future*. Alabama: The University of Alabama Press, 1975.

——, ed. *Basic Documents of American Public Administration*. New York: Holmes & Meier, 1976.

Nigro, Felix A., and Lloyd D. Nigro. *Modern Public Administration*, 5th ed. New York: Harper & Row, 1980.

O'Donnell, Maurice E., ed. *Readings in Public Administration*. Boston: Houghton Mifflin, 1966.

Presthus, Robert. *Public Administration*, 2nd ed. New York: Ronald, 1975.

Reagan, Michael D., ed. *The Administration of Public Policy*. Riverside, Calif.: Scott, Foresman, 1969.

Rehfuss, John. *Public Administration as Political Process*. New York: Scribner's, 1973.

Richardson, Ivan L., and Sidney Baldwin. *Public Administration: Government in Action*. Columbus: Merrill, 1976.

Rourke, Francis E., ed. *Bureaucratic Power in National Politics*, 2nd ed. Boston: Little, Brown, 1972.

Shafritz, Jay M., and Albert C. Hyde, eds. *Classics of Public Administration*. Oak Park, Ill.: Moore, 1978.

Sharkansky, Ira. *Public Administration: Policy-Making in Government Agencies*, 4th ed. Chicago: Rand McNally, 1978.

Simmons, Robert H., and Eugene P. Dvorin. *Public Administration: Values, Policy and Change*. Los Angeles: Alfred, 1977.

Simon, Herbert A., Donald W. Smithburg, and Victor A. Thompson. *Public Administration*. New York: Knopf, 1950.

Starling, Grover. *Managing the Public Sector*. Homewood, Ill.: Dorsey, 1977.

Stillman, Richard J., II. *Public Administration: Concepts and Cases*. Boston: Houghton Mifflin, 1976.

Uveges Jr., Joseph A.,.ed. *The Dimensions of Public Administration*, 2nd ed. Boston: Holbrook, 1975.

Waldo, Dwight, ed. *Public Administration in a Time of Turbulence*. Scranton: Chandler, 1971.

Williams, J. D. *Public Administration: The People's Business*. Boston: Little, Brown, 1980.

C. PROFESSIONAL JOURNALS

Administrative Science Quarterly, Graduate School of Business and Public Administration, Malott Hall, Cornell University, Ithaca, N.Y. 14853.

American Behavioral Scientist, Sage Publications, Inc., 275 South Beverly Drive, Beverly Hills, CA 90212.

American Journal of Public Health, The American Public Health Association, New York, N.Y. 10021.

American Journal of Sociology, Subscription Dept., Journals Division, University of Chicago Press, 5801 South Ellis Avenue, Chicago, IL 60637.

American Political Science Review, American Political Science Association, 1527 New Hampshire Avenue, N.W., Washington, D.C. 20036.

American Sociological Review, American Sociological Association, 1722 North Street N.W., Washington, D.C. 20036.

Canadian Public Administration, Institute of Public Administration of Canada, 1205 Fewster Dr. Unit 14, Mississauga, Ontario L4W 1A2, Canada.

Foreign Affairs, Council on Foreign Relations, New York, N.Y. 10021.

Government Employee Relations Report, The Bureau of National Affairs, Inc., 1231 25th Street, N.W., Washington, D.C. 20037.

Harvard Business Review, Harvard University, Graduate School of Business Administration, Soldiers Field, Boston, MA 02163.

Indian Journal of Public Administration, Indian Institute of Public Administration, Indraprastha Estate, Rind Road, New Delhi 110002, India.

Industrial and Labor Relations Review, New York State School of Industrial and Labor Relations, Cornell University, Ithaca, N.Y. 14853.

International Review of Administrative Sciences, International Institute of Administrative Sciences, 25 rue de la charite, 1040 Brussels, Belgium.

Journal of the American Institute of Planners, The American Institute of Planners, Baltimore, MD.

Journal of Applied Behavioral Science, Institute for Applied Behavioral Science, 1501 Wilson Blvd., Arlington, VA 22209.

Journal of Politics, Southern Political Science Association, University of Florida, Gainesville, FL 32611.

Public Administration Review, American Society for Public Administration, 1225 Connecticut Avenue N.W., Washington, D.C. 20036.

Public Management, International City Management Association, 1140 Connecticut Avenue, N.W., Washington, D.C. 20036.

Public Personnel Management, International Personnel Management Association, 1313 East 60th Street, Chicago, IL 60637.

Public Welfare, The American Public Welfare Association, Chicago, IL 60637.

State Government, Council of State Governments, Box 11910 Iron Works Pike, Lexington, KY 40511.

Public Interest, National Affairs, Box 542 Old Chelsea Post Office, New York, N.Y. 10011.

D. SPECIALIZED REFERENCE SOURCES

Dubin, Robert. *Handbook of Work, Organization, and Society*. Chicago: Rand McNally, 1976.

Dunnette, Marvin D. *Handbook of Industrial and Organizational Psychology*. Chicago: Rand McNally, 1976.

Grazia, Alfred De, Carl E. Martinson, and John B. Simerone. *Administrative Management: Public and Private Bureaucracy*. Princeton: Princeton Research Publishing Co., 1969.

Heady, Ferrel, and Sybil L. Stokes. *Comparative Public Administration: A Selected Annotated Bibliography*, 2nd ed. Ann Arbor: The University of Michigan, 1960.

Henderson, Francine I. *Public Policy Studies in The South: A Selected Research Guide*. Atlanta: Clark College 1975.

Heyel, Carl, ed. *The Encyclopedia of Management*. New York: Van Nostrand Reinhold, 1973.

Hoselitz, Bert F., ed. *A Readers' Guide to the Social Sciences*, rev. ed. New York: Free Press, 1970.

Johnson, George W., ed. *American Political Science Research Guide*. New York: IFI/Plenum Data Co., 1977.

March, James G. *Handbook of Organizations*. Chicago: Rand McNally, 1965.

McCurdy, Howard E. *Public Administration: A Bibliography*. Washington, D.C.: American University Press, 1972.

Seckler-Herdson, Catheryn. *Bibliography on Public Administration Annotated*, 4th ed. Washington, D.C.: American University Press, 1953.

Sills, David L., ed. *International Encyclopedia of the Social Sciences*. New York: MacMillan and Free Press, 1968.

Simpson, Antony E. *Guide to Library Research in Public Administration*. New York: Ctr. Productive Public, 1976.

Spitz, Alan A., and Edward W. Weidner. *Development Administration; An Annotated Bibliography*. Honolulu: East-West Center, 1963.

Stogdill, Ralph M. *Handbook of Leadership*. New York: Free Press, 1974.

Tompkins, Dorothy Campbell. *Research and Service: A Fifty Year Record*. Berkeley: University of California, 1971.

Whittick, Arnold, ed. *Encyclopedia of Urban Planning*. New York: McGraw-Hill, 1974.

The Book of the States. Council of State Governments. Lexington, KY.

The County Yearbook. National Association of Counties. Washington, D.C.

The Municipal Yearbook. International City Management Association. Washington, D.C.

E. CAREER AWARENESS INFORMATION

Books and periodicals on careers are excellent sources of information. *The Occupational Outlook Handbook* published annually by the Bureau of Labor Statistics (U.S. Department of Labor) describes occupations, entry requirements, projected earnings, and the outlook for employment in each occupation. A similar reference, *The Encyclopedia of Careers and Vocational Guidance,* describes over 600 occupations.

The Bureau of Labor Statistics also publishes the *Occupational Outlook Quarterly* which includes articles of interest to job seekers as well as "how-to" items on career planning. Individual career pamphlets available through the BLS, the U.S. Government Printing Office, and from specific professional associations (e.g., nursing, legal, information sciences, engineering, and many others) describe particular careers.

Computerized information. A U.S. government document, *Computer-Based Vocational Guidance Systems,** gives an overview of the computerized information available on career planning. Various systems provide data on selected occupations and their outlook and some even allow an individual to estimate his or her potential for a given occupation.

The Educational Resources Information Center (ERIC) which is coordinated by the National Institute of Education, an agency of HHS, is a clearing house for all kinds of educational information including data on careers. Monthly indexes of more than 750 journals list available information which is accessible in microfiche form at more than 600 locations throughout the country.**

Self-help guides are available commercially and are used by some agencies in their career planning programs. These guides or workbooks serve to help people decide on a career and help them in setting objectives along the lines. Following is a sampling:

1. *Career Dimensions I and II* by Walker Storey, General Electric Company, Croton-on-Hudson, New York (about $6.75 each).
2. *A Life Planning Workbook for Guidance in Planning and Personal Goal Setting* by George A. Ford and Gordon L. Lippitt, NTL Learning Resources Corporation, Fairfax, Virginia.
3. *How to Decide: A Guide for Women,* by Nelle Scholz, Judith Prince, and Gordon Miller, College Entrance Examination Board, Princeton, New Jersey ($5.95)

Computer-Based Vocational Guidance Systems (Washington, D.C.: U.S. Government Printing Office, 1969).
**Neal Baxter, "Ask ERIC," *Occupational Outlook Quarterly* (Spring 1977), pp. 18–21.

Appendix 3

Organizations and Associations for Public Managers

Airport Operators Council International, Inc.
    1700 K Street, N.W., Suite 602
    Washington, D.C. 20006
American Association of Port Authorities
    1612 K Street, N.W., Suite 502
    Washington, D.C. 20006
American Association of School Administrators
    1801 North Moore Street
    Arlington, VA 22209
American Association of State Highway and Transportation Officials
    444 North Capitol Street, Suite 225
    Washington, D.C. 20001
American Correctional Association
    4321 Hartwick Road, Suite L-208
    College Park, MD 20740
American Institute of Certified Planners
    1776 Massachusetts Avenue, N.W.
    Washington, D.C. 20036
American Planning Association
    1313 East 60th Street
    Chicago, IL 60637
American Public Health Association
    1015 18th Street, N.W., 7th Floor
    Washington, D.C. 20036
American Public Power Association
    2600 Virginia Avenue, N.W., Room 212
    Washington, D.C. 20037
American Public Welfare Association
    1155 16th Street, N.W., Suite 201
    Washington, D.C. 20036

American Public Works Association
    1313 East 60th Street
    Chicago, IL 60637
American Society for Public Administration
    1225 Connecticut Avenue, N.W., Room 300
    Washington, D.C. 20036
American Public Transit Association
    1100 17th Street, N.W., Suite 1200
    Washington, D.C. 20036
American Water Works Association, Inc.
    6666 West Quincy Avenue
    Denver, CO 80235
Council of State Governments
    Iron Works Pike
    P.O. Box 11910
    Lexington, KY 40511
Council of State Planning Agencies
    444 North Capitol Street
    Washington, D.C. 20001
International Association of Chiefs of Police
    11 Firstfield Road
    Gaithersburg, MD 20760
International Association of Fire Chiefs
    1329 18th Street, N.W.
    Washington, D.C. 20036
International City Management Association
    1140 Connecticut Avenue, 2nd Floor
    Washington, D.C. 20036
International Personnel Management Association
    1850 K Street, N.W., Room 870
    Washington, D.C. 20006
Municipal Finance Officers Association
    180 North Michigan Avenue
    Chicago, IL 60601
National Academy of Public Administration
    1225 Connecticut Avenue, Room 300
    Washington, D.C. 20036
National Association of Counties
    1735 New York Avenue, N.W., 5th Floor
    Washington, D.C. 20006
National Association of Housing and Redevelopment Officials
    2600 Virginia Avenue, N.W., Room 404
    Washington, D.C. 20037
National Association of Regional Councils
    1700 K Street, N.W., Room 1306
    Washington, D.C. 20036

National Association of Schools of Public Affairs and Administration
    1225 Connecticut Avenue
    Washington, D.C. 20036
National Association of State Budget Officers
    444 North Capitol Street, Suite 204
    Washington, D.C. 20001
National Conference of State Legislatures
    1405 Curtis Street, 23rd Floor
    Denver, CO 80202
National Governors' Association
    444 North Capitol Street, 2nd Floor
    Washington, D.C. 20001
National Institute of Public Affairs
    1225 Connecticut Avenue, N.W., Room 300
    Washington, D.C. 20036
National League of Cities
    1620 Eye Street
    Washington, D.C. 20006
National Municipal League
    47 East 68th Street
    New York, N.Y. 10021
National Training and Development Service
    5028 Wisconsin Avenue, N.W., Room 321
    Washington, D.C. 20016
Public Administration Service
    1776 Massachusetts Avenue, N.W.
    Washington, D.C. 20036
United States Conference of Mayors
    1620 Eye Street, 4th Floor
    Washington, D.C. 20006
Urban Institute
    2100 M Street, N.W.
    Washington, D.C. 20037

Index

Unions (See Public sector
  organization)
Unit cost information   47
Unity of command   97–98
Urwick, Lyndal   41

V

Van Adelsberg, Henry   133
Vroom, Victor H.   128

W

Wage issues   111, 130–133
Waldo, Dwight   240
Walton, Richard   142
Wanat, John   165
Weber, Max   42–43

Weyland, Fred C.   83–84
Wholey, Joseph S.   198
Wildavsky, Aaron   162, 164, 170,
  201
Wilson, Woodrow   6–7, 178
Women, in management   125–126
Wright, Deil S.   32

Y

Yetton, Philip W.   128

Z

Zero-Base Budgeting
  (ZBB)   175–177
Ziegler, Harmon   63

About the Authors

Donald P. Crane, Ph.D. (Georgia State University), is Professor of Management and Urban Life at Georgia State University. Dr. Crane is a consultant to government and business. He has published numerous articles on administration, and his textbook, *Personnel: The Management of Human Resources*, 3rd ed., will be released in 1982 by Wadsworth Publishing Co. Dr. Crane has had extensive experience in personnel/industrial relations and serves as an arbitrator of union-management grievances in both the private and public sectors. Dr. Crane is a member of the Academy of Management, the American Association for Public Administration, and the National Academy of Arbitrators and served as Distinguished Lecturer in Personnel and Labor Relations at the U.S. Army War College and as Manpower Fellow at the U.S. Department of Labor.

William A. Jones, Jr., D.P.A. (University of Georgia), is Professor of Management, Political Science, and Governmental Administration at Georgia State University. He served for eight years as founding Director of the University's Institute of Governmental Administration. Dr. Jones earlier held administrative positions in a variety of government agencies, most recently as Deputy Administrator of the Southeastern Region, Law Enforcement Assistance Administration, U.S. Department of Justice. His other public sector management positions were with the National Aeronautics and Space Administration, the U.S. Public Health Service, the Social Security Administration, and the Office of the Secretary, Department of HEW. He is consultant to various state and federal agencies. Dr. Jones served for three years as a member of the National Council of the American Society for Public Administration. He is also past President of the Georgia Chapter and past national Chairman of ASPA's section on Criminal Justice Administration. He is a member of the Academy of Management's Public Sector Division and editor of *Annals of Public Administration: Criminal Justice*.